NEWCASTLE WEST END
The Complete Record 1882-1892

The season-by-season record & who's who of a forgotten football club

Paul Joannou
with
Alan Candlish & Bill Swann

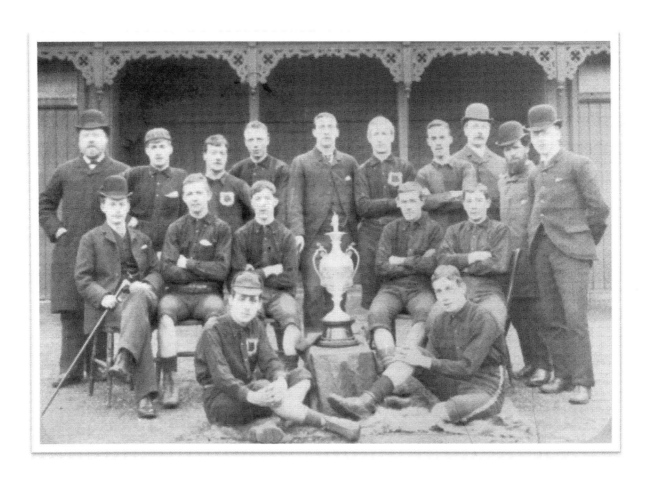

Newcastle West End with the Northumberland Senior Cup in 1888. The photograph was kept by long serving forward Jack Barker, unfortunately player names are not captioned. West End's red-and-black halved shirts are worn as are the county caps and badges.

NEWCASTLE WEST END
The Complete Record 1882-1892

The season-by-season record & who's who of a forgotten football club

Paul Joannou
with
Alan Candlish & Bill Swann

First edition published November 2023 in Great Britain by Novo Publishing Ltd.

Text & Data © 2023 Paul Joannou.
Design © 2023 Novo Publishing.
Cover by Novo Publishing & Mitchell A Joannou.
ISBN 9780956815644

Photographs & Illustrations: P Joannou Archive.
Printed and bound by 4Edge, Hockley, Essex.
www.4edge.co.uk

Although Newcastle West End brought many footballers from Scotland to Tyneside during their short period in the game, there were several local players to serve the club with distinction. Jack Barker became a stalwart and totalled in excess of 150 matches, scoring 44 goals over eight seasons. Barker enjoyed a well-supported benefit match during April 1891 against Sunderland, the VIP admission card to St James' Park survives, illustrated. After he stopped playing football, Jack lived in the Benwell area and for a time ran the Turks Head Inn, pictured outside his pub (centre with the white bar coat). Several of his photographs survive, now a historic archive of the era.

CONTENTS

FOREWORD

By JOHN GIBSON
who has reported on Newcastle United for the Chronicle over the last 57 years.

Gibbo now, and as a young West Ender growing up in Elswick & Benwell.

Like thousands upon thousands of Geordie disciples before me and no doubt still to come in an endless future, the consistent unbreakable love of my life has without question been Newcastle United. It is a cradle to grave obsession not in the slightest dictated by success or failure. Birthright decides our fate.

Having been born and brought up in the west end of the city the emergence of a great institution takes on even greater significance. Because when west and east became united 130 years gone the outcome was the Magpies we love.

I was born on Benwell's Adelaide Terrace when it was a very different place to today. Sutton's Dwellings stood to the immediate right of our house which was above a grocery store opposite a pub and the back yard housed an outside toilet, an aviary lovingly created from an old air raid shelter by my grandad, and a rabbit hutch created by me when I was knee high to a corner flag. The rabbit was inevitably black and white!

I used to walk with my uncle Frank from our house along Elswick Road to the Big Lamp and down to St James' Park to faithfully support United. I loved Joe Harvey and Bobby Mitchell, big Frank Brennan and George Robledo, but above all I hero worshipped Wor Jackie.

The history of Newcastle United we all know well of course. It is the Geordies' bible. But what of the West End, my roots and part of the roots of a mighty football club rising as a great power once again? Paul Joannou, a personal friend who shares the same west end upbringing as me, is unquestionably Newcastle's most authoritative historian and he paints a vivid picture of small beginnings which grew into a mighty obsession.

West End's short 10-year life started when they were formed in 1882 from Crown Cricket Club of Elswick, based at Crown Street off Elswick Road. They fielded many noted players including the very first international footballers to play for a Tyneside club when Scots flooded across Hadrian's Wall from the amateur-only game north of the border. Ralph Aitken was the trailblazer in 1886, Bob Kelso the first true idol of the fans.

The West End were backed by several Elswick and Benwell worthies including Joseph Cowen, founder of my own newspaper, the Evening Chronicle in 1885, who to this day has a statue standing in his honour at the bottom of Westgate Road, and Arthur Henderson MP who uniquely served three separate terms as Leader of the Labour Party in three different decades as well as winning the Nobel Peace Prize in 1934. Two mighty men of North East and national significance in at the birth of association football.

Maybe the West End became defunct leaving the East End temporarily Newcastle's dominant force but they did give us St James' Park, our treasured cathedral on the hill where Geordies still go to worship.

The research of a forgotten football club has as usual been carried out in painstaking detail and genuine love by Paul Joannou, a fellow Benwell boy. What Paul and his team has produced is not only the first stirrings of our beloved Newcastle United but a realisation of my own roots buried in the Victorian West End. For both I am eternally grateful.

INTRODUCTION

The *Complete Record of Newcastle West End* generally follows the same format as previous similar titles on Newcastle United. Bringing together the same team which produced *Newcastle United: The Ultimate Record* was a natural step to compile the history of the other half of the city's football heritage. The West Enders are very much linked to Newcastle United, of course when they were known as Newcastle East End, and a memorable East versus West rivalry developed during the 1880s. Having completed the story of United's early period it was fitting to do the same for Newcastle West End.

Over many years, indeed going back decades, both myself and Alan Candlish have researched United's history to their origins in Byker during 1881. At the same time, we both took a keen interest in other clubs on Tyneside during those formative years. And that study resulted in relating the story of how football arrived and developed in the North East and on Tyneside in particular; during 2009 *Pioneers of the North* was published. Newcastle West End was a part of that text, but now we have taken the story of the West Enders a stage further using much of the material from many years past.

The era of the 1880s is significantly different in football research than from 1890s onwards. There are very few official football records in England or Scotland for the early seasons of West End's time in the game, while there are no club ledgers or meeting documents. The main source of tracing the West Enders history has been contemporary newspapers, searching through the many North East titles and from around the country, including sporting dailies and weeklies such as the local *Northern Athlete* and nationwide *Athletic News, Scottish Referee* and *Football & Cricket.*

Photographs are rare from the decade while a few newspaper sketches provide images of games and players. Several used are poor definition, taken from old groups and vintage newspapers, but are precious in illustrating teams and players. Two or three West End team-groups previously owned by stalwart player Jack Barker have survived and are reproduced. All are in monochrome rather than colour of course. Only Victorian collector cards exist in full colour and illustrate West End's distinctive red (or maroon) & black kit.

Apart from West End's significant connection with Newcastle East End/Newcastle United, readers should note that there were other sides in the region to be prominent, and like West End, also now long gone and largely forgotten football clubs. Included were pathfinders of the game, Tyne and Rangers, the likes of Elswick Rangers, Rendel and Shankhouse Black Watch, as well as smaller clubs such as Trafalgar.

The book is split into two sections and comprehensively covers West End over their 10 years existence:
Part 1: The season-by-season and match-by-match record.
Part 2: The who's who, which includes all footballers and officials.
(See further *Introduction* notes on both sections, pages 19 and 52).

Any reader with new information on the West Enders, especially photographs of the team, players or officials, please contact the publisher at paul@novopublishing.co.uk

Acknowledgements
Firstly, I must thank my co-authors Alan Candlish and Bill Swann for their dedicated commitment to compile this history. Both are life-time supporters of Newcastle United like myself and have a deep interest in the region's football origins and past. Alan, with his painstaking research and eye for detail, and Bill for his meticulous production of the statistics, have been invaluable in producing the book.

Thanks to well-known journalist John Gibson – another west end lad – for his Foreword, and to my son Mitchell for designing the cover artwork. Many individuals have helped in past years. Two are worthy of special mention. The late John Allan, sadly one of the victims of the Covid pandemic, was a constant source of information and a near resident of Newcastle's Central Library as he spent week by week delving through past newspapers. It is a great pity he cannot see the finalised text. Another Geordie, Jordan Tinniswood, also spent countless hours on football research and his booklets on East End and West End, *Before They Were United*, were a great bedrock for study.

Many football historians around the country have assisted, notably; Rod Evans, John Litster, Martin O'Connor and David Wherry. Thanks to William Sheridan at the Partick Thistle Archive (www.thethistlearchive.net) for exchanging information when it was discovered, somewhat remarkably, that seven past Thistle men also played in the colours of West End.

Rob Mason, Mike Gibson and Paul Days, all Sunderland historians, have produced much on the Wearsiders and they have all helped in piecing together West End's history. Finally longstanding Scottish historian Andy Mitchell has been an essential contact for all things north of the border.

Over the period of research contact has been made with a few descendants of West End's players and officials. Thanks to the following: Julie Brunton (ref Tom Queen), Stuart Fitzgerald (John Fitzgerald), Chris I'Anson (William I'Anson), Derek Graham (Alexander Graham), Jock McCann (McCann brothers), Glenn Renforth (Ryder brothers), John Shaw (John Ferguson), D Waggott (Waggott brothers).

The Scottish Football Museum at Hampden Park has an on-going project to digitise their vast collection of historical material and the official Minutes of the Scottish FA were a valuable source of information, reviewing players that had crossed the border as the ban on professionalism took hold in Scotland. The Museum also managed to find a rare photograph showing Bobby Calderwood, while the archive of St John's College, Cambridge, located an equally scarce team group featuring Henry Newbery. My appreciation for allowing those illustrations to be reproduced.

Newcastle's Central Library, Local Studies Dept has been a principal point of reference both recently and over the last few decades. Information Officer, Sarah Mulligan is thanked for her help.

The British Newspaper Archive (www.bitishnewspaperarchive.co.uk) has been used extensively and is a vital asset to football research, an on-line collection of over 70 million newspaper pages which includes numerous titles from Newcastle and the wider North East. Family history sites such as Ancestry, Findmypast and ScotlandsPeople have all been essential when piecing together the lives of players and officials.

Paul Joannou, September 2023.

Cover illustrations
Front
Newcastle West End with the Northumberland Senior Cup.
Rear
Top left: A match ticket from Jack Barker's benefit match in 1891.
Top right: A Victorian collector card featuring West End.
Below: West End pictured in hooped jerseys, colourised from an original photograph owned by Jack Barker.

NEWCASTLE'S WEST END
On Victorian Tyneside

Newcastle West End Football Club belongs to the city districts of Westgate, Arthur's Hill, Elswick and its bordering Benwell community, as well parts of the neighbourhoods of St Thomas' and St Andrew's, especially around Nun's Moor and Castle Leazes, where now of course Newcastle United is based.

Westgate, as the name suggests, is where one of the old fortified entrances of Newcastle was located, and the principal route of Westgate Road ran into the city-centre with important sites around Corporation Street and Bath Lane, including the Tyne Brewery. Arthur's Hill overlooked the town and ran down to where St James' Park is located. The Arthur's Hill estate was developed around 1826 and named after the developer's son.

Contemporary sketches of Newcastle upon Tyne during the 1880s.

Elswick was originally a separate township and is where the club was founded. By the 1880s, Elswick was part of the city and growing enormously as heavy industry flourished on the slopes leading to the River Tyne. The adjoining Benwell district was semi-rural, an area of fields and a few collieries. It was also consumed in the westward spread of the industrial development, led by the Armstrong empire of shipbuilding, armament production and the manufacturing of engines and heavy equipment of all kinds. There were coal staithes, dry-docks, chemical and glass works, forges and railway works, all jam-packed into the riverside.

The Armstrong Elswick Works (left), and Westgate Road (right), both at the turn of the century.

Thousands of workers, managers and their families settled in the west end of Newcastle and lived in the vast array of housing developed on the slopes between Scotswood Road along the river, and Westgate Road running west. There were basic workers' terraces and flats, as well as more up-market executive dwellings, some very grand indeed. There were pleasant green spaces as well, notably Elswick Park, while the Royal Grammar School and the College of Medicine at the stunning Surgeon's Hall, were both situated on Rye Hill.

Newcastle upon Tyne's population in 1801 was only around 28,000. By the time the industrial revolution had fully taken hold in 1900, it was 215,000. Awarded city status during 1882 – as football started to make an impact – Newcastle upon Tyne became a powerhouse of the country.

The city's west end became a breeding ground for football and produced several clubs in those developing years of the game. Newcastle West End were joined by teams from Elswick Leather Works and Elswick Ordnance Works, two large factories alongside the river. Elswick Rangers were formed too, noted as being linked to the enormous Armstrong Works, as were the Ordnance line-up. And Rendel – originating from Rendel Street in Elswick – made a home in Benwell, not far from Rangers. For a few years, within a distance of only a couple of miles, three grounds staged regular football; St James' Park, Mill Lane and Normount Road.

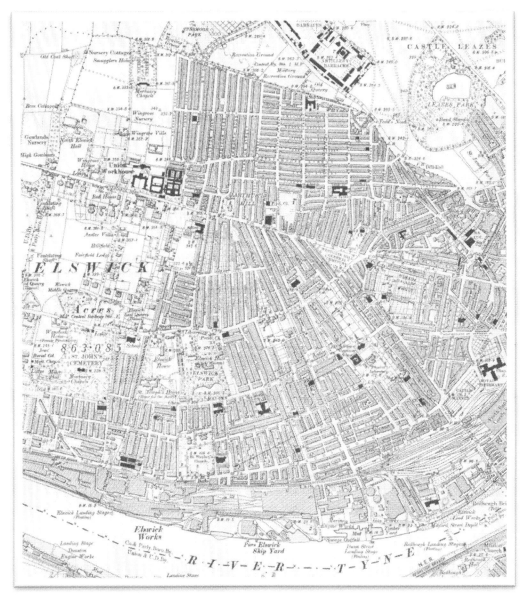

Newcastle's west end as shown on the 1899 OS map; Castle Leazes and St James' Park (top right), Elswick riverside (bottom), Arthur's Hill (centre) with Westgate Road & West Road running from the city-centre (right) towards the west. The Benwell district is to the left of Elswick off the plan. (Courtesy of National Library of Scotland.)

FOOTBALL IN THE 1880s

It may have been the same game, but over 140 years ago on Victorian Tyneside football was a bit different to the modern money-spinning sport watched by millions all over the world. The style of football belonged to the pioneering age; formations were something of a charge on the opponent's goal with outfield set-ups such as 1-1-8, 2-2-6 or 1-2-7. Dribbling skills and dashes of the forwards were features of play. As the decade moved forward a pyramid formation of 2-3-5 evolved – two defenders in front of the goalkeeper, three midfielders and five forwards of two wide-men, two inside-forwards and a leader of the attack, the centre-forward. It became the norm by the end of the decade, and largely stayed that way for nearly 40 years.

Rules were still evolving. Cross-bars replaced a tape between the posts from 1875, but there were instances of clubs still using the inadequate tape into the 1880s. That caused many quarrels on the field when goals were scored – or not scored. The same applied to goal-nets, introduced by 1882 but not compulsory for Football League and FA Cup matches until season 1891-92. In one Northern League fixture with West End, Sheffield United made a protest that there were no nets fixed to the posts.

The penalty-kick wasn't introduced until 1891 while durations of matches were not always the regulation 90 minutes. It should be noted that games were often less, some with 20- or 30-minute periods. During the winter months, back then well before the advent of floodlighting, growing darkness caused several disputes over goals. During 1884-85, West End played 11 fixtures during November to January and played only one game with two periods of 45 minutes. In addition, often the length of matches (and especially kick-off times) were dependant on train timetables, the principal mode of transport for travelling sides of the era.

Pitches were bumpy patches of grass, roughly marked out and not well-maintained until later in the decade when clubs found proper grounds. Umpires initially took control of fixtures, one nominated from each side, who often were far from being impartial. Consequently, as could be expected, disputes were frequent and arguments raged, even to the point where one side walked off the pitch! During the early 1880s, a referee could be appointed to stand on the touchline as a sort of 'neutral observer', a 'mediator' with certain powers to restrict squabbles. By season 1891-92 the FA decided that referees should become all-powerful – the man in charge in the middle. Umpires were reassigned to the touchline and there to assist the referee – eventually labelled as linesmen in 1898. Gradually all three officials became independent and not linked to the competing sides in any way.

Newspaper sketches of typical football matches during the 1880s, including a match played on Tyneside, right.

On a national basis football was more developed elsewhere in the country, especially in the North West and Midlands. The North East around Tyneside and Wearside had lagged way behind until the sport was introduced by the well-to-do sons of the city's upper-class when they returned from football-playing public-schools and universities with the 'association code'. Tyne Association were formed in 1877 and from that point football took off, slowly at first, then briskly during the 1880s and 1890s. The creation of the Northumberland & Durham FA as 1880 began, then as two separate organisations by May 1883, acted as a stimulus to growth.

As Tyne led the way, the game was an amateur one at first, played by the well-educated and affluent. But then the working-class became gripped by the round ball and quickly took over, Newcastle Rangers being the first grass-roots club. Those pioneering sides, Tyne and Rangers, had, by the mid-1880s, given way to a new group of teams which took the development of football a stage further. Most prominent of those new outfits as the decade progressed were Newcastle West End and Newcastle East End. There were other good teams in the city as well notably Elswick Rangers, Rendel and, on the outskirts in South Northumberland, Shankhouse.

Shankhouse Black Watch with the Northumberland Senior Cup. The Northumbrians were one of the top sides in the region during the 1880s. Included in this illustration is Billy Matthews (back row, second from left) who guested for West End during 1887.

On Wearside, clubs also followed Tyne's lead, but on a smaller scale. Yet that district saw Sunderland and Sunderland Albion become more progressive than their counterparts on Tyneside, both joining the new league competitions which were formed. Such was their development, Sunderland quickly advanced to become the country's foremost club by the mid-1890s.

Competitions

Until the later years of the 1880s, up and down the country football was largely played in what would these days be termed 'friendly' matches, or as described by the Tyneside press, "ordinary matches". During later seasons many top sides from the North West of England and from Scotland arrived on Tyneside to face West End and East End – and usually gave an exhibition of the game by defeating the area's best, showing that a large gap then existed in development.

There was knock-out competitive football in the shape of local Football Association sanctioned tournaments. Initially in the North East region, the Northumberland & Durham FA's Challenge Cup was the premier silverware, and when the two bodies went their separate ways during 1883, clubs battled for their respective trophies; the *Northumberland Senior Cup* and *Durham Senior Cup*. The Northumberland FA's original rules stated that the competition "shall be called The Northumberland Football Association Challenge Cup". But it became known as the Senior Cup and remains in play well over a century later.

A prestigious *Inter County Championship* was also created for season 1884-85 when the trophy winners from Northumberland and Durham competed for the North East title. Other competitions of lesser importance began too, such as the *Tyne Charity Shield* and *Temperance Festival* football tournament which took place on the Town Moor as part of the holiday attraction. There were also similar competitive tests for reserve and junior sides.

The *FA Challenge Cup,* which was known more commonly back then as the *English Cup*, kicked off during 1871 but it was some time before Tyneside clubs entered the draw. Scottish teams at first took part until the Scottish FA barred their entry in 1888. Regional stages kicked-off the competition and West End made their debut during October 1886. By 1888-89 a qualifying structure was introduced to reach what was termed the FA Cup 'proper'.

League football did not arrive until a meeting during April 1888 at the Royal Hotel in Manchester inaugurated the *Football League*. A total of 12 clubs took part in the opening championship season of 1888-89, Preston North End being the first title winners. There were no clubs from the North East. But the region was quick to grasp the necessity for regular competitive action and the following season during March 1889 the *Northern League* was founded at the Three Tuns Hotel in Durham. The league is one of the oldest around, still on the go in the 2020s. West End, East End and Elswick Rangers were founder members of a group of 10 clubs from Northumberland, Durham and Cleveland. Soon other competitions followed, the *North Eastern Counties* and *Northern Alliance* leagues. Like the Northern League, the Northern Alliance remains part of football's pyramid. Elsewhere other regions followed with their own league structures such as the *Midland League* and *Lancashire League*.

The national Football League – although made up with clubs from the North West and Midlands – was very much a success. With a title trophy and prestige at stake, rival leagues were formed as more and more clubs wanted football with a competitive edge. *The Combination* started for season 1888-89 as well, with 20 sides, but was a failure and didn't last the campaign. The *Football Alliance* with 12 clubs was its replacement, running for three seasons from 1889-90. Sunderland Albion were members but resigned after having to pay half of the train fare of visiting clubs to Wearside. But the Alliance couldn't compete against the prospering Football League and in 1892 they merged to create a Second Division. Newcastle clubs were not ready in terms of maturity for any of the so-called national leagues, although the original Sunderland club were to join the Football League in 1890.

In Scotland, relevant due to the many footballers who headed to Tyneside, similar regional knock-out competitions took place. The *Scottish Cup* began in 1873 and the *Scottish League* arrived later than its English counterpart, for season 1890-91 with Dumbarton and Rangers sharing the title. A *Scottish Football Alliance* ran from 1891 to 1897 while a short-lived *Scottish Football Federation* also introduced league football. A structure for Scottish 'Junior' football existed as well, the term 'junior' being something of a misnomer, not juvenile sides, but for what could be classed as modern-type 'non-league' clubs, at a standard below the 'seniors' of the game.

Professionalism

Football began as an amateur sport but its evolution brought in professionalism; payments for playing the game. The Football Association sanctioned a professional deal for players in July 1885, although conditions had to be met to appear in the FA Cup or any other FA-affiliated competitions, such as the Northumberland Senior Cup. Rules such as qualification by birth or residential status were included. Known as "Native Players", footballers who had lived long enough in the district were allowed to play. Yet, it was still a momentous decision in football's development. Players could now be paid and regulations would quickly be relaxed by the end of the decade. A few clubs in the North East fully embraced the professional model, including West End. As 1888 began the club started to make all their native players professionals.

There was an important difference in Scotland, a hugely significant one. The Scottish Football Association was staunchly amateur and totally against professionalism. They stubbornly refused to endorse playing football for money and brought in draconian rules which resulted in any footballers playing for English clubs without permission were suspended from the Scottish game. Black-lists appeared and it became a hot topic north of the border. Although at times a shady form of payment did exist, the new rules saw an exodus south until the authorities finally conceded and allowed professionalism during 1893. Up to then, Scots eyed rich pickings across the border and flocked south, especially to clubs in the North West and North East.

The Scottish Invasion

By the mid-1880s, Newcastle West End decided on a strategy of engaging players from other regions, notably Scotland. Newcastle East End followed, as did newly formed Elswick Rangers. Sunderland Albion did likewise on Wearside along with Ironopolis in Cleveland. As professionalism took hold, West End – together with their North East rivals – advertised for players in *Athletic News* and *Scottish Sport*. As a result, a constant flow of footballers from Scotland arrived. West End had a liking for the Scots, fielding nearly 40% of all their footballers. Not as many pulled on East End's colours, while there were plenty more on Wearside. West End were to field no fewer than six Scotland international players during their period in the game, a remarkable number for a club just in their early stages of development.

Some were good, many though were patently second-rate. One comment in the local *Northern Magpie* weekly questioned the arrival of more Scots to West End during December 1888 and compared them to the home-produced Jack Barker: "What! More players from the Land O'Cakes. Go on West End! Though all the men you bring, there is not one that can beat the Newcastle production – Little Barker as he is generally termed."

A match report on one FA Cup fixture between West End and Sunderland Albion during October 1888 highlighted that no fewer than 16 Scottish players were on the field. The entire Albion side were from north of the border while five West Enders were Scots as well. Without doubt the men from the north had a big influence on the development of the game in the region.

RENTON FOOTBALL TEAM
"Champions of the World"

Above: *The Scotland team pictured at the Oval before a clash with England in March 1886. Two players to appear for West End are pictured, Watty Arnott (back, second from left) and Bobby Calderwood (back, third from right). (Courtesy of Scottish Football Museum.)*

Left: *The region around Renton in Dunbartonshire was a hotbed of football during the period. Renton FC, pictured, were arguably the best in the country, and became "Champions of the United Kingdom and the World" when they defeated West Bromwich Albion during 1888. Many of West End's Scottish footballers came from this area. Two stars of the Renton side, Bob Kelso and Donald McKechnie joined the West Enders, while both Johnny Campbell and John McNee later appeared with Newcastle United. All are pictured. Players only, left to right. Back: Kelso, Hannah, Lindsay, McCall A, McKechnie. Front: McCallum, Campbell H, Kelly, Campbell J, McCall J, McNee.*

Occasionally reports of how players were paid surfaced in the news columns. During season 1889-90, West End's footballers were usually paid 10 shillings (50p) for a win or draw in Northern League matches, 7s 6d (38p), if they lost. While for a more important match £1 was on the table to win the contest. Examples of such games that season included the FA Cup tie at Stockton, which West End duly won 1-0, and a 3-0 victory over Newcastle East End at St James' Park on Christmas morning.

PART 1

SEASON by SEASON RECORD

THE WEST ENDERS: FORMATION

As the 1880s began, the region's pathfinder clubs Tyne and Rangers had gradually brought the game of football to the public. Interest was stirred. New teams began playing the sport all over Tyneside and beyond. In the east of Newcastle, in South Byker, a new club was founded during November 1881 called Stanley FC – situated at Stanley Street on Walker Road. Formed by cricketers, they were to become Newcastle East End – and ultimately Newcastle United. As more and more sides took to kicking a ball around on rough-and-ready patches of grass, almost a year later during August 1882, in the west of the city, the cricketers of Crown Cricket Club of Elswick, also formed a football eleven.

Crown Street was located in the heart of Elswick, running between Westgate Road and Elswick Road down towards the River Tyne. Close by were Elswick Park and Westgate Hill Cemetery, both still there over a century later. The cricketers of Crown CC were playing the summer game by 1881, and maybe as early as 1878. They played on the Town Moor, at Nun's Moor and Castle Leazes.

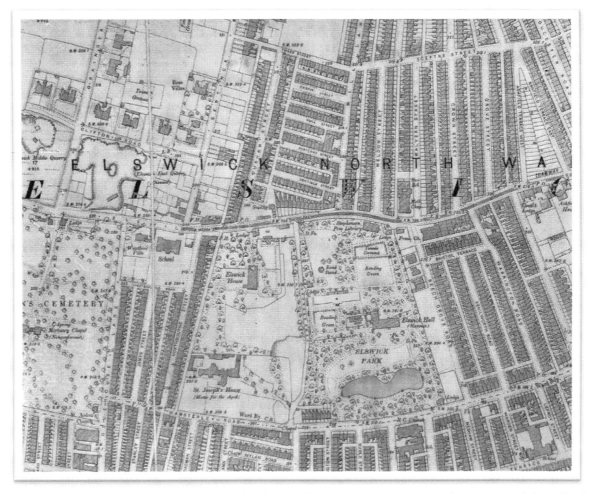

Elswick Road runs through the centre of the plan with Elswick Park to the south. Crown Street is situated running upwards from Elswick Road, one of the many terraces in the district.

During August 1881, a meeting at Lockhart's Cocoa Rooms took place and Crown CC changed their title to West End Juniors CC, shortly dropping the 'Juniors' tag. Their captain was Thomas Waggott and treasurer, John Waggott – both to soon appear as footballers – with Robert White as secretary. A year later, on 21st August 1882 they decided to create a footballing side to be known as *West End Football Club*.

A nostalgic feature in Newcastle's *Sunday Sun* newspaper during 1933 contained memories from Tom Bell, a former local footballer and later long serving secretary of the Northumberland FA. He recalled that it was Billy Tiffin who prompted the cricketers to try the 'association code' noting that he "started the Newcastle West End club when he took a football to the Leazes Park when a cricket match was in progress". Bell added that "the cricketers all dropped their bats and pads and started playing football".

Many football clubs originated from cricket clubs during the years of the 1880s, including several on Tyneside – notably Newcastle West End and Newcastle East End. The summer game was popular on Tyneside, pictured is a scene at the Bath Road ground in Newcastle with the Church of St Thomas in the background. The arena was also an early venue for football until 1881.

Tiffin was appointed secretary and treasurer of the new club, while skipper of the side was William Scott, although he isn't recorded as playing a game but was a noted cricketer and footballer who resided in Elswick. John Waggott was vice-captain and a committee was formed comprising William Mather, Charles Wray and John Blair.

Key Moments
Aug 1881: *Crown Cricket Club change their name to West End Cricket Club.*
Aug 1882: *The cricketers form West End Football Club.*
May 1886: *West End move to a new home at St James' Park.*
Jan 1888: *West End become a semi-professional club.*
May 1889: *West End turn fully professional.*
Sept 1889: *West End join the Northern League.*
July 1890: *West End become a Limited Company.*
May 1892: *West End fold and are disbanded.*

First game: *7 Oct 1882 v Rosewood (a) L0-2 (Fr).*
First victory: *2 Dec 1882 v Marlborough (a) W1-0 (Fr).*
First game at St James' Park: *2 Oct 1886 v Newcastle East End W3-2 (Fr).*
First FA Cup fixture: *30 Oct 1886 v Sunderland (a) L1-2 (replay ordered, (h) W1-0).*
First trophy: *24 March 1888 v Shankhouse Black Watch W6-3 (NSC).*
First league fixture: *14 Sept 1889 v Newcastle East End (h) W2-0 (NL).*
Last fixture: *23 April 1892 v Stockton (a) L0-1 (NL).*
Biggest victory: *15-0 v North Eastern (h) 4 Feb 1888 (NSC).*
Heaviest defeat: *1-12 v Bootle (a) 12 Jan 1889 (Fr).*

Illustrations of any kind featuring football were rare during the 1880s, however the Tyneside-based Northern Magpie newspaper contained a sketch from the West End versus Sunderland Albion FA Cup tie during 1888-89 at St James' Park. Featured are the two captains, Albion's Sam McClennan (left, in their colours of black & white stripes) and Billy Swinburne (right, wearing West End's halved shirts). From the caricaturist's depiction, the game looks a touch full-blooded! The Wearsiders won 5-2, but West End lodged a successful protest and the match was replayed, Albion winning again, this time by 2-1 after extra-time in front of a 4,000 crowd.

Introduction & Notes

West End's season-by-season record includes only games considered to be first-team matches, although a few fixtures are debatable. The only exception is the inclusion of the club's Reserve XI winning the Northumberland Senior Cup in 1892, West End's very last trophy just prior to the club disbanding. Match details of this victory are included, but appearances and goals are not added to the biography totals.

Match reports in the contemporary newspapers covering football during the earliest seasons were meagre and lacked detail. Both Newcastle West End's and Newcastle East End's games were often covered only by two or three lines. Team line-ups are given in the traditional 1-11 format, but it should be noted that during the first two campaigns, certain reports often published a list of names for the team which played, and not in the later customary presentation of goalkeeper, full-backs, half-backs and forwards. So, on occasion, the first named player may not have been an actual 'keeper for those initial games. Thankfully the universal system was soon used and match reports in the North East's press of the day began using the 1-2-3-5 formation to inform readers instead of simply a list of 11 names. Sometimes newspapers even gave a pitch arrangement showing playing positions of both sides.

Discrepancies in team line-ups from newspaper to newspaper existed. Of course, identifying players was not at all easy, decades before numbering systems were introduced, and prior to formal team returns by the clubs. Where these occur a consensus has been reached to judge which is the most likely correct line-up. A few instances in team line-ups exist where certain players with the same surname is documented, but his initial is not identified. These players are notated with an 'X' eg, *Waggott X*.

Where data has not been traced, especially for the early seasons when newspaper reports were scant of information, results, scorers, attendances, and teams are left blank. In this period, goals were often described as arriving from a "scrimmage" and where no definite goalscorer has been reported and that term used, it is included in the statistics. Appearances and goals are summarised for each season, but it should be noted that teams and scorers are derived from contemporary reports and are incomplete, especially for West End's early campaigns. Dismissals in matches were rare, but where found these are highlighted on the season record as *(d)* in team lists.

Average home attendances are included from season 1886-87 determined from the gates traced and showing the number obtained for the season, eg 12 attendances found of the 19 games played, shown as, *(12/19 games)*. However, many of the individual attendances were estimates by the reporter present at the game.

There were several instances of disputed goals and scores. Against Heaton Association during January 1885, the Heaton club won 4-2 but the score could have been 5-3 with contested goals for both sides. Typically, results were reported as "West End won by one goal to one offside goal (disputed)" or "a win for West End by 5 goals to two goals plus one disputed"! Where events such as these examples occur, a consensus of the result and scorers has been taken based sometimes on three or four versions. By 1885-86 match information started to become more comprehensive without frequent inconsistencies.

At times West End, and their opponents, played matches with only 10 men, sometimes even nine. Where this happens the team listing leaves one position vacant. Throughout, names of certain clubs have been used which are not quite the correct titles of the day. *Tyne Association* were named "Tyne AFC" and *Newcastle Rangers*, simply "Rangers AFC". Even *Newcastle West End* and *Newcastle East End*, were "West End FC" and "East End FC". But to avoid confusion, these names have been generally used. The add-on of "Association" was often employed to distinguish teams from rugby organisations until the association code held its own. Also, *The Wednesday*, was the formal title of Sheffield Wednesday up to 1929, but the city addition was generally used well before that date.

An Appendix section in the book gives an outline of the majority of now long-gone football clubs associated with West End, as opponents or connected to players.

1882-83
A MODEST BEGINNING

Newcastle West End kicked-off their football in a low-key fashion facing other relatively new clubs of a similar standing. The side's first game was an away fixture against Rosewood on 7 October 1882. There are no newspaper reports of the meeting, only the result noted, a 2-0 defeat. During November, West End played their first home game and faced the region's top club, Tyne Association, but not against the first-eleven, rather Tyne's junior side. That took place on the Town Moor near Leazes Park where West End had found a pitch, like several recently formed outfits. West End drew 0-0.

The West Enders had a modest beginning, they didn't win a game until their fifth match during early December, a 1-0 victory against Marlborough. Season 1882-83 proved a difficult first campaign in football, only winning three contests all told. Press reports were limited but they indicate that a total of 14 matches were played, mostly fixtures against humble opponents, or the second-eleven of more established clubs. Included was their first 'derby' encounter against the club West End were to be huge rivals with in the coming seasons – Byker-based, Newcastle East End. Facing their reserve line-up at the end of March, West End lost by 3-0.

As noted in the Newcastle Journal, a West End meeting was held in August 1882 to elect officers for the club's first season.

Classed as a minor or junior club, West End were allowed to enter the Northumberland & Durham Second XI Junior Competition and during February met Newcastle Association in the first round of the tournament. The outcome was another defeat, by 2-1. During the summer of 1883, the new outfit also took part in another knock-out competition, the Temperance Festival Junior Football Competition. That was played out on the Town Moor as one of several sporting activities at what was to become a hugely popular holiday carnival, to be later famously known as The Hoppings. There was no victory for West End, being eliminated at the first hurdle by Hebburn. Once more though they were not humiliated, losing 1-0 in a rather close defeat.

Key personalities during that maiden season were Billy Tiffin, the Waggott brothers – Ned and Thomas, Henry and John – as well as another pair of siblings to be involved with West End from the start, John and Walter Mather. All were born and bred in the club's neighbourhood and lived within a mile of each other around Elswick, Arthur's Hill and Westgate.

The new club held its annual meeting at Lockhart's Cocoa Rooms in Newcastle during July. There was satisfaction that while not making headlines or performing to any high standard, at least the new club from the heart of the city's west end was now up and running.

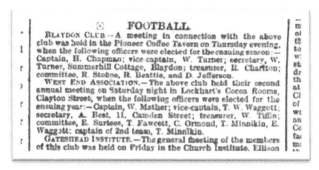

During July 1883 the Newcastle Journal reported on West End's second annual meeting at Lockart's Cocoa Rooms.

Note: West End's first captain is stated as "W Scott" however he does not appear to have played for the club, although several team line-ups are not traced. William Scott did play cricket for West End Juniors that year, also likely to be the same person who was skipper at the Newcastle Association club, joining West End's new set-up briefly before returning by the end of 1882. The father of later player William Scott (junior), both residing at Shumac Street in the heart of Elswick, Scott (senior) was described as a "bowler of repute" and "ardent supporter and diligent worker on behalf of Association football". He later became President of the Northumberland FA.

- For West End's second fixture against Heaton, unusually the press noted a 1-2-2-2-4 formation; two backs, two half-backs, two centres, two at left wing, and two at right wing. Later reports started to show a more familiar 1-2-3-5 line-up.
- Offside 'goals' even then were reported; Newcastle Association having a goal disallowed during February.
- The fixture with Hebburn Juniors at Christmas was only a nine-a-side match; West End played two backs, two half-backs and four forwards.
- West End's first venture in a cup tournament was in the Northumberland & Durham 2nd XI Junior Competition. They faced Newcastle FA 2nd XI and lost 2-1 to a contentious offside winner during the second-half.

Captain: William Scott, John Waggott.
Ground: Town Moor.

Appearances: Tiffin WWT 9, Waggott H 9, Waggott JA 9, Fawcett T 8, Surtees E 8, Best A 7, Mather W 6, Minnikin T 6, Henderson J 5, Waggott TW 5, Irwin T 4, Waggott E 4, Storey T 3, Brown X 2, Davidson R 2, Lightfoot R 2, Storey E 2, Atkinson FO 1, Brymer R 1, Graham G 1, Laws H 1, Moat W 1, Simm JT 1.
Goals: none traced.

Season 1882-83

Match			1	2	3	4	5	6	7	8	9	10	11	Match	Referee
1	07 Oct A Rosewood	L 0 2	Fawcett	Waggott J	Henderson	Waggott T	Surtees	Waggott H	Lightfoot	Mather W	Tiffin	Simm J	Best	1	
2	14 Oct A Heaton Association	L 0 1	Henderson	Waggott J	Waggott H	Brown X	Surtees	Best	Irwin	Waggott T	Waggott E	Tiffin	Fawcett	2	
3	11 Nov H Tyne Association Juniors	D 0 0 (0 0)		Waggott J	Waggott H			Waggott T	Mather W	Tiffin	Best	Tiffin		3	
4	25 Nov H Elswick Leather Works Juniors	L 0 1	Irwin	Lightfoot	Waggott H	Minnikin	Surtees	Waggott H	Waggott T	Fawcett	Tiffin	Waggott J	Best	4	
5	02 Dec A Marlborough	W 1 0	Waggott H	Mather W	Waggott J	Waggott E	Minnikin	Fawcett		Tiffin	Best		Best	5	
6	23 Dec A Hebburn Juniors	D 1 1						Fawcett		Tiffin				6	
7	30 Dec A St Cuthbert's	L 0 1												7	
8	06 Jan H Brandling	D 1 1												8	
9	13 Jan H St Cuthbert's	W 4 0	Irwin	Mather W	Waggott H	Surtees	Graham G	Storey T	Fawcett	Henderson	Tiffin	Waggott J	Best	9	
10	03 Feb A Rendel	W 1 0	Waggott H	Surtees	Waggott J	Minnikin	Laws	Henderson	Storey E	Fawcett	Tiffin	Storey T	Davidson	10	
11	17 Mar A Elswick Leather Works Juniors	D 1 1	Brinner	Waggott T	Mather W	Surtees	Minnikin	Waggott H	Fawcett	Tiffin	Best	Waggott J	Waggott E	11	
12	31 Mar A Newcastle East End 2nd XI	L 0 3												12	

Round	Northumberland & Durham FA 2nd XI Junior Competition													Round	
1	10 Feb A Newcastle FA 2nd XI	L 1 2 (1 1)	Henderson	Waggott J	Mather W	Atkinson	Surtees	Waggott H	Fawcett	Tiffin	Storey T	Storey E	Minnikin	1	J.Eden

Round	Temperance Festival Junior Competition													Round	
1	12 Jun A Hebburn	L 0 1	Irwin	Waggott J	Surtees	Minnikin	Davidson	Waggott H	Waggott E	Moat	Tiffin	Brown X	Best	1	

Match 4: Result reported as Elswick won by 1 goal to one disputed goal

Match 6: Press records show only 9 players listed for each team

Match 7: Result also reported as drawn 0-0, St.Cuthbert's goal disputed

N&D FA 2nd XI Junior Competition

Round 1: Newcastle FA also had a goal disallowed for offside in the first half

Temperance Festival Junior Competition

Round 1: Press records give two different dates for this match, 12 or 13 June

1883-84
TROPHY UP FOR GRABS

During West End's second programme of action, the club headed in the right direction, starting to look like a football club. They developed well and played almost double the number of fixtures, 24 all told. And they started to win games; recording 15 victories. Included were 7-0 and 10-0 results at Christmas and New Year against now inferior opponents, Drysdale and Brunswick, both record victories at the time. West End had moved from being one of those junior-like sides to establish the club as a developing outfit. Perhaps they had even caught up in terms of development with Newcastle East End on the other side of the city. During November they drew 1-1 with the East Enders in Byker and then won 2-0 at the end of the season in March on the Town Moor. On that occasion captain William Mather scored twice, although one of his goals was disputed.

There was little to choose between West End and East End then. The Byker club had a modicum of revenge by inflicting a 2-0 defeat on the West Enders in the Temperance Festival competition that summer. They went onto reach the final of the tournament only to lose to Sunderland

The original Northumberland Senior Cup; now a prize for local clubs.

Typical of games during those early seasons were disputes over goals. On no fewer than five occasions press reports noted arguments between the teams over the scoreline with at times the officials, then umpires – one for each side – also failing to agree. Conflicts and disagreements between clubs were not restricted to contested goals. A meeting of the Northumberland FA at the club rooms on Dean Street during October considered the alleged case of a team wanting to literally fight its opponents during the progress of a match. It was decided that in future strong measures would be taken against clubs offending in that way. Neither side was named in reports. It may have still been an amateur game, but passions ran high during those early days of football.

A representative view of football during the early 1880s showing a tape crossbar.

There was still a substantial gap with the best on Tyneside though. During January, West End faced the first-eleven of Tyne in the club's very first senior competitive match. That was a second-round tie in the newly formed Northumberland Senior Cup. West End now had silverware up for grabs, and what was at the time, a major trophy to play for. West End received a bye for the first-round but at Tyne's base at Warwick Place in Jesmond, the home side ran out handsome winners. They led 3-0 at half-time and cruised to victory scoring another four goals in the second period to win by 7-0. That heavy defeat was hardly a surprise. West End were outclassed and still had work to do.

- West End's Billy Tiffin and John Waggott earned recognition by being called up for Northumberland County trial matches during September, but were not selected. West End players though would soon be capped.
- Against Hebburn during November, West End were reported as having used illegal tape between the posts instead of the required crossbar.
- When the Drysdale club lost 7-0 to West End, they included two future stars for the West Enders, Harry Jeffrey and Jack Barker.
- Away from the football pitch, at Christmas the club enjoyed an annual dinner at the Black Bull on Barrack Road and "a capital spread was partaken by a goodly company".

Captain: Walter Mather.
Senior Cup: R2 (Winners: Tyne).
Ground: Town Moor.

Appearances: Mather W 18, Tiffin WWT 18, Waggott TW 18, Minnikin T 17, Fawcett T 16, Ormond C 16, Surtees E 16, Waggott JA 16, Best A 15, Mather JA 15, Henderson J 12, Lowe JD 5, Moat W 4, Longbottom H 2, Robson E 2, Findlay WS 1, Irwin T 1, Lawther C 1, Mason W 1, Schubert A 1, Waggott X 1, Welford JA 1.
Goals: Mather W 2, Mather JA 1.

Season 1883-84

Match	Date		Opponent	Result	1	2	3	4	5	6	7	8	9	10	11	Match	Referee
1	29 Sep	A	Birtley 2nd XI	L 0-4 (0 0)	Lawther	Waggott J	Ormond	Waggott T	Minnikin	Surtees	Mather W	Moat	Tiffin	Mather J	Fawcett	1	
2	06 Oct	A	Rendel	W 1 0	Minnikin	Ormond	Best	Schubert	Surtees	Waggott T	Fawcett	Mather J	Tiffin	Moat	Mather W	2	
3	20 Oct	H	St Cuthbert's	W 3 1	Minnikin	Waggott J	Ormond	Surtees	Waggott T	Mather J	Tiffin	Mather W	Tiffin	Fawcett	Best	3	
4	27 Oct	H	Jarrow	W 4 0	Minnikin	Waggott J	Ormond	Henderson	Waggott T	Mather J	Tiffin	Mather W	Fawcett	Best	Surtees	4	
5	03 Nov	H	Eswick Leather Works	D C 0 (0 0)	Minnikin	Waggott J	Ormond	Surtees	Waggott T	Henderson	Mather W	Tiffin	Best	Mather J	Fawcett	5	
6	10 Nov	A	Newcastle East End	D 1 1		Waggott J	Ormond	Henderson	Waggott T	Surtees	Mather J	Mather W	Tiffin	Fawcett	Longbottom	6	
7	17 Nov	A	Marlborough	D 1 1												7	
8	24 Nov	H	Hebburn	W 4 0	Minnikin	Waggott J	Ormond	Surtees	Waggott T	Henderson	Mather J	Fawcett	Tiffin	Best	Mather W	8	
9	01 Dec	A	Newcastle Rangers 2nd XI	W 1 0 (0 0)	Minnikin	Waggott J	Ormond	Surtees	Waggott T	Henderson	Mather W	Fawcett	Mather W	Best	Mather W	9	
10	08 Dec	H	Rendel	W 5 1	Minnikin	Waggott J	Ormond	Surtees	Henderson	Henderson	Lowe	Fawcett	Tiffin	Best	Finday W	10	
11	15 Dec	A	Jesmond 2nd XI	D 1 1 (1 0)	Minnikin	Waggott J	Ormond	Surtees	Waggott T	Henderson	Mather W	Tiffin	Tiffin	Best	Robson	11	
12	22 Dec	H	Drysdale	W 7 0	Minnikin	Best	Ormond	Surtees	Waggott T	Henderson	Mather W	Tiffin	Fawcett	Waggott J	Fawcett	12	
13	29 Dec	A	Jesmond 2nd XI	D 0 0 (0 0)	Minnikin	Waggott J	Lowe	Surtees	Waggott T	Ormond	Mather W	Mather W	Tiffin	Best	Fawcett	13	
14	01 Jan	H	Brunswick	W 10 0	Minnikin	Waggott J	Lowe	Waggott T	Henderson	Ormond	Mather W	Mather J	Tiffin	Best	Fawcett	14	
15	19 Jan	H	Hebburn	W 3 0	Minnikin	Waggott J	Ormond	Surtees	Waggott T	Henderson	Mather W	Mather J	Tiffin	Best	Fawcett	15	
16	02 Feb	A	St Cuthbert's	W 1 0	Minnikin	Waggott J	Ormond	Irwin	Waggott T	Henderson	Mather W	Surtees	Tiffin	Best	Best	16	
17	16 Feb	A	Eswick Leather Works	W 3 1	Minnikin	Lowe	Waggott J	Waggott T	Henderson	Waggott X	Mather W	Best	Fawcett	Mather J	Tiffin	17	
18	23 Feb	H	Birtley	W 1 0		Ormond	Best		Waggott T			Mather J				18	
19	01 Mar	A	All Saints	W 5 2						Moat						19	
20	08 Mar	A	Rosehill	L 0 1	Minnikin	Ormond	Best	Robson	Waggott T	Moat	Mather W	Mather J	Tiffin	Fawcett	Surtees	20	
21	22 Mar	H	Newcastle East End	W 2 0	Mason	Waggott J	Ormond	Longbottom	Moat	Waggott T	Tiffin	Mather W	Best	Mather J	Surtees	21	
22	11 Apr	H	Lemington Rangers	W 4 1					Waggott T	Henderson		Fawcett	Surtees			22	

Northumberland FA Senior Cup

Round					1	2	3	4	5	6	7	8	9	10	11	Round
1			bye													1
2	12 Jan	A	Tyne Association	L 0 7 (0 3)	Minnikin	Waggott J	Lowe	Wexford	Tiffin	Mather J	Mather J	Fawcett	Tiffin	Best	Fawcett	2

Temperance Festival

					1	2	3	4	5	6	7	8	9	10	11	
1	14 Jun	N	Newcastle East End	L 0 2	Minnikin	Ormond	Waggott J	Wexford	Tiffin	Mather J	Best	Fawcett	Surtees	Waggott T	Mather W	1

Match 16: Only 10 WE players listed in reports

Temperance Festival

Played on Town Moor

1884-85
SEMI-FINAL & DISPUTES

West End's improvement continued during the 1884-85 campaign. They became a stronger eleven on the pitch and were becoming noticed in the North East's rapidly expanding football scene. Once more the side won most of their programme of fixtures, still at this time mainly non-competitive friendly, or "ordinary games" as the press called them. They lost only six matches of the 26 played.

West End even defeated Tyne by 3-2 in Jesmond just before Christmas, and only lost by a solitary goal to Newcastle Rangers, although by then both pioneer clubs were on the decline and would soon be overtaken by East End and West End.

The club's small, but growing, band of supporters also enjoyed a cup run for the first time. In the Northumberland Senior Cup the West Enders reached the semi-final. Taking care of minor side North Tyne Swifts 6-1, then Newcastle Association by 2-1, they met East End in what was a cracking semi-final during March. At Dalton Street in Byker, West End were 3-1 behind at half-time to their city rivals, but battled back to earn a 3-3 draw. However, in the replay played at a neutral venue of Tyne's pitch at Warwick Place, West End collapsed and lost 5-0. Attendances for some fixtures were now being recorded in the news columns. In Byker a crowd of 1,500 saw that Senior Cup meeting, while in Jesmond for the replay an estimated 600 gathered around the pitch.

Newcastle East End (later Newcastle United) pictured with the Senior Cup in 1885, they were the first of the city rivals to lift a trophy. West End would soon follow.

There were plenty of disputes on the field again. One fixture against Heaton as January began, illustrates the frequent quarrels which took place at that time. From a number of newspapers that reported on the game, it appears the home side defeated West End by 4-2, but the West Enders disputed one of their goals and also claimed one which the umpire did not allow. West End's

own report noted that their goal, "was undoubtedly obtained in a fair manner but the shot being low and darkness setting in, the goalkeeper protested that the ball went past a post instead of through".

The umpire, who was nearest at the time, gave it as a goal, but the other umpire would not give his decision in favour of the point. The captains could not agree either and play was not continued, both sides waiting until the call of time before leaving the field. West End maintained the score should have been 3-3. Heaton emphatically disagreed. Seemingly, goal nets were not being used, even though Football Association rules dictated they should be in place.

Another fixture against Newcastle FA 'B' resulted in a 5-0 West End victory but it was reported that they had placed the ball through the posts on no fewer than 10 occasions, yet only five goals were awarded. The other five were ruled out for offside.

West End also took part for the third time in the Temperance Festival football tournament during the summer. They reached the semi-final stage again, but lost to Bedlington Burdon in what could be termed an end-to-end meeting that finished 5-4.

The Waggotts and Mathers as well as Billy Tiffin continued to be at the core of the side. Tommy Minnikin, Joe Welford and Ed Surtees were also now regulars.

- Against Rendel in December, West End played with only 10 men and still won 3-2 with disputed goals for each side.
- Following the visit to play Shankhouse Blues in mid-December, it was reported that after the match the home side "kindly entertained the West End to an excellent tea and a pleasant evening was spent".
- The Senior Cup match during February, against Newcastle FA, was the subject of a Newcastle protest about the referee, but West End's opponents lost their petition.
- When Rosehill faced West End at the start of November, they included "T Watson" in the side, to become West End and East End secretary and later renowned with both Sunderland and Liverpool.

Captain: John Mather, John Waggott.
Senior Cup: Semi-final (Winners: Newcastle East End).
Ground: Town Moor.

Appearances: Tiffin WWT 22, Waggott TW 21, Waggott E 20, Welford JA 19, Best A 17, Mather W 17, Waggott JA 16, Minnikin T 15, Fawcett T 14, Ormond C 12, Surtees E 12, Mather JA 8, Stewart E 8, Amory J 6, Lambert G 5, Moat W 4, Barker J 2, Douglas JR 2, Laws H 2, Lawther C 2, McDougall R 2, Oldham RA 2, Storey E 2, Fish A 1, Frazer JW 1, Harrison W 1, Irwin T 1, Jones JS 1, Lowe JD 1, Proctor D 1, Smith X 1, Tindle 1, Waggott H 1, Wynn E 1.
Goals: Tiffin WWT 5, Mather W 3, Welford JA 2, Surtees E 1, (unknown 1).

Season 1884-85

Match	Date		Opponent	Result		1	2	3	4	5	6	7	8	9	10	11	Notes
1	20 Sep	A	Heaton Association	W 3-2		Laws	Waggott J	Ormond	Waggott T	Minnikin	Waggott E	Welford	Fawcett	Tiffin	Best	Surtees	
2	27 Sep	H	Lemington Rangers	D 1-1		Laws	Waggott J	Ormond	Waggott T	Minnikin	Waggott E	Welford	Surtees	Tiffin	Best	Fawcett	
3	04 Oct	H	Rendel	W 3-1		Minnikin	Amory	Ormond	Harrison	Lowe	Smith X	Waggott E	Surtees	Tiffin	Best	Fawcett	
4	11 Oct	H	Newcastle Rangers	L 0-1		Minnikin	Wynn	Ormond	Amory	Waggott E	Waggott T	Welford	Tiffin	Mather W	Best	Frazer	Mather W
5	01 Nov	A	Rosehill	W 1-0		Minnikin	Amory	Ormond	Waggott T	Waggott E	Waggott T	Moat	Fish	Mather W	Tiffin	Fawcett	
6	08 Nov	A	Lemington Rangers	W 4-0		Stewart E	Amory	Ormond	Waggott T	Waggott E	Minnikin	Moat	Fish	Mather W	Best	Fawcett	
7	15 Nov	H	Whitburn	W 5-2		Stewart E	Douglas	Best	Waggott T	Minnikin	Waggott E	Tiffin	Waggott J	Mather W	Lawther	Fawcett	
8	22 Nov	A	Ovingham	W 1-0 (1 0)		Minnikin	Waggott J	Best	Waggott T	Moat	Waggott E	Welford	Tiffin	Mather W	Moat	Fawcett	Tiffin
9	06 Dec	A	Rendel	W 3-2 (3 1)		Minnikin	Waggott J	Stewart E	Waggott T	Storey E	Waggott E	Welford	Tiffin	Mather W	Best	Fawcett	
10	13 Dec	A	Shankhouse Blues	W 1-0 (0 0)		Minnikin	Waggott H	Stewart E	Waggott T	Amory	Waggott E	Welford	Tiffin	Irwin	Best	Fawcett	Tiffin
11	20 Dec	H	Tyne Association	W 3-2 (2 1)		Minnikin	Waggott J	Proctor	Waggott T	Stewart E	Waggott E	Welford	Tiffin	Mather W	Best	Fawcett	Tiffin
12	27 Dec	H	Newcastle FA B	W 5-0 (3 0)		Minnikin	Waggott J	Douglas	Waggott T	Surtees	Waggott E	Welford	Tiffin	Mather W	Best	Fawcett	
13	03 Jan	A	Heaton Association	L 2-4 (1 2)		Minnikin	Waggott J	Waggott T	Mather J	Waggott E	Surtees	Welford	Tiffin	Mather W	Best	Fawcett	
14	24 Jan	H	North Eastern	W 5-1 (2 0)		Minnikin	Waggott J	Lambert	Mather J	Waggott E	Waggott E	Welford	Tiffin	Mather W	Best	Lawther	Tiffin 2, Mather W 2, Welford
15	31 Jan	H	Newcastle FA	W 2-1		Fawcett	Waggott J	Lambert	Waggott T	Best	Waggott E	Welford	Tiffin	Mather W	Stewart E	Jones J	
16	04 Apr	H	Heaton Athletic	W 5-2		Oldham	Amory	Ormond	Waggott T	Moat	Storey E	Welford	Tiffin	Mather W	Stewart E	Lawther	
17	06 Apr	A	Tantobie	W 4-1		Oldham	Amory	Best	Waggott T	Moat	Waggott E	Welford	Tiffin	Mather W	Stewart E	Jones J	

Northumberland FA Senior Cup

Round	Date		Opponent	Result		1	2	3	4	5	6	7	8	9	10	11	Notes	Referee
1			bye															
2	07 Feb	N	North Tyne Swifts	W 6-1		Waggott E	Ormond	Lambert	Mather J	Waggott J	Waggott T	Welford	Tiffin	Mather W	Best	Surtees		
3	21 Feb	N	Newcastle FA	W 2-1		Ormond	Lambert	Waggott J	Waggott T	Mather J	Waggott E	Welford	Tiffin	Mather W	Surtees	Best		J Morrison
sf	07 Mar	A	Newcastle East End	D 3-3 (1 3) 1500		Ormond	Waggott J	Lambert	Waggott T	Mather J	Waggott E	Welford	Tiffin	Mather W	Surtees	Best	Welford, Surtees, unknown	
sfr	14 Mar	N	Newcastle East End	L 0-5 (0 2) 600		Ormond	Waggott J	Lambert	Mather J	Waggott E	Waggott T	Welford	Tiffin	Mather W	Surtees	Fawcett		

Northumberland & Tyne Charity Shield

	Date		Opponent	Result													Referee
	26 Mar	A	Rosehill	L 0-1													J Phillips

Temperance Festival

Round	Date		Opponent	Result		1	2	3	4	5	6	7	8	9	10	11
p1	13 Jun	A	Shankhouse Blues	W 2-1		Minnikin	Waggott J	McDougall	Waggott T	Mather J	Waggott E	Welford	Tiffin	Mather W	Barker	Surtees
p2	27 Jun	H	Rendel	W 3-0		Minnikin	Waggott J	McDougall	Waggott T	Mather J	Waggott E	Welford	Tiffin	Mather W	Barker	Surtees
sf	01 Jul	N	Bedlington Burdon	L 4-5												
3 place	01 Jul	N	Newcastle East End B	L 1-3												

Northumberland FA Senior Cup
Round 2: Played at Abbotsfield Terrace
Round 3 and sfr: Played at Warwick Place

Temperance Festival
sf: Played as two halves of 30 mins
sf and 3 place: Played on Town Moor

1885-86
NEW TYNESIDE FORCE

Times were changing in Newcastle as the old guard of Tyne and Rangers were all but dead and buried. Football was developing fast and several of the new breed of clubs started to become a force in the region. Newcastle West End were one of three or four clubs on Tyneside to show up well – alongside the East Enders who were to shortly move to a new ground on the Heaton and Byker border. Three years ago, Tyne were pre-eminent in the whole North East and gave West End a lesson in how the association code should be played. Now West End were the ones in the ascendancy; they won 6-0 in a meeting during October.

On Wearside, the Sunderland club was now evolving rapidly and West End first played them during February and March. Sunderland were just too strong, but not by much, winning both encounters by a single goal. Overall though, the side's record was more than decent during the campaign; winning 12 of the 24 fixtures, although a 6-1 defeat by East End during November was a chastening experience.

West End enjoyed another excellent run in the Northumberland Senior Cup, this time reaching their first final. They had to face East End during January en-route and West End were out for revenge. They had drawn 2-2 in another meeting on Boxing Day so the team was in a confident mood. And West End started with a bang, Walter Mather scoring after only two minutes of play. His brother John made it 2-0 and although their Byker rivals pulled a goal back, West End held out for a 2-1 victory.

RULES

1 – That this Club be called "THE NEWCASTLE WEST END FOOTBALL CLUB".

2 – That this Club play according to the Rules of the English Football Association.

3 – That the Club be governed by a Committee, consisting of the Captain and Vice-Captain of each Team, Secretary and Treasurer, and six ordinary Members, five of whom shall form a quorum.

4 – That the subscription for the Season be 4s for seniors, and 1s 6d, for juniors, payable on or before September 30th.

5 – Anyone not paying his Subscription, within the time specified, will become liable to be debarred from playing until he has paid.

6 – That the Captain, Vice, and another Member choose the Eleven to play in Matches.

7 – That the Captain, or in his absence, the Vice-Captain shall have control of the Team while playing and shall have power to suspend any Member for refusing to obey his orders, until the offence has been brought before the Committee.

8 – That the Committee meet every alternative Wednesday, commencing the first Wednesday in October.

9 – That a General Meeting be held in April or May each year, when all Officers for the ensuing Season shall be elected.

10 – That no foul language be allowed on the field.

Newcastle West End's official rules in 1886.

Rendel were taken care of in the next round then West End were tied with Backworth in the semi-final. On a snow-covered pitch, West End eased into the final to be played on 10th April. A crowd of 2,000 gathered at Tyne's arena in Jesmond for the showpiece final with Shankhouse, one of region's best line-ups at the time. Although West End performed with credit, the pitmen were superior and won by 3-2.

One player stood out and began to make an impact over season 1885-86, forward Jack Barker. He was to serve the club in sterling fashion over the next five seasons. Jack Taylor at full-back was also a fixture in the line-up, another long-serving player.

West End found a new ground during the season. Following a contentious ban on playing football on the Town Moor, the club was one of several that had to search for a new base. West End relocated to the old Jesmond FC ground near Brandling Park. It was only a short stopover though, as they found another home for the start of the following season.

At the end of a satisfying campaign, club officials gathered to carry out the usual election of management. There was an important appointment, that of Tom Watson as secretary – effectively the man to control affairs. He was to have a huge influence on West End. When Tom arrived, while the club were performing well on the field, they had what was described as "neither a sou in the bank nor an enclosed ground to play on". That changed rapidly with Watson in control.

- During September West End took part in the Benwell seven-a-side tournament. They won the first tie against North Eastern 3-0, but were eliminated in the next round by Elswick Ordnance Works.
- Paired with Cathedral in the Senior Cup opening round during January, on the day of the match, only nine of the opposition turned up and they refused to play. West End were duly awarded a bye.
- When Shankhouse faced West End in the Senior Cup final, they were deemed to also be representing Morpeth Harriers after the two clubs could not be separated in the semi-final having played five games. Black Watch and Harriers eventually shared the trophy.
- Temperance Festival Football during June saw 15 clubs compete in the senior competition, 16 for the Second XI and 19 at Junior level. While West End lost in the seniors, their 'A' side reached the final but fell to Bedlington Burdon.

Captain: John Waggott, Joseph Welford.
Senior Cup: Final (Winners: Shankhouse Black Watch).
Ground: Town Moor & Abbotsfield Terrace, Jesmond.

Appearances: Barker J 20, McDougall R 20, Waggott E 20, Mather JA 18, Mather W 18, Waggott JA 18, Tiffin WWT 17, Taylor J 16, Welford JA 16, Douglas JR 10, Surtees E 8, Telford W 8, Pape R 4, Angus JW 3, Miller C 3, Minnikin T 3, Moat W 3, Waggott TW 3, Brown WE 2, Best A 1, Bouckley J 1, Davison W 1, Forster X 1, Jeffrey H 1, Mason W 1, Morris A 1, Waggott X 1, Watson WJ 1.
Goals: Welford JA 3, Mather JA 2, Mather W 2, Mather JA or W 1, Tiffin WWT 1.

Season 1885-86

Match	Date	V	Opponent	Result	Att/Note	1	2	3	4	5	6	7	8	9	10	11	Match	Referee
1	12 Sep	H	Brunswick														1	
2	19 Sep	N	North-Eastern	W 3 0													2	
3	19 Sep	N	Elswick Ordnance Works	L 1 2	1000												3	
4	26 Sep	A	Shankhouse Black Watch	L 1 2		Miller C	Waggott J	Taylor	McDougall	Mather J	Waggott E	Welford	Tiffin	Barker	Moat	Mather W	4	
5	03 Oct	H	Newcastle FA	W 4 0		Miller C	Waggott J	Taylor	McDougall	Mather J	Waggott E	Welford	Tiffin	Mather W	Surtees	Barker	5	
6	17 Oct	A	Tyne Association	W 6 0 (6 0)		Miller C	Waggott J	Taylor	McDougall	Mather J	Surtees	Welford	Tiffin	Mather W	Barker	Waggott E	6	
7	07 Nov	A	Ovingham			Telford	Waggott J	Taylor	McDougall	Mather J	Bouckley	Welford	Tiffin	Best	Surtees	Barker	7	
8	14 Nov	N	Newcastle East End	L 1 6		Telford	Waggott J	Taylor	McDougall	Mather J	Waggott E	Welford	Tiffin	Mather W	Surtees	Barker	8	
9	21 Nov	A	Rosehill	W 5 1 (1 0)		Telford	Waggott J	Waggott X	McDougall	Mather J	Waggott T	Welford	Tiffin	Mather W	Surtees	Barker	9	
10	28 Nov	H	Morpeth Harriers	D 1 1 (0 1)	Welford	Telford	Waggott J	Taylor	Waggott E	McDougall	Waggott T	Welford	Tiffin	Mather W	Surtees	Barker	10	
11	05 Dec	H	Elswick Ordnance Works	W 6 0		Telford	Waggott J	Taylor	Waggott E	McDougall	Waggott T	Surtees	Barker	Mather W	Welford	Tiffin	11	
12	26 Dec	A	Newcastle East End	D 2 2 (1 2)		Telford	Douglas	Taylor	Waggott E	McDougall	Waggott T	Mather J	Surtees	Mather J	Tiffin	Tiffin	12	
13	01 Jan	H	Melbourne (Middlesbrough)	W 2 0		Jeffrey	Taylor	Douglas	Waggott E	Waggott J	McDougall	Welford	Barker	Mather W	Tiffin	Barker	13	
14	02 Jan	A	Heaton Association	W 3 0		Mason	Waggott J	Brown W	McDougall	Mather J	Waggott E	Welford	Moat	Mather W	Pape	Barker	14	
15	13 Feb	A	Sunderland	L 0 1 (0 0)		Douglas	Waggott J	Davison	McDougall	Waggott E	Taylor	Pape	Waggott E	Mather W	Barker	Tiffin	15	
16	09 Mar	A	Sunderland	L 1 2 (1 0)	Mather W	Minnikin	Taylor	Moat	McDougall	Waggott J	Douglas	Welford	Waggott J	Mather W	Pape	Barker	16	
17	13 Mar	H	Elswick Leather Works	L 1 3 (0 0)	500, Mather X	Minnikin	Waggott T	Douglas	McDougall	Mather J	Waggott E	Welford	Waggott J	Mather W	Pape	Barker	17	
18	27 Mar	A	Steelburn Wanderers	W 3 1		Waggott E	Forster X	Douglas	McDougall	Mather J	Waggott J		Angus	Mather W	Tiffin	Barker	18	

Northumberland FA Senior Cup

Round	Date	V	Opponent	Result	Att/Note	1	2	3	4	5	6	7	8	9	10	11	Round	Referee
1	16 Jan	H	Cathedral	W	be awarded to WE												1	
2	30 Jan	A	Newcastle East End	W 2 1 (2 1)	300, Mather W, Mather J	Telford	Waggott J	Douglas	McDougall	Mather J	Waggott E	Welford	Taylor	Mather W	Tiffin	Barker	2	W Wood
3	06 Feb	H	Rendel	W 3 2 (1 2)		Telford	Waggott J	Douglas	McDougall	Mather J	Taylor	Welford	Waggott E	Mather W	Tiffin	Barker	3	
sf	20 Feb	N	Backworth Hotspur	W 2 0 (0 0)	400, Welford, Mather J	Minnikin	Taylor	Douglas	McDougall	Mather J	Waggott E	Welford	Waggott J	Mather W	Tiffin	Barker	sf	G Hall
f	10 Apr	N	Shankhouse Black Watch	L 2 3 (1 1)	2000, Welford, Tiffin	Waggott E	Taylor	Douglas	McDougall	Mather J	Waggott J	Welford	Angus	Mather W	Tiffin	Barker	f	W Scott.

Northumberland & Tyne Charity Shield

	Date	V	Opponent	Result		1	2	3	4	5	6	7	8	9	10	11		Referee
sf	24 Apr	N	Morpeth Harriers	L 0 2 (0 0)		Watson	Taylor	Brown W	McDougall	Waggott E	Morris	Mather J	Angus	Mather W	Tiffin	Barker	sf	W/A Lochhead

Temperance Festival

	Date	V	Opponent	Result														Referee
1	12 Jun	A	Shankhouse Black Watch	L 0 2													1	R Bellwood

Matches 1 and 11 : Played on Town Moor

Matches 2 (sf) and 3 (f) : Benwell Football Tournament, played at Benwell

Match 8 : Played at Warwick Place

Match 13 : Played at Moor Edge, Brandling

Match 17 : WE disputed Elswick's third goal and left the field 5 mins before time was up

Match 18 : WE turned up 2 men short. Forster of Steelburn played as one substitute and WE played with 10 men throughout

Northumberland FA Senior Cup

Round 1 : Cathedral turned up with 9 men and refused to play. Tie awarded to WE

Rounds 2, sf, f : Played at Warwick Place

Round 3 : Played at Abbotsfield Terrace

Northumberland & Tyne Charity Shield

Played at Warwick Place. After extra time, score at full-time 0-0

1886-87
ST JAMES' PARK HOME

Up to now the West Enders had relied on local footballers, mainly born and bred in the neighbourhood. By the summer of 1886, the club had grown to such a level that ambitions were much greater and as a result they attracted footballers from not only the wider Tyneside area, but from the rest of the country...notably from Scotland. As a result of strict amateur rules north of the border, Scottish players – big names included – began to transfer to England where they could be paid for playing football.

West End made headlines when they signed up Scotland capped winger Ralph Aitken during September. It was a huge coup; he was the very first international footballer to arrive on Tyneside. It was noted by the pen-named correspondent *Custos* in the *Newcastle Daily Journal* that "West End seem determined to make themselves the 'boss' club of the area and I am sure the plucky West Enders will deserve every bit of success they get".

Other Scots began to land on Tyneside for that season to join Aitken, including Jack Angus, two McDonalds, James Raylstone and J Chalmers. All were relatively successful, Glaswegian Angus hitting 13 goals for West End during the programme. More, many more were to follow. One comment in the *Newcastle Daily Chronicle* noted "the public prefer good foreign to bad native talent". One notable local addition to the ranks was Alnwick's full-back James Duns. He was a top defender.

There was an added development at the club too. During the close-season West End moved from their temporary pitch in Jesmond to the former ground of Newcastle Rangers, St James' Park. That was a major event, at last the club had somewhere they could call a real home. Another factor that showed West End's increasing stature was that opponents to their new base now included clubs from out of the North East. To arrive were noted Scottish teams, Dumbarton Athletic, Albion Rovers and St Bernard's. Derby St Luke's also travelled from the Midlands. And Britain's very top clubs were soon to take to the field at St James' Park, especially for Easter and festive holiday attractions.

For the second year running West End met Shankhouse in the final of the Senior Cup – and once more they lost to the Northumbrians, this time heavily by 5-1. On the way, Tyne were given another hiding as West End won 6-0.

Perhaps the most notable point in the season was the club's first entry into the FA Cup – or as it was termed back then, the "English Cup". At the end of October, they were paired with Sunderland and a controversial tie was played out at the Wearsiders' Newcastle Road ground. West End lost narrowly 2-1 in front of a big 4,500 crowd, but they lodged a successful protest due to a late winning goal being scored in failing light as extra-time was being played.

The Sunderland Echo advertised the 'English Cup' match between Sunderland and West End.

In the replay at St James' Park, a headed goal in the last 10 minutes from Jack Angus sent the Geordies through, Sunderland protesting unsuccessfully this time. The attendance was a very healthy 4,000, the biggest for a home game by some distance. Then West End faced Gainsborough Trinity, a strong team from Lincolnshire, but lost 6-2.

- West End's first game at their new base of St James' Park took place on 2nd October 1886 against East End. Thomas Bell, the Sheriff of Newcastle, formally opened the ground and 2,000 watched a 3-2 victory with Jack Barker striking a hat-trick.
- In that debut match at St James' Park, some reports noted that Barker registered the opening goal with a high shot, but others related that the honour fell to Ralph Aitken.
- When West End defeated Sunderland in the FA Cup, the Wearsiders lodged a three-point objection; that the winning goal was scored direct from a corner, the Cup Committee having no right to order a replay, and that West End's side was partly comprised of professionals who were not qualified. All were rejected.

Captain: John Mather, James Duns.
FA Cup: R2 (Winners: Aston Villa).
Senior Cup: Final (Winners: Shankhouse Black Watch).
Ground: St James' Park.
Average Home Attendance: 1,442, top crowd 4,000 (12/19 games).

Appearances: Taylor J 27, Angus JW 26, Barker J 26, Chalmers J 25, Oldham RA 21, Duns J 20, Raylstone JB 18, Campbell A 17, Swinburne W 15, Tiffin WWT 15, McDonald J 11, Aitken RA 10, McDonald A 10, Mather JA 9, Waggott JA 8, Boswell W 5, Mather W 5, Waggott E 5, Welford JA 5, Dobson TK 4, Laing W 4, Minnikin T 4, Wardale JD 4, Thompson H 3, Douglas JR 2, Surtees E 2, Thompson John 2, Wardropper JosW 2, Amory J 1, Beattie JW 1, Cameron J/W 1, Dewar J 1, Ferguson J 1, Figures WH 1, Forster R 1, Fotheringham J 1, Galbraith J 1, Gall J 1, Gardiner S 1, Guild G 1, Hayes J 1, Hendry A 1, Jeffrey H 1, Matthews W 1, Morris A 1, McGirl E 1, McLeod D 1, Rule WY 1, Sutherland DJ 1, Thompson WP 1, Waggott TW 1, Williams J 1, (others 1).
Goals: Angus JW 13, Raylstone JB 9, Barker J 8, McDonald J 7, Tiffin WWT 7, Aitken RA 4, McDonald A 4, Boswell W 3, Campbell A 2, Dobson TK 1, Laing W 1, Mather W 1, Minnikin T 1, Oldham RA 1, Swinburne W 1, Taylor J 1, Thompson WP 1, og 1.

Season 1886-87

Match	Date		Opponent	Result						Att	Scorers	1	2	3	4	5	6	7	8	9	10	11	Match	Referee
1	18 Sep	A	Morpeth Harriers	W	4	1	(1	0)			Aitken 2, Tiffin, Angus	Oldham	Taylor	Chalmers	Waggott E	Mather J	Campbell	Barker	Tiffin	Mather W	Angus	Aitken	1	
2	25 Sep	A	Newcastle FA	W	2	1						Cameron	Chalmers	Douglas	Waggott E	Mather J	Campbell	Figures	Morris	Mather W	Barker	Angus	2	
3	02 Oct	H	Newcastle East End	W	3	2	(2	0)		2000	Barker 3	Oldham	Taylor	Chalmers	Waggott E	Mather J	Campbell	Angus	Tiffin	Mather W	Barker	Aitken	3	J Phillips
4	09 Oct	H	Elswick Rangers	W	4	1	(0	1)		600	Barker, Mather W, Angus, Aitken	Oldham	Taylor	Ferguson J	Campbell	Mather J	Chalmers	Angus	Tiffin	Mather W	Barker	Aitken	4	AP Arnold
5	16 Oct	A	Bishop Auckland Church Institute	L	0	4	(0	1)		800		Oldham	Duns	Douglas	Welford	Mather J	Chalmers	Angus	Tiffin	Mather W	Barker	Aitken	5	J Wilkinson
6	23 Oct	H	Gateshead Association	W	10	1	(8	0)		500	Angus, unknown 9	Oldham	Duns	Taylor	Campbell	Mather J	Chalmers	Dobson	Welford	Angus	Barker	Aitken	6	
7	27 Nov	A	Sunderland	L	0	1	(C	0)		6000		Minnikin	Duns	Taylor	Waggott J	Beattie	Chalmers	Angus	Tiffin	McGirl	Barker	Aitken	7	
8	04 Dec	H	Newcastle FA	W	2	0				400		Minnikin	Waggott J	Duns	Hayes	Taylor	Waggott E	Welford	Barker	Angus	Tiffin	Gardiner	8	
9	11 Dec	A	Elswick Rangers	L	1	5	(C	2)			Barker	Oldham	Taylor	Duns	Chalmers	Waggott J	Waggott J	Barker	Tiffin	Angus	Surtees	Gall	9	
10	18 Dec	H	Bishop Auckland Church Institute	W	1	0					Laing	Oldham	Duns	Taylor	Swinburne	Laing	Chalmers	Barker	McDonald A	Raylstone	Tiffin	Angus	10	
11	25 Dec	H	Shankhouse Black Watch	W	2	1	(1	1)		1500	Tiffin, Raylstone	Oldham	Taylor	AN Other	Waggott J	Laing	Campbell	Barker	McDonald A	Raylstone	Tiffin	Waggott E	11	RM Bellwood
12	29 Dec	H	Darlington St Augustine's	L	1	2																	12	
13	01 Jan	H	Dumbarton Athletic	D	1	3	(1	3)		1000	Angus	Forster R	Warcropper Jos	Duns	Swinburne	Laing	Campbell	Barker	McDonald A	Raylstone	Angus	Aitken	13	RM Bellwood
14	04 Jan	H	Albion Rovers	W	4	0	(E	0)			Angus	Minnikin	Taylor	Hendry	Dewar J	Campbell	Fotheringham	Angus	McDonald A	Raylstone	McLeod D	Galbraith	14	J Phillips
15	12 Feb	H	Durham University	W	2	1	(1	1)		800	McDonald A, Raylstone 2, Angus	Oldham	Jeffrey	Taylor	Swinburne	Campbell	Chalmers	Barker	Barker	Boswell	McDonald J	Angus	15	J Oliver
16	02 Apr	H	Middlesbrough	L	1	3	(1	2)		2000	Boswell, Angus	Oldham	Duns	Taylor	Swinburne	Raylstone	Chalmers	Warcaile	Barker	Boswell	McDonald J	Angus	16	J Phillips
17	08 Apr	H	Edinburgh St Bernard's	W	5	1	(3	1)			McDonald J	Oldham	Duns	Taylor	Swinburne	Raylstone	Chalmers	Warcaile	Barker	Boswell	McDonald J	Angus	17	J Phillips
18	09 Apr	H	Redcar	W	5	1	(3	1)			McDonald J, Barker, og, unknown 2	Thompson H	Chalmers	Taylor	Swinburne	Guild	Sutherland	Barker	Thompson Jn	Raylstone	McDonald J	Angus	18	
19	12 Apr	H	Derby St Luke's	L	0	2	(0	0)		1000		Oldham	Taylor	Chalmers	Swinburne	Raylstone	Waggott T	Warcaile	Welford	Surtees	McDonald J	Thompson Jn	19	J Phillips
20	16 Apr	A	Darlington	D	2	2	(2	2)			Boswell, McDonald J 2	Thompson H	Duns	Taylor	Swinburne	Raylstone	Chalmers	Boswell	Waggott J	Matthews	McDonald J	Williams	20	J Glover
21	02 May	H	Gateshead Association	W	4	1	(:	0)		500	Angus, Taylor	Oldham	Duns	Warcropper Jos	Swinburne	Raylstone	Chalmers	Barker	Taylor	Tiffin	McDonald J	Angus	21	
22	07 May	H	Darlington St Augustine's	W	4	1	(:	0)		500	Barker, Angus, McDonald J 2	Oldham	Duns	Warcaile	Rule	Raylstone	Chalmers	Barker	Taylor	Boswell	McDonald J	Angus	22	
23	09 Jul	A	Ashington Rising Star	W	4	1	(:	4)		4000	Thompson W, Boswell, Minnikin, McDonald J	Thompson H	Taylor	Taylor	Swinburne	Raylstone	Minnikin	Barker	Tiffin	Boswell	McDonald J	Thompson W	23	EH Metcalf

FA Cup

Match	Date		Opponent	Result					Att	Scorers	1	2	3	4	5	6	7	8	9	10	11	Match	Referee
1	30 Oct	A	Sunderland	L	1	2	(:	1)	4500	Campbell	Oldham	Duns	Waggott J	Campbell	Mather J	Chalmers	Dobson	Welford	Angus	Barker	Aitken	1	
1r	13 Nov	H	Sunderland	W	1	0	(0	0)	4000	Angus	Oldham	Taylor	Duns	Swinburne	Mather J	Dobson	Dobson	Campbell	Angus	Tiffin	Aitken	1r	Mr Darley
2	20 Nov	N	Gainsborough Trinity	L	1	6	(3	4)	3000	Aitken, Dobson	Armory	Taylor	Duns	Waggott J	Mather J	Chalmers	Dobson	Campbell	Angus	Barker	Aitken	2	J Glover

Northumberland FA Senior Cup

Match	Date		Opponent	Result					Att	Scorers	1	2	3	4	5	6	7	8	9	10	11	Match	Referee
1	22 Jan	A	Tyne Association	W	6	0	(1	0)		Raylstone 3, McDonald A, Oldham, Tiffin	Oldham	Taylor	Swinburne	Campbell	Chalmers	Barker	McDonald A	Raylstone	Tiffin	Angus		1	G Hall
2	29 Jan	H	Prudhoe Rovers	W	6	0	(0	0)		Angus, Tiffin 2, Raylstone 2, Campbell	Oldham	Taylor	Swinburne	Campbell	Chalmers	Barker	McDonald A	Raylstone	Tiffin	Angus		2	NP Pattinson
3	05 Feb	A	Rendel	W	3	1	(3	0)	600	Tiffin 2, Barker	Oldham	Duns	Taylor	Swinburne	Campbell	Chalmers	Barker	McDonald A	Raylstone	Tiffin	Angus	3	J Phillips
sf	05 Mar	H	Morpeth Harriers	W	5	0	(0	0)	3000	Angus 2, McDonald A 2, Raylstone	Oldham	Duns	Taylor	Swinburne	Campbell	Chalmers	Barker	McDonald A	Raylstone	McDonald J	Angus	sf	W Scott
f	19 Mar	N	Shankhouse Black Watch	L	1	5	(0	3)	5000	Swinburne	Oldham	Duns	Taylor	Swinburne	Campbell	Chalmers	Barker	McDonald A	Raylstone	McDonald J	Angus	f	W Scott

Temperance Festival

Match	Date		Opponent	Result			Referee
	12 Jun	A	Shankhouse Black Watch	L	0	2	RM Bellwood

FA Cup
Round 1: After extra-time, score at full-time 1-1. WE lodged a complaint about having to play extra-time in darkness, upheld by the FA who ordered a replay
Round 1 replay: Sunderland lodged a complaint, rejected by FA
Round 2: Some reports record the score as 2-5

Northumberland FA Senior Cup
Round 1: By the time goalkeeper Oldham scored, he and Duns had exchanged positions
sf and sf r: Played at Heaton Junction
sf: Goals by A McDonald, may be J McDonald, reports differ

1887-88
FIRST TROPHY WIN

For season 1887-88 more Scots arrived at St James' Park. Ralph Aitken headed back to Dunbartonshire but in his place came four more than decent players; goalkeeper Tom Fyfe, Bob McDermid at the back as well as forwards Donald McColl and Tom Nicholson. Jack Angus continued to be a danger up front, scoring 20 goals in the campaign. Hexham-born Billy Swinburne became an automatic choice at half-back, an important player over the next three seasons.

The club's new line-up showed up well for the most part and West End did lift their first trophy after a successful run in the Senior Cup – their third final in a row. Remarkably they met Shankhouse again and it was third time lucky for the West Enders during March. They won 6-3 in front of 7,000 at the Heaton Junction Ground. On the way to that victory, West End recorded the club's highest ever scoreline when they thrashed North Eastern 15-0. It was noted that they "bombarded the North Eastern goal" and that 'keeper Fyfe joined the forward-line during the closing minutes. As a bonus, soon afterwards, West End also secured the Tyne Charity Shield, again winning against Shankhouse.

There was now a double Tyne versus Wear clash, West End had not only Sunderland to face, but breakaway and bitter rivals Sunderland Albion as well. Five games were played against the two clubs, including another FA Cup tie. A huge crowd for the time of 8,000 saw Sunderland defeat West End 3-1 at their Newcastle Road base, this after Donald McColl had put the Geordies in front. The pick of those early derby matches though was in the Northumberland & Durham Inter County Challenge Cup. At the end of April with home advantage in West End's favour and with the backing of a 6,000 crowd, the Wearsiders still won 2-0.

West End now faced two clubs from Wearside, Sunderland and Sunderland Albion. Pictured are Sunderland in September 1887, a line-up which included West Ender Sam Stewart (second left, front row).

More clubs from Scotland faced West End on Tyneside, including Scottish Cup holders Hibernian. But the management's biggest feat was arranging the visit of West Bromwich Albion during April. They had reached the FA Cup final three times in succession and had lifted the trophy only 10 days before. The Midland side gave a football lesson by winning 5-1 in front of 6,000.

West End also ventured out of the North East that season, first to Edinburgh to face St Bernard's then a longer trip to Lincolnshire where they met last season's FA Cup opponents Gainsborough Trinity during November. There was still a way to go to compete with the rest of the country's better teams, West End losing most of the exhibition-style games. But they were on the right tracks as the 1-1 draw with Trinity showed. As a huge bonus attendances were on the rise, and with it cash receipts. Gates almost doubled now they were settled at St James' Park.

West End's future looked bright. They were undoubtedly at that point the best on Tyneside, superior that season than now arch rivals, Newcastle East End. Their policy of bringing in imports from Scotland was working. Yet they lost the influential Tom Watson just before Christmas when he decided to join their foes at Heaton. The club's management never really found an adequate replacement to look after business on and off the field. And those Caledonians on the pitch would not always be the answer.

- Season-tickets were available to West End supporters at a price of 4s 0d (20p).
- A meeting with neighbours Elswick Rangers during November was never finished as rage among spectators saw a crowd invasion after an on-pitch confrontation between George McKay of Rangers and Jack Barker. The game was abandoned at 2-2.
- During the season West End announced they were going to make all 'native' players professionals – a native footballer being one who had lived in the district long enough to qualify to play in Cup matches.
- During December against Shankhouse, West End fielded one of the game's foremost players, Scotland's Watty Arnott who was visiting Newcastle. He played only around an hour before he had to catch a train north.

Captain: John Wardale, William Swinburne, Edward Surtees, Jack Barker.
FA Cup: R2 (Winners: West Bromwich Albion).
Senior Cup: Winners.
Ground: St James' Park.
Average Home Attendance: 2,689, top crowd 6,000 (9/21 games).

Appearances: McDonald J 36, Fyfe T 34, Swinburne W 34, McColl D 32, Raylstone JB 32, Barker J 31, Angus JW 30, McDermid R 28, Taylor J 27, Nicholson T 24, Smart J, 22, Jeffrey H 11, Davidson R 10, Duns J 9, Brady A 8, Grant J 5, Scott D 5, Waggott E 4, Waggott JA 4, Chalmers J 3, Knight W 3, Findlay J 2, Gardiner S 2, Minnikin T 2, Stokoe W 2, Surtees E 2, Arnott W 1, Atkinson FO 1, Bennett W 1, Brown W 1, Collier G/J 1, Davison W 1, Hamilton T 1, Hunter 1, Nugent J 1, Oldham RA 1, Scott J 1, Scott W 1, Tiffin WWT 1, Wardale JD 1, White AH 1, (others 1).
Goals: Angus JW 20, Nicholson T 18, McDonald J 13, Barker J 11, Raylstone JB 9, Brady A 7, McColl D 7, Gardiner S 1, Jeffrey H 1, Scott W 1, Stokoe W 1, Surtees E 1, Taylor J 1, og 1, (scrimmage 3), (unknown 8).

Season 1887-88

Match	Date		Opponent	Result	Score	Att	Scorers	1	2	3	4	5	6	7	8	9	10	11	Match	Referee
1	10 Sep	A	Edinburgh St Bernard's	L	2 4 (0 3)		Angus 2	Oldham	Duns	Taylor	Swinburne	Smart	Chalmers	Wardale	Barker	Raylstone	McDonald J	Angus	1	Mr Sheddon
2	24 Sep	H	Darlington	W	3 1 (1 0)	1600	Raylstone, Angus, Barker	Minnikin	Duns	Taylor	Swinburne	Raylstone	Smart	Barker	Surtees	Davidson	McDonald J	Angus	2	R Bellwood
3	01 Oct	A	Redcar	W	4 1 (2 0)		unknown (scrimmage), Scott W, Raylstone, Angus	Collier	Duns	Taylor	Swinburne	Raylstone	Smart	Barker	Scott W	Davidson	McDonald J	Angus	3	
4	08 Oct	H	Sunderland	L	2 3 (1 3)	2000	Raylstone, McDonald	Fyfe	Duns	Taylor	Swinburne	Raylstone	Smart	Barker	Tiffin	Davidson	McDonald J	Angus	4	J Phillips
5	22 Oct	H	Newcastle East End	D	0 0 (0 0)			Fyfe	Davidson	Taylor	Swinburne	Raylstone	Smart	McColl	AN Other	Nicholson	McDonald J	Angus	5	
6	29 Oct	A	Darlington St Augustine's	W	4 2 (3 1)		Nicholson, Angus, McColl, Raylstone	Fyfe	Duns	Taylor	Swinburne	Raylstone	Smart	Barker	McColl	Nicholson	McDonald J	Angus	6	
7	12 Nov	A	Gainsborough Trinity	D	1 1 (1 1)	1200	Nicholson	Fyfe	Duns	Taylor	McDermid	Hamilton	Smart	Barker	McColl	Nicholson	McDonald J	Angus	7	T Saxilby
8	19 Nov	H	Eswick Rangers	D	2 2 (2 1)		Barker 2	Minnikin	Taylor	Waggott J	McDermid	Waggott E	Smart	Barker	McColl	Nicholson	McDonald J	Angus	8	A Peters
9	26 Nov	H	Morpeth Harriers	W	1 0 (1 0)		Surtees	Fyfe	Findlay J	Waggott J	Waggott E	Smart	Scott J	Scott D	Stokoe	Davidson	Surtees	Surtees	9	
10	03 Dec	A	Whitburn	D	1 1 (0 0)		Angus	Fyfe	Taylor	McDermid	Swinburne	Smart	Knight	Scott D	McColl	McDonald J	Davidson	Angus	10	T Morpeth
11	10 Dec	H	Shankhouse Black Watch	D	1 1 (1 1)		McDonald	Fyfe	Arnott	Taylor	Swinburne	Raylstone	Smart	Scott D	McColl	McDonald J	McDermid	Angus	11	R Bellwood
12	24 Dec	H	Notts Mellors	W	4 1 (0 1)		Nicholson, McColl, McDonald, Raylstone	Fyfe	Taylor	McDermid	Swinburne	Raylstone	Smart	Scott D	McColl	Nicholson	McDonald J	Angus	12	
13	26 Dec	H	Hibernian	L	0 6 (0 3)	2000		Fyfe	Taylor	McDermid	Swinburne	Raylstone	Waggott J	Barker	McColl	Nicholson	McDonald J	Angus	13	
14	31 Dec	H	Cambuslang	L	0 4 (0 1)			Fyfe	Taylor	Duns	Smart	Raylstone	McDermid	Barker	Gardiner	Swinburne	Davidson	Nugent	14	R Bellwood
15	02 Jan	H	Dumbarton Athletic	L	2 5 (2 3)	2000	Gardiner, Barker	Fyfe	Taylor	Raylstone	Swinburne	McDermid	Knight	Barker	Gardiner	Davidson	McColl	Scott D	15	
16	03 Jan	H	Motherwell	L	0 2 (0 1)	2000		Fyfe	Taylor	McDermid	Waggott E	Swinburne	Raylstone	Bennett	McColl	Gardiner	Gardiner	Brown W	16	
17	07 Jan	H	Rendel	L	0 1 (0 0)			Fyfe	Taylor	Findlay J	Waggott E	Swinburne	Waggott J	Barker	McColl	Davidson	McDonald J	Angus	17	
18	14 Jan	H	Stockton	W	5 0 (1 0)		McDonald, Brady 2, Barker, Angus	Fyfe	Taylor	McDermid	Swinburne	Raylstone	Smart	Barker	McColl	Brady A	McDonald J	Angus	18	
19	28 Jan	A	Newcastle East End	W	3 0 (1 0)		Brady, McDonald, Barker	Fyfe	Taylor	McDermid	Swinburne	Raylstone	Smart	Barker	McColl	Brady A	McDonald J	Angus	19	A Peters
20	11 Feb	A	Sunderland	W	3 2 (0 1)	5000	og (Kirtley), Nicholson, Raylstone	Fyfe	McDermid	McDermid	Swinburne	Raylstone	Smart	Barker	McColl	Nicholson	McDonald J	Angus	20	
21	18 Feb	H	Whitburn	W	5 0 (4 0)		Nicholson 2, Angus 3	Fyfe	Taylor	McDermid	Swinburne	Raylstone	Smart	Barker	McColl	Nicholson	McDonald J	Angus	21	
22	03 Mar	A	Morpeth Harriers	W	3 1 (3 1)		Stokoe, unknown 2	Fyfe	McDermid	Jeffrey	Swinburne	Raylstone	Atkinson	Stokoe	McColl	Davidson	Brady A	McDonald J	22	
23	30 Mar	H	Edinburgh St Bernard's	W	3 1 (2 0)	600	Nicholson 2, Barker	Fyfe	McDermid	Jeffrey	Swinburne	Raylstone	Knight	Barker	McColl	Nicholson	McDonald J	Angus	23	
24	03 Apr	H	West Bromwich Albion	L	1 5 (1 1)	6000	Nicholson	Fyfe	McDermid	Jeffrey	Swinburne	White	Raylstone	Barker	McColl	Davidson	McDonald J	Angus	24	D Crawford
25	21 Apr	A	Darlington	W	4 1 (2 1)		Barker, McDonald, McColl, Jeffrey	Fyfe	McDermid	Jeffrey	Swinburne	Raylstone	Grant	Barker	McColl	Taylor	Brady A	McDonald J	25	
26	05 May	H	Birtley	W	5 0 (2 0)		McDonald, Brady 2, McColl 2	Fyfe	McDermid	Jeffrey	Swinburne	Raylstone	Grant	Barker	McColl	Brady A	Nicholson	McDonald J	26	
27	12 May	A	Sunderland Albion	L	1 3 (0 1)	2000	unknown (scrimmage)	Fyfe	McDermid	Taylor	Swinburne	Grant	Jeffrey	Barker	McColl	Nicholson	McDonald J	Angus	27	
28	21 May	A	Bishop Auckland Town	D	2 2		unknown 2	Fyfe	McDermid	Jeffrey	Swinburne	Grant	Raylstone	Barker	McColl	Nicholson	McDonald J	Angus	28	

FA Cup

Round	Date		Opponent	Result	Score	Att	Scorers	1	2	3	4	5	6	7	8	9	10	11	Round	Referee
1	15 Oct	H	Redcar	W	5 1 (2 0)	8000	Barker, Angus 2, Nicholson, McDonald	Fyfe	Duns	Chalmers	Swinburne	Raylstone	Smart	Barker	Davidson	Nicholson	McDonald J	Angus	1	Dr Wilson
2	05 Nov	A	Sunderland	L	1 3 (1 0)	8000	McColl	Fyfe	Duns	Chalmers	Swinburne	Raylstone	Smart	Barker	McColl	Nicholson	McDonald J	Angus	2	JC Stacey

Northumberland FA Senior Cup

Round	Date		Opponent	Result	Score	Att	Scorers	1	2	3	4	5	6	7	8	9	10	11	Round	Referee
1	bye																			
2	21 Jan	A	Berwick Rangers	W	5 0 (3 0)	3000	Angus, unknown 4	Fyfe	Taylor	McDermid	Swinburne	Raylstone	Smart	Barker	McColl	Nicholson	McDonald J	Angus	2	R Warburton
3	04 Feb	H	North Eastern	W	15 0 (6 0)		unknown (scrimmage), McDonald 2, Raylstone 3, Angus 4, Nicholson 4, Taylor	Fyfe	Taylor	Chalmers	Swinburne	Raylstone	Smart	Barker	McColl	Nicholson	McDonald J	Angus	3	F Knott
sf	25 Feb	N	Eswick Rangers	D	1 1 (0 1)		Nicholson	Fyfe	Taylor	McDermid	Swinburne	Raylstone	Smart	Barker	McColl	Nicholson	McDonald J	Angus	sf	Dr Wilson
sfr	10 Mar	N	Eswick Rangers	W	3 0 (2 0)	3000	McDonald 2, Barker	Fyfe	Taylor	McDermid	Swinburne	Raylstone	Jeffrey	Barker	McColl	Nicholson	McDonald J	Angus	sfr	G Miller
f	24 Mar	N	Shankhouse Black Watch	W	6 3 (4 0)	7000	McColl, Barker, McDonald, Nicholson 2, Angus	Fyfe	Taylor	McDermid	Swinburne	Raylstone	Jeffrey	Barker	McColl	Nicholson	McDonald J	Angus	f	G Miller

Northumberland & Tyne Charity Shield

Round	Date		Opponent	Result	Score	Att	Scorers	1	2	3	4	5	6	7	8	9	10	11	Round	Referee
sf	07 Apr	A	Newcastle East End	W	2 0 (2 0)	4000	Angus, Brady	Fyfe	Jeffrey	Swinburne	Raylstone	McDonald J	Barker	McColl	Nicholson	Brady A	Angus		sf	G Miller
f	14 Apr	H	Shankhouse Black Watch	W	3 0 (2 0)	2000	Brady, Nicholson, Angus	Fyfe	Jeffrey	Swinburne	Raylstone	McDonald J	Barker	McColl	Nicholson	Brady A	Angus		f	W Scott

Northumberland & Durham Inter County Challenge Cup

	Date		Opponent	Result	Score	Att	Scorers	1	2	3	4	5	6	7	8	9	10	11		Referee
	28 Apr	H	Sunderland	L	0 2 (0 2)	6000		Fyfe	McDermid	Hunter	Swinburne	Raylstone	Grant	Barker	McColl	Nicholson	Brady A	McDonald J		Dr Wilson

Match 8: When Eswick equalised at 2:2 the crowd encroached on the pitch, and by the time they had been cleared it was too dark to complete the match

FA Cup
Round 2: After extra-time, score at full-time 1:1. At the time biggest crowd ever for any match in Northumberland & Durham

Northumberland FA Senior Cup
sf, sfr, f: All played at Heaton Junction
sf: WE played most of the game with 10 men, Smart having been carried off early in the first-half

1888-89
SCOTS INVADE TYNESIDE

With the professionalism row in Scotland reaching a peak, footballers north of the Cheviots began to invade the north of England, principally to the North West and North East. Tyneside and Wearside were favourite destinations, in Newcastle at West End, East End and now with Elswick Rangers too, all three clubs willing to pay wages and importantly having connections to find players work alongside the Tyne.

Scottish international full-back Bob Kelso was a star arrival at St James' Park from Renton. One of the game's very best defenders, he joined the West Enders and became the idol of the crowd. He was joined by team-mates in Dunbartonshire, Donald McKechnie and Billy Jardine. Dan Kennedy was signed from neighbours Vale of Leven while Neil Hannah and John Downes were notable additions from Glasgow.

That season West End fielded almost 20 different Scots in their red-and-black shirts. Westgate-born Harry Jeffrey became a regular defender in the side. He remained on Tyneside for most of his career playing over 150 times for the West Enders – the most by any player – and later 55 for Newcastle United.

West End began the season with two high-scoring victories at St James' Park as friendly encounters continued. They defeated Notts District 7-0 and Glaswegians, Kelvinside Athletic by 8-0. Plenty of goals were scored in the programme with Donald McColl – who hit 16 goals – and Tom Nicholson both potent up front. Rendel were beaten 6-1 and Bishop Auckland Church Institute walloped 9-0.

The Geordie lads made another rare excursion out of the region, this time to Merseyside during January to face Bootle, then ranked highly alongside Everton. It wasn't a happy trip as West End lost heavily by 12-1. It had been something of a gruelling journey through the night and one report noted that the players "reached their destination more inclined to sleep than play football". West End finished the game with only seven players on the field!

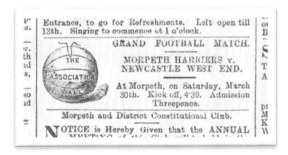

The Morpeth Herald included an advert for the visit of West End in March 1889.

In FA Cup action, now with a revamped qualifying stage, West End cruised through the opening match and faced a tie with Sunderland Albion on Tyneside. The Wear men won 5-3, or so they thought, as West End lodged a successful appeal claiming that Albion had fielded Bob Gloag, an ineligible player. But in the ordered replay,

Sunderland won again by 2-1. A good crowd of 4,000 watched the rerun, for a second time at St James' Park.

West End controversially decided not to defend their Senior Cup title when they chose not to compete due to a perceived lack of drawing power by local opponents. Instead, they looked to arrange more attractive-looking games. Sheffield Wednesday, to soon become Football Alliance champions, came to Tyneside, so too did West Bromwich Albion again, and from Scotland, Vale of Leven and Scottish Cup finalists Celtic. The highlight though from a supporters' point of view that season was the 4-1 Christmas Day victory over Newcastle East End. An elated St James' Park crowd of 5,000 saw their Heaton rivals demolished, a striking result as the East Enders were without doubt top dogs in Newcastle that year. Towards the end of the season during April another challenge match took place at St James' Park against FA Cup runners-up Wolves. That contest showed a mismatch remained with the élite elsewhere in the country as West End lost 9-2.

- For the visit to face Middlesbrough in December at Linthorpe Road, it was reported that West End's travelling support numbered around 600 in the 4,000 attendance.
- The West End and Sunderland Albion cup-tie incredibly saw no fewer than 16 Scots take part in the tie.
- During January 1889 the club's management fully adopted professionalism and declared they would sign any players deemed necessary to reclaim the tag of best on Tyneside.
- The 1888-89 season was marked by the introduction of the very first league competition as the Football League kicked off. It would be a while before a Newcastle side reached that level, but for the following campaign, the North East would see its own league tournament launched.

Captain: William Swinburne.
FA Cup: R2q (Winners: Preston North End).
Senior Cup: Did not compete (Winners: Newcastle East End).
Ground: St James' Park.
Average Home Attendance: 2,667, top crowd 5,000 (18/27 games).

Appearances: Jardine W 38, Swinburne W 37, McColl D 36, Barker J 35, Jeffrey H 33, Taylor J 33, McDonald J 32, Kelso RR 31, Kennedy DC 16, Hannah N 15, Nicholson T 12, Downes J 11, Watts J 11, Brown W 10, McKechnie D 9, Hardman HG 8, Sadler T 7, McDonald W 6, McCrimmon J 4, McQuillan P 4, Waggott E 4, Dewar W 3, Porterfield A 3, Stanger TW 3, Davidson R 2, Miller P 2, McCombie W 2, Nugent J 2, Baxter J 1, Fitzgerald JE 1, Fowler G 1, Gardiner S 1, Greener JW 1, Jefferson J 1, Jones B 1, Knight W 1, Millar G 1, McDermid R 1, McFarlane J 1, McIntyre JJ 1, Sawers A 1, Shaw G 1, Stewart S 1, Thompson J/D 1, Tiffin WWT 1, Tinn W 1, Wilde GM 1, Wilson J 1.
Goals: McColl D 16, Nicholson T 15, Barker J 13, Kennedy DC 13, McDonald J 9, Hannah N 7, Brown W 5, Downes J 3, Kelso RR 3, Davidson R 2, McCrimmon J 2, Swinburne W 2, Baxter J 1, Dewar W 1, Hardman HG 1, Jeffrey H 1, McCombie W 1, (scrimmage 6), (unknown 16).

Season 1888-89

Match	Date		Opponent	Scorers	Result			Att	1	2	3	4	5	6	7	8	9	10	11	Match	Referee
1	01 Sep	H	Notts District	Swinburne, McDonald J 3, Nicholson, Barker 2	W	7 0	(3 0)		Jardine	McQuillan	Taylor	Kelso	Swinburne	McKechnie	Barker	McColl	Nicholson	Brown W	McDonald J	1	
2	08 Sep	H	Kelvinside Athletic	McColl 2, Brown, Nicholson 2, Kelso, McDonald J, unknown	W	8 0	(2 0)		Jardine	McQuillan	Taylor	Kelso	Swinburne	McKechnie	Barker	McColl	Nicholson	Brown W	McDonald J	2	
3	15 Sep	A	Halliwell (Bolton)	Brown, Nicholson	L	2 3	(1 2)	1500	Jardine	McQuillan	Taylor	Kelso	Swinburne	McKechnie	Barker	McColl	Nicholson	Brown W	McDonald J	3	Dr Wilson
4	22 Sep	H	Glasgow University	Nicholson	D	1 1	(1 0)	3000	Jardine	Jeffrey	Taylor	Shaw G	Swinburne	McKechnie	Barker	McColl	McQuillan	Nicholson	McDonald J	4	AH White
5	29 Sep	H	Shankhouse Black Watch	McDonald J 2, Brown, Barker	W	4 1	(1 1)		Jardine	Jeffrey	Taylor	Kelso	Swinburne	McKechnie	Barker	McColl	Brown W	McDonald J	Gardiner	5	R Bellwood
6	13 Oct	H	Middlesbrough	McDonald J, Barker	W	2 0	(0 0)	2000	Jardine	Jeffrey	Taylor	Kelso	Watts	McKechnie	Barker	McColl	Nicholson	McDonald J	Kennedy D	6	W Scott
7	20 Oct	A	Shankhouse Black Watch	Nicholson	L	1 2	(1 2)		Jardine	Jeffrey	Taylor	Watts	Swinburne	McKechnie	Barker	McColl	Nicholson	Sadler	McDonald J	7	J Cowens
8	03 Nov	A	Stockton		L	0 1	(0 0)		Jardine	Sadler	Knight	Kelso	Swinburne	Brown W	Brown W	Wilson J	Jones B	McDonald J	Stanger	8	J Reed jnr
9	17 Nov	H	Bishop Auckland Town	Brown, McColl	D	2 2	(0 2)		Jardine	Sadler	McIntyre J	Kelso	Swinburne	Jeffrey	Barker	McColl	Miller P	Brown W	Brown W	9	J Oliver
10	24 Nov	A	Birtley	McColl, Hannah 2	W	3 1	(3 1)		Jardine	Sadler	Miller P	Fitzgerald	Watts	Waggott E	Kelso	McColl	Hannah N	Brown W	Thompson J/D	10	Mr Shaw
11	01 Dec	A	Middlesbrough	Hannah, Barker 2	W	3 2	(0 1)	4000	Jardine	Jeffrey	Taylor	Kelso	Swinburne	Sadler	Barker	McColl	Hannah N	McDonald J	McFarlane J	11	T Bradbury
12	08 Dec	H	Rendel	McColl 2, Barker, Swinburne, Kennedy, unknown (scrimmage)	W	6 1	(4 0)	1500	Jardine	Jeffrey	Taylor	Kelso	Swinburne	Sadler	Barker	McColl	Hannah N	Kennedy D	McDonald J	12	F Knott
13	15 Dec	A	Bishop Auckland Church Institute	unknown 9	W	9 0	(4 0)		Jardine	Jeffrey	Taylor	Kelso	Swinburne	Waggott E	Barker	McColl	Hannah N	Kennedy D	McDonald J	13	
14	22 Dec	H	Birtley	unknown (scrimmage), Kennedy	W	2 1	(1 0)		Jardine	Jeffrey	Taylor	Kelso	Swinburne	Dewar W	Barker	McColl	Hannah N	Kennedy D	Kennedy D	14	R Bellwood
15	25 Dec	H	Newcastle East End	Kennedy, Barker 2, Brown	W	4 1	(2 0)	5300	Jardine	Jeffrey	Taylor	Kelso	Swinburne	Watts	Barker	McColl	Hannah N	Brown W	Kennedy D	15	F Knott
16	29 Dec	H	Sheffield Wednesday		L	0 1	(0 1)	2000	Jardine	Jeffrey	Taylor	Kelso	Swinburne	McDonald W	Barker	McColl	Hannah N	Brown W	Brown W	16	Mr Emery
17	01 Jan	H	Vale of Leven	McColl, Kennedy, Hannah	D	3 3	(1 2)	2000	Jardine	Jeffrey	Taylor	Kelso	Swinburne	McDonald W	Barker	McColl	Hannah N	Brown W	Kennedy D	17	F Knott
18	05 Jan	H	Elswick Rangers	Kennedy, Hannah, Barker	W	3 1	(3 0)	2000	Jardine	Jeffrey	Taylor	Watts	Swinburne	McDonald W	Barker	McColl	Hannah N	Kennedy D	Davidson	18	G Phillips
19	12 Jan	A	Bootle	Hannah	L	1 12	(1 5)	1200	Jardine	Jeffrey	Taylor	Kelso	Swinburne	Watts	Barker	McColl	Hannah N	Kennedy D	McDonald J	19	
20	02 Feb	A	Newcastle East End	Hannah	L	1 2	(0 2)	3000	Jardine	Jeffrey	Fowler	Kelso	Swinburne	McDonald W	Barker	McColl	Nicholson	Downes	Hannah N	20	F Knott
21	09 Feb	H	West Bromwich Albion	Baxter	L	0 2	(0 2)	2000	Jardine	Jeffrey	Taylor	Kelso	Swinburne	Dewar W	Barker	McColl	Hannah N	McDonald J	Downes	21	F Knott
22	16 Feb	H	Morpeth Harriers	McColl 2, Downes 2, Dewar	W	5 2	(4 1)	2000	Jardine	Jeffrey	Taylor	Kelso	Swinburne	Watts	Barker	McColl	Hannah N	McDonald J	Downes	22	F Knott
23	23 Feb	H	Sunderland Albion	McColl	D	1 1	(1 1)	3000	Jardine	Jeffrey	Taylor	Wilde	Swinburne	Dewar W	Barker	McColl	Dewar W	McDonald J	Downes	23	J Mackay
24	02 Mar	A	Darlington	McColl, Barker	W	2 1	(2 0)		Porterfield	Swinburne	Taylor	Waggott E	Watts	Waggott E	Barker	McColl	Hardman	McDonald J	Downes	24	S Kemp
25	09 Mar	A	Sunderland Albion	McColl	L	1 4	(0 3)	4000	Jardine	Jeffrey	Sawers A	Waggott E	Swinburne	McDonald W	Barker	McColl	McCrimmon	McDonald J	Downes (d)	25	J R Douglas
26	16 Mar	H	West Hartlepool	McCrimmon, McCombe, McColl, Kennedy, Jeffrey	W	5 0	(2 0)	4000	Jardine	Jeffrey	Taylor	Kelso	Swinburne	McDonald J	McCombe	McColl	McCrimmon	Kennedy D	Downes	26	T Woof
27	23 Mar	H	Glasgow Celtic	Kelso, McDonald J, McCrimmon	L	3 4	(1 3)	4000	Jardine	Jeffrey	Taylor	Kelso	Swinburne	McDonald J	Barker	McColl	McCrimmon	Kennedy D	Kennedy D	27	Dr Wilson
28	30 Mar	A	Morpeth Harriers	Barker, Downes	L	1 2	(1 0)	1000	Jardine	Jeffrey	Taylor	Kelso	Swinburne	McDonald J	Hardman	McColl	McCrimmon	McCombie	Downes	28	J Pyke
29	06 Apr	A	Bishop Auckland Town	Kennedy, Barker, unknown 6	W	8 3	(3 2)		Jardine	Jeffrey	Taylor	Kelso	Swinburne	Hannah N	Barker	McColl	Hardman	McDonald J	Downes	29	R Hay
30	13 Apr	A	Edinburgh St Bernard's	Kennedy 2	W	2 1	(2 0)		Jardine	Swinburne	Taylor	Kelso	McDonald J	McDonald W	Barker	McColl	Hardman	Kennedy D	Downes	30	
31	19 Apr	H	Elswick Rangers	Kennedy 2, unknown (scrimmage)	W	3 0	(2 0)	4000	Jardine	Jeffrey	Taylor	Kelso	Swinburne	Porterfield	Barker	McColl	Hardman	McDonald J	Kennedy D	31	T Woof
32	22 Apr	H	Wolverhampton Wanderers	McColl, Kennedy	L	2 9	(1 5)	4000	Jardine	Jeffrey	Taylor	Kelso	Swinburne	McDonald J	Barker	McColl	Jefferson	Nugent	Kennedy D	32	Dr Wilson
33	23 Apr	H	Derby Junction	Baxter	W	1 0	(1 0)	2000	Jardine	Jeffrey	Taylor	Kelso	Swinburne	McDonald J	Hardman	McColl	Hardman	Nugent	Baxter J	33	F Knott
34	27 Apr	H	Bishop Auckland Church Institute	unknown (scrimmage)	D	1 1	(1 1)		Porterfield	Jeffrey	Taylor	Jardine	Swinburne	Watts	Barker	McColl	Tinn	McDonald J	Nicholson	34	J Sheldon
35	11 May	H	Ashington	Hardman, Kennedy, Nicholson 3	W	5 0			Jardine	McDermid	Taylor	Watts	Swinburne	McDonald J	Barker	Greener	Hardman	Nicholson	Kennedy D	35	
36	25 May	H	Elswick Rangers	Nicholson 2, unknown (scrimmage)	D	3 3	(1 2)		Jardine	McDermid	Millar	Jeffrey	McDonald J	Taylor	Barker	Stewart S	Nicholson	McDonald J	Nicholson	36	Dr Wilson

Round			FA Cup																	Round	
1q	06 Oct	H	Bishop Auckland Church Institute	McColl, McDonald J, unknown (scrimmage), Nicholson 3, Kelso	W	7 2	(1 1)	1000	Jardine	Jeffrey	Taylor	Kelso	Swinburne	McKechnie	Barker	McColl	Nicholson	McDonald J	Tiffin	1q	J R Douglas
2q	27 Oct	H	Sunderland Albion	Davidson 2, McColl	L	3 5	(2 1)	3000	Jardine	Jeffrey	Taylor	Kelso	Swinburne	McKechnie	Barker	McColl	Davidson	McDonald J	Stanger	2q	R W Gosson
2qr	10 Nov	H	Sunderland Albion	Nicholson	L	1 2	(1 1)	4000	Jardine	Jeffrey	Taylor	Kelso	Swinburne	Sadler	Barker	McColl	Nicholson	McDonald J	Stanger	2qr	Mr Hastie

Match 7 : WE played the second-half with 9 men through injuries

Match 19 : WE lost. McDonald to injury in the first-half, and in the second, first Kennedy, then Hannah and Watts, ending with 7 men

Match 21 : One of Albion's goals was deflected in off WE's umpire Phillips

Match 25 : Both sides had a player sent off , Downes (WE), and Richardson (Sunderland Albion)

FA Cup

Round 2 : Referee blew for half-time 10 mins early, and the players having left the field had to return to complete the half

WE lodged a complaint that one of Albion's players was ineligible. The FA upheld the complaint and ordered a replay

Round 2qr : After extra-time, score at full-time 1:1

1889-90
LEAGUE ACTION KICKS OFF

With the introduction of competitive weekly football as the Football League took hold, several parts of the country began to launch regional leagues. Locally, the new Northern League began during mid-September with ten clubs. West End's opening fixture was against Newcastle East End at St James' Park on 14th September and football supporters from both sides of the city packed the arena. A crowd of 4,000 saw the West Enders victorious by 2-0 in a feisty encounter – with two players ordered off after a brawl, John Barker and James Miller.

West End took a liking to the format, and the additional edge it gave to matches. They surged to the top of the table and were leaders for much of the campaign. The red-and-blacks were unbeaten in their first nine matches, winning eight. Included was an 8-1 rout of Elswick Rangers. Their main rivals for the Northern League title were Stockton and St Augustine's of Darlington.

The West Enders should really have lifted the championship trophy, but they dropped points in January, losing to Middlesbrough and East End, before a crucial meeting with St Augustine's at their new Chestnut Grove ground at the end of April in which the Saints won 4-1. Then on the last day of the season when a draw would have secured the title, West End faced the other club from the town, Darlington, this time at Feethams. They lost again, 3-0, and bizarrely only fielded ten men in what was a trophy decider. West End finished level on points with St Augustine's and with identical records but lost the race for silverware on goal-average.

The St James' Park club also did well in the FA Cup. They eased through the four game qualifiers and faced Grimsby Town of the Football Alliance in Round 1 during January. West End dominated the tie but missed chances and were knocked out by a much-debated offside goal.

Players came and went as management continually juggled with team selection. After a full season with West End, Bob Kelso moved on, to win honours with Preston and Everton. Other Scots spent time in Newcastle; Dave Whitton a new goalkeeper, William Brady and three of the McKay clan who joined the St James' Park ranks at the same time. Tom Nicholson continued to net goals for the third season in a row, 19 in the programme.

On the local scene, the club returned to action in the Senior Cup and for a second time lifted the trophy by defeating amateur outfit Rendel in a replayed final by 5-0. Big match friendlies continued with Burnley and Renton arriving at St James' Park. So too did Aston Villa, West End winning 1-0, against so-called weakened opponents yet a side which still included five internationals. The club also brought Everton to Tyneside for an end of season finale. West End were boosted by no fewer than five Sunderland Albion players, and another from Elswick Rangers, pulling on their colours. They still fell, by 2-1, but against a side to become

Football League champions in 1891 it wasn't a bad result at all.

Season 1889-90 perhaps had been the West End club's finest campaign in their eight-year existence so far. And away from the football pitch the club made a bold decision, making plans to follow East End's path to become a Limited Company.

- Admission to St James' Park that season was recorded; 6d (3p) plus another 3d (1p) for entry into a special reserved area while ladies were admitted free.
- Late in the season West End players became annoyed when they found they were being paid less than East Enders who earned a superior bonus. Both sets of players received 15s 0d (75p) for a win and 10s 0d (50p) for any other result, but the East Enders were also paid 1s 0d (5p) for every goal scored.
- When the West Enders travelled to face Sunderland during September 1889, a crowd of 9,000 were at the Newcastle Road ground, the highest to watch the club.

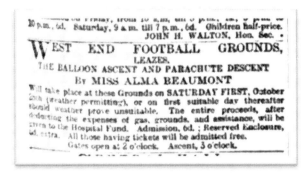

- During October 1889, St James' Park hosted a novel display by American adventurist Miss Alma Beaumont who made a dare-devil jump by parachute from a balloon.

Captain: William Swinburne.
Northern League: P18 W12 D2 L4 F44 A24 Pts 26.
Position: Runners-up (Champions: St Augustine's).
FA Cup: R1 (Winners: Blackburn Rovers).
Senior Cup: Winners.
Ground: St James' Park.
Average Home Attendance: 3,375, top crowd 6,000 (16/27games).

Appearances: Jeffrey H 43, Whitton DR 43, Swinburne W 41, Raylstone JB 40, Barker J 37, Nicholson T 31, McColl D 30, McKay G 30, Brady W 28, Wilson WA 27, Marshall J 22, McKay J 16, McDonald J 15, McKay T 14, Carnelley F 13, Moore I 12, Lindsay A 11, Kennedy DC 10, Robertson WW 9, Taylor J 9, Kirkham F 8, Dixon H 5, Angus JW 4, Jardine W 4, Hardman HG 2, Bewley WH 1, Hannah J 1, Hunt 1, Knox W 1, Minnikin T 1, McDermid R 1, McKechnie D 1, Nugent J 1, Sawers W 1, Smith J 1, Waggott E 1, Walker J 1.
Goals: Nicholson T 19, McDonald J 14, Brady W 13, Barker J 12, McColl D 9, McKay T 9, Marshall J 8, McKay J 6, Raylstone JB 6, McKay G 4, og 3, Angus JW 2, Dixon H 2, Kennedy DC 2, Swinburne W 2, Carnelley F 1, Lindsay A 1, Moore I 1, Robertson WW 1, Smith J 1, (scrimmage 2), (unknown 3).

Season 1889-90

Northern League

#	Date	V	Opposition	Result	Att	Scorers	1	2	3	4	5	6	7	8	9	10	11	Ref
1	14 Sep	H	Newcastle East End	W 2-0 (2-0)	4000	McDonald, McKay T	Whitton	Jeffrey	Swinburne	McKay T	Kirkham	McKay J	Barker (d)	Brady W	McColl	McDonald J	Angus	F Hardisty
2	21 Sep	A	South Bank	W 4-1 (2-0)	1000	Nicholson, McDonald 2, McKay T	Whitton	Jeffrey	Wilson W	McKay G	Kirkham	Raystone	Barker	Brady W	McDonald	Nicholson	McKay T	W Hurst
3	28 Sep	H	Darlington St Augustine's	W 3-2 (1-2)	1000	McDonald 2, Brady	Whitton	Jeffrey	Taylor	Kirkham	Raystone	McKay G	Barker	Brady W	McDonald J	Marshall	McKay T	S Kemp
4	12 Oct	H	Birtley	W 3-1 (1-0)		McDonald, Kennedy, Marshall	Whitton	Wilson W	Taylor	Kirkham	Raystone	McKay G	Marshall	Brady W	McKay T	McDonald J	Kennedy D	A Grundy
5	02 Nov	A	Auckland Town	D 1-1 (0-1)		og (Brown)	Whitton	Jeffrey	Swinburne	McKay T	Raystone	McKay G	Marshall	McColl	Nicholson	McDonald J	Kennedy D	J Glover
6	09 Nov	A	Stockton	W 1-0 (0-0)	7000	Nicholson	Whitton	Jeffrey	Swinburne	McKay T	Raystone	McKay G	Brady W	McColl	Nicholson	Barker	Kennedy D	Mr Howcroft
7	23 Nov	H	Elswick Rangers	W 8-1 (5-0)		McKay T 2, Brady 2, Nicholson, Raystone 2, Barker	Whitton	Jeffrey	Swinburne	McKay T	Raystone	McKay G	Brady W	McColl	Nicholson	McKay J	Barker	W Hurst
8	14 Dec	A	Auckland Town	W 4-2 (1-0)		Nicholson, Marshall, unknown 2	Whitton	Jeffrey	Swinburne	Robertson	Raystone	McKay G	Brady W	McColl	Nicholson	Marshall	Barker	J Glover
9	28 Dec	A	Elswick Rangers	W 2-0 (1-0)		Marshall, Nicholson	Whitton	Jeffrey	Swinburne	Robertson	Raystone	McKay G	Marshall	Brady W	Nicholson	Kennedy D	Barker	A Grundy
10	11 Jan	H	Middlesbrough	L 1-2 (0-1)	1000	McKay J	Jardine	Jeffrey	Swinburne	Swinburne	Raystone	McDonald J	Marshall	McColl	Dixon	McKay J	Barker	J Glover
11	25 Jan	A	Newcastle East End	W 3-1 (1-1)	3000	Swinburne	Whitton	Jeffrey	Taylor	Swinburne	Robertson	Wilson W	Barker	Brady W	Moore	Nicholson	Hunt	J Mackay
12	08 Feb	H	Stockton	W 1-0 (0-0)	6000	Lindsay, Nicholson, Raystone	Whitton	Jeffrey	Wilson W	Swinburne	Raystone	Carmelley	Lindsay	McColl	Moore	Nicholson	Barker	Mr O'Hara
13	15 Mar	H	Birtley	D 1-1 (0-1)		Moore	Whitton	Jeffrey	Wilson W	Swinburne	Raystone	McKay G	Lindsay	McColl	Moore	Marshall	Barker	Mr O'Hara
14	22 Mar	A	Middlesbrough	W 2-1 (2-1)	3000	McColl	Whitton	Jeffrey	Swinburne	McDonald J	Raystone	Carmelley	Lindsay	McColl	Moore	McKay J	Barker	Mr Potts
15	12 Apr	A	Darlington	W 2-1 (1-2)	2000	Barker, og (Withington)	Whitton	Jeffrey	Wilson W	Swinburne	Raystone	Carmelley	Marshall	McColl	Moore	Nicholson	Barker	W Hurst
16	26 Apr	A	Darlington St Augustine's	L 1-4 (1-2)		unknown (scrimmage)	Jardine	Jeffrey	Wilson W	Swinburne	Raystone	Carmelley	Marshall	McColl	Nicholson	Robertson	Brady W	S Kemp
17	29 Apr	H	South Bank	W 6-2		Brady, Nicholson 3, Robertson, McColl	Whitton	Jeffrey	Wilson W	Swinburne	Raystone	Carmelley	Brady W	McColl	Robertson	McKay J	McKay J	S Kemp
18	03 May	A	Darlington	L 2-3			Whitton	Jeffrey	Wilson W	Swinburne	Raystone	McKay G	Marshall	McColl	Moore (abs)	Nicholson	Barker	S Kemp

FA Cup

Round	Date	V	Opposition	Result	Att	Scorers	1	2	3	4	5	6	7	8	9	10	11	Ref
1q	05 Oct	H	Port Clarence	W 9-1 (5-1)	2000	McDonald 4, McKay T 3, McKay J, Marshall	Whitton	Jeffrey	Taylor	Kirkham	Raystone	McKay G	Marshall	McKay J	McKay T	McDonald J	Kennedy D	W Hurst
2q	26 Oct	A	Birtley	W 2-0 (2-0)	800	Nicholson, Brady	Whitton	Jeffrey	Swinburne	McKay T	Raystone	McKay G	Marshall	McColl	Nicholson	McDonald J (d)	McDonald J (d)	A Grundy
3q	16 Nov	H	South Bank	W 5-0 (1-2)	6000	Nicholson 3, Kennedy, McColl	Whitton	Jeffrey	Swinburne	Robertson	Raystone	McKay G	Brady W	McColl	Nicholson	Barker	Kennedy D	J Glover
4q	07 Dec	A	Stockton	W 1-0 (1-0)	3000	Nicholson	Whitton	Jeffrey	Swinburne	Wilson W	Raystone	McKay G	Brady W	McColl	Nicholson	Marshall	McKay J	Mr Hirst
1	18 Jan	H	Grimsby Town	L 1-2 (0-2)	3000	McColl	Whitton	Jeffrey	Swinburne	Wilson W	Raystone	Robertson	McColl	Brady W	Barker	McKay J	Barker	Mr Gregson

Northumberland FA Senior Cup

Round	Date	V	Opposition	Result	Att	Scorers	1	2	3	4	5	6	7	8	9	10	11	Ref
sf	22 Feb	H	Elswick Rangers	W 3-1 (2-0)	1000	McDonald, Barker, Nicholson	Whitton	Jeffrey	Taylor	Swinburne	Raystone	Carmelley	Marshall	McColl	McDonald J	Nicholson	Barker	J Allan
f	29 Mar	N	Rendel	D 3-3 (2-0)	4300	Barker, unknown (scrimmage), McDonald	Whitton	Jeffrey	Wilson W	Swinburne	Raystone	McKay G	Marshall	McColl	McDonald J	Nicholson	Barker	F Hardisty
fr	19 Apr	N	Rendel	L 3-5 (3-0)	5000	Nicholson, McColl, McKay G 3	Whitton	Jeffrey	Wilson W	Swinburne	Raystone	McKay G	McColl	Marshall	McKay G	Nicholson	Barker	F Hardisty

Northumberland & Tyne Charity Shield

Round	Date	V	Opposition	Result	Att	Scorers	1	2	3	4	5	6	7	8	9	10	11	Ref
sf	23 Apr	H	Elswick Rangers	D 1-1 (1-0)	1000	Brady	Whitton	Jeffrey	Wilson W	Swinburne	Raystone	McKay G	Lindsay	McColl	Moore	Nicholson	Brady W	NP Pattison
sfr	05 May	N	Elswick Rangers	L 0-3 (0-2)			Whitton	Jeffrey	Taylor	Swinburne	Raystone	McKay G	Brady W	Hardman	Dixon	Nicholson	Barker	V Pratt

Other matches

#	Date	V	Opposition	Result	Att	Scorers	1	2	3	4	5	6	7	8	9	10	11	Ref
19	02 Sep	H	Fifth Kirkudbright Rifle Volunteers	D 3-3 (1-0)	3000	McKay T 2, Angus	Whitton	Jeffrey	Swinburne	Wilson W	Kirkham	McKay G	Barker	McColl	McKay J	McKay T	Angus	
20	04 Sep	H	Elswick Rangers	W 6-0 (0-0)	5000	Brady 4, Angus, Barker	Whitton	Jeffrey	Swinburne	Wilson W	Kirkham	McKay G	Barker	Brady W	McKay J	Angus	Angus	
21	07 Sep	A	Sunderland	L 0-2 (0-2)	4000		Whitton	Jeffrey	McKay G	Kirkham	Kirkham	Wilson W	Barker	Barker	Barker	McKay T	McKay T	
22	19 Oct	A	Ashington	W 2-0 (1-0)	9000	Marshall, McKay J	Whitton	Minnikin	Swinburne	Wilson W	Raystone	Kirkham	Waggott E	Kennedy D	Waggott E	Brady W	Marshall	W Anderson
23	30 Nov	H	Dumfries	W 11-1 (6-0)		Marshall, McKay J, Dixon 2, Carmelley, Raystone 2, Barker 3, unknown	Whitton	Bewley	Taylor	McKay T	Raystone	Carmelley	Marshall	McColl	Marshall	Walker J	Barker	
24	21 Dec	H	Sunderland Albion	D 0-3 (0-2)	3000	Brady	Whitton	Jeffrey	Swinburne	Robertson	Raystone	McKay G	Brady W	Marshall	Nicholson	McKay J	Barker	
25	25 Dec	H	Newcastle East End	W 3-2 (0-2)	5000	McKay J 2, Brady	Whitton	Jeffrey	Swinburne	Wilson W	Kirkham	McKay G	Brady W	McColl	Nicholson	McKay J	Barker	
26	01 Jan	H	Burnley	L 2-3 (2-2)	4000	Brady, Marshall	Whitton	Jeffrey	Wilson W	Wilson W	Raystone	McKay G	Marshall	Brady W	Nicholson	McDonald J	Barker	
27	02 Jan	H	Renton	L 1-6 (1-1)	3000	Brady	Whitton	Jeffrey	Wilson W	Wilson W	Raystone	McDonald J	Hardman	Brady W	Nicholson	Barker	Nugent	
28	01 Feb	H	Gainsborough Trinity	W 4-2 (2-0)	2000	Nicholson 2, McColl, Barker	Whitton	Jeffrey	Swinburne	Robertson	Robertson	Carmelley	Lindsay	McColl	Moore	McKay J	Barker	
29	15 Feb	A	Middlesbrough Ironopolis	L 2-3 (1-1)		Barker 2	Whitton	Jeffrey	Wilson W	Swinburne	Raystone	Carmelley	Lindsay	McColl	Moore	Nicholson	Barker	
30	01 Mar	A	Darlington	D 3-3 (0-2)		McColl, McDonald 2	Jardine	Swinburne	Taylor	McKay G	Raystone	Carmelley	Lindsay	Dixon	Dixon	McDonald J	Kennedy D	
31	08 Mar	H	Newcastle West End Reserves	W 4-3 (1-2)		Barker, Swinburne, Nicholson, Marshall	Whitton	Jeffrey	Taylor	Swinburne	Raystone	Carmelley	Marshall	McColl	McDonald J	Nicholson	Barker	
32	04 Apr	H	Aston Villa	L 1-2 (1-2)	6000	McColl	Whitton	Jeffrey	Wilson W	Wilson W	Raystone	McKay G	Lindsay	McColl	Nicholson	Nicholson	Barker	J Oliver
33	05 Apr	H	Newcastle East End	D 0-0 (0-0)	3000	og (Smith), McColl	Whitton	Jeffrey	Wilson W	Wilson W	Raystone	McKay G	Kennedy D	Barker	Nicholson	Barker	Barker	G Young
34	07 Apr	H	Long Eaton Rangers	L 1-3 (0-3)	2000	McKay G	Whitton	Jeffrey	Wilson W	Wilson W	Raystone	McKay G	Barker	Barker	Moore	McColl	Marshall	
35	08 Apr	H	Corinthians	D 0-3 (0-3)	2000	Raystone	Whitton	Jeffrey	Wilson W	Wilson W	Raystone	McKay G	Brady W	McColl	Moore	Lindsay	Barker	F Knott
36	26 Apr	A	Sunderland	L 1-4 (1-1)	6000		Jardine	Jeffrey	McDermid	McDermid	Raystone	McKay G	Brady W	Nicholson	Moore	McColl	Lindsay	
37	08 May	H	Everton	L 1-2 (1-2)		Smith	Whitton	Jeffrey	Smith	Knox	Knox	Carmelley	Barker	Smith J	Sawers W	Marshall	Hannah J	F Knott

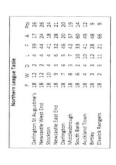

Northern League Table

	P	W	D	L	F	A	Pts
Darlington St Augustine's	18	12	2	4	39	17	26
Newcastle West End	18	12	2	4	24	18	26
Stockton	18	10	4	4	41	18	24
Newcastle East End	18	9	3	6	32	28	21
Darlington	18	7	6	5	46	20	20
Middlesbrough	18	8	3	7	42	37	19
South Bank	18	6	2	10	33	60	14
Auckland Town	18	4	4	10	41	49	12
Birtley	18	3	3	12	28	48	9
Elswick Rangers	18	2	5	11	21	66	9

Northern League
Match 4 - due to be played at Birtley, but switched to Newcastle at request of Birtley
Match 18 - Moore was absent so WE played with 10 men for whole game

Northumberland FA Senior Cup
Matches f and fr: played at Jesmond

Northumberland & Tyne Charity Shield
sf: Played at Jesmond
sfr: Played at Heaton Junction

1890-91
A DOWNWARD SPIRAL

The close-season of 1890 saw West End go through an upheaval on and off the pitch. Senior figures were not happy how the previous campaign had ended, missing out on the Northern League title while there was conflict behind the scenes too. Consequently, they made wholesale changes to the playing staff. Only a handful of regulars were retained as a new batch of Scots came in. Capped by his country, Bobby Calderwood led the way, joined by the McCann brothers, as well as Byrne, Merrilees and Dowling, six of almost a dozen from north of the border that campaign. West End used numerous players in the programme as they tried to knit together a winning combination. Even the late arrival of two of Tyneside's foremost names, Joe Wardropper and Sam Wood from Rendel, made little difference. Local lad Rodger Patten was perhaps the only new face to finish the season with credit.

West End's makeover didn't work and their second season in the Northern League was much tougher. They did win the opening encounter handsomely by 5-1 against champions St Augustine's at St James' Park, but very quickly the red-and-blacks were one of the also-rans, finishing in seventh position, one place above bottom club, surprisingly St Augustine's, who had deteriorated rapidly. West End had to apply for re-election to the league. There was much unrest among shareholders and supporters. West End were on a downward spiral.

Knockout action did not bring any joy either. In the FA Cup, West End didn't even progress from the qualifying rounds. Although thrashing Southwick 8-1 in an earlier qualifier, they lost to a much stronger Sunderland Albion line-up, 3-0 on Tyneside with Scottish international 'Blood' Hannah scoring two of the goals. While in the Senior Cup, once more the club decided to withdraw to the frustration of many.

But most disappointing of all was a complete humiliation by their rivals East End from Heaton, by then what could be termed a fervent local derby. In six matches against the East Enders – league and friendlies – they lost five and drew one. Included were four heavy defeats; 7-1, 5-0, 4-1 and 4-0. By now, supporters of both clubs wanted to see the city derby and 6,000 watched the Christmas Day meeting at St James' Park. But gates of that size for West End were few and far between due to a mix of poor displays and inferior opponents. Finances also began to be a major concern.

The mediocre season was only lifted by an occasional victory in challenge matches. Included was an entertaining 8-4 success facing the famed Corinthians at the end of March when former West Ender Henry Newbery appeared at centre-forward for the visitors. That was an amazing game as West End trailed 4-1 at half-time. They won well against lesser opponents such as Carlisle and Blackpool Olympic, but were outclassed when they met a higher grade of club as shown against the illustrious Preston North End (0-4), Sunderland (0-5) and Scottish joint-champions Rangers (0-3). Preston included past favourite Bob Kelso (left) in their ranks along with several other top names.

Kelso. (Captain.

Off the field of play, matters were going from bad to worse. The club was on the verge of collapse, the limited company was wound up and four enthusiastic directors announced they would now run West End as a private enterprise.

- Gate receipts for the festive meeting with East End on 25th December were £115, a record for the club.
- West End protested that the FA Cup defeat by Sunderland Albion should not have stood, claiming a player was ineligible. But their appeal was thrown out.
- With West End leading 6-0 against Blackpool Olympic, goalkeeper Dave Whitton left his posts to join in with the forwards while it was reported that fans started to walk out of the ground in disgust due to the total one-sided nature of the contest.
- A Northern League match against Stockton was scheduled to be played on 20th December but was staged only as a friendly after West End objected to the state of their own St James' Park pitch! They went onto win 9-0 but lost the re-arranged league clash 4-0.

Captain: Robert Calderwood, William Dempsey, Harry Jeffrey, John McCann.
Northern League: P14 W3 D4 L7 F21 A38 Pts 10.
Position: 7th (Champions: Ironopolis).
FA Cup: R3q (Winners: Blackburn Rovers).
Senior Cup: Did not compete (Winners: Shankhouse).
Ground: St James' Park.
Average Home Attendance: 2,745, top crowd 6,000 (22/31 games).

Appearances: Calderwood R 41, Dowling P 41, Jeffrey H 39, Patten R 36, McCann J 30, Whitton DR 30, Byrne F 29, McCann E 27, McKenzie T 18, Graham AT 16, Dempsey W 13, Ross J 13, Walker D 13, Kennedy A 12, Ryder W 12, McCrory M 11, Gillespie JS 10, McKellar D 8, McLucas RR 7, Taylor J 7, Hardman HG 6, Heslop J 6, Ryder J 6, Wood SP 6, Fitzgerald JE 5, Raylstone JB 5, Wardropper JosW 5, Barker J 4, Johnstone RT 4, Merrilees HF 3, Jardine W 2, Newbery HC 2, Cattell C 1, Collins J 1, Cowan R 1, Dixon H 1, Halliday R 1, Kirkpatrick J 1, Mackie RW 1, Martin 1, Mathieson A 1, McInnes TFM 1, McIntyre R 1, Penny A 1, Redpath JG 1, Thompson J/D 1, Walton J 1.
Goals: Calderwood R 20, Patten R 18, McCann E 9, Dempsey W 8, McKenzie T 7, McCrory M 5, Newbery HC 5, McKellar D 4, Hardman HG 3, Kennedy A 3, McLucas RR 3, og 3, Heslop J 2, Jeffrey H 2, Wood SP 2, Byrne F 1, Johnstone RT 1, McCann J 1, Raylstone JB 1, Ross J 1, Walker D 1, (scrimmage 4), (unknown 3).

Season 1890-91

Northern League — results

Match	Date		Opponent	Res	FT	(HT)	Att	Pos	Scorers
1	06 Sep	H	Darlington St Augustine's	W	5 1	(1 0)	3000	1	McKellar, Ross, Walker og (Neill), Johnstone
2	13 Sep	A	Middlesbrough Ironopolis	L	1 5	(1 4)	2000	2	Mckellar
3	27 Sep	A	Newcastle East End	L	1 7	(3 4)	5000	5	McKellar
4	11 Oct	H	Middlesbrough	W	4 0	(1 0)	4000		unknown (scrimmage)
5	01 Nov	A	Darlington	W	2 1	(3 1)	2500		Dempsey 2
6	22 Nov	A	Stockton	L	0 5	(0 2)	3000		
7	27 Dec	A	Darlington	W	4 1	(1 1)	1500	3	Calderwood, McKenzie, Hardman, McCann E
8	31 Jan	A	Middlesbrough	L	0 1	(0 0)	3000		
9	07 Feb	H	Stockton	L	0 4	(0 4)	4000	5	
10	04 Apr	H	Middlesbrough Ironopolis	D	2 2	(0 1)		6	Byrne, McCann E
11	11 Apr	A	Darlington St Augustine's	D	1 1	(1 1)		6	Calderwood
12	15 Apr	A	Sunderland Albion	L	1 4	(0 2)	2000	7	Wood
13	25 Apr	A	Sunderland Albion	L	3	(0 2)	3000	7	Heslop
14	29 Apr	H	Newcastle East End	D	2 2	(0 2)	2000	7	Calderwood, Jeffrey

FA Cup — results

Round	Date		Opponent	Res	FT	(HT)	Att	Scorers
1q	04 Oct	H	Elswick Rangers	W	5 2	(1 1)	1500	Calderwood 2, Patten 2, Dempsey
2q	25 Oct	H	Southwick	W	8 1	(5 0)	1500	Patten 2, Kennedy 2, Dempsey 2, Calderwood, unknown
3c	15 Nov	A	Sunderland Albion	L	0 3	(0 1)	3000	

Northumberland FA Senior Cup

Round	Date		Opponent		
1	24 Jan	H	Rendel	L	WE withdrew, Rendel awarded walkover

Northumberland & Tyne Charity Shield

Match	Date		Opponent	Res	FT	(HT)	Scorers
1	27 Apr	H	Rendel	W	8 1	(5 0)	McCrory 2, Patten 3, Calderwood, McCann E 2
sf	02 May	N	Willington Athletic	D	1 1	(1 0)	unknown (scrimmage)
sfr	05 May	N	Willington Athletic	L			WE withdrew, Willington awarded walkover

Other matches — results

Match	Date		Opponent	Res	FT	(HT)	Att	Scorers
15	04 Sep	H	Preston North End	L	0 4	(0 1)	4000	
16	20 Sep	A	Albion Rovers	W	3 0	(0 0)	2000	Patten, Dempsey, McKellar
17	18 Oct	A	West Hartlepool NER	W	5 2	(3 2)		Calderwood 2, Dempsey 2, Patten
18	08 Nov	H	Motherwell	W	6 1	(2 1)		McKenzie 2, Calderwood 2, Hardman 2
19	29 Nov	A	Sunderland	L	0 5	(0 3)		
20	06 Dec	H	Mossend Swifts	L	1 3	(0 2)		Kennedy
21	13 Dec	A	Carlisle	W	8 0	(5 0)		McKenzie 3, og (Carr) 2, Calderwood, Patten, Jeffrey
22	20 Dec	H	Stockton	W	9 0	(5 0)	6000	Patten, Newbery 5, McKenzie, unknown, McCann J
23	25 Dec	H	Newcastle East End	L	0 5	(0 3)		
24	26 Dec	A	Middlesbrough Ironopolis	W	4 1	(1 0)	1000	Calderwood 2, McCann E, unknown (scrimmage)
25	01 Jan	H	Glasgow Rangers	L	0 3	(0 0)	4000	
26	02 Jan	H	Clyde	D	1 1	(0 0)	2000	Patten
27	03 Jan	H	Corinthians	L	1 4	(0 2)	4000	Calderwood
28	10 Jan	H	Newcastle East End	W	3 0	(0 4)	4000	Patten
29	14 Feb	H	Wishaw Thistle	D	0 0	(0 0)	2000	
30	21 Feb	A	Blackpool Olympic	W	6 0	(4 0)	1000	McCann E, Patten, McLucas 2, Raylstone, unknown
31	28 Feb	H	Middlesbrough	L	0 1	(0 0)	1000	
32	14 Mar	H	Newcastle East End	L	2 3	(2 1)		Calderwood, McLucas
33	21 Mar	A	Rendel	W	4 0	(4 0)	4000	Patten, Calderwood 2
34	27 Mar	A	Newcastle East End	L	0 4	(0 4)	400	Patten, Calderwood, McCann J
35	28 Mar	A	London Caledonians	W	3 0	(2 0)		Calderwood, McCrory, McCann E
36	30 Mar	H	Burnley	W	3 1	(2 0)	1000	Calderwood, McCrory, McCann E
37	31 Mar	H	Corinthians	W	8 4	(1 4)	3000	McCann E 2, Patten 3, McCrory 2, Calderwood
38	20 Apr	H	Sunderland	W	2 0	(1 0)	5000	Wood
39	22 Apr	A	Rendel	W	2 0	(2 0)		unknown (scrimmage), Heslop

Line-ups

Match	1	2	3	4	5	6	7	8	9	10	11	Referee
1	Whitton	Jeffrey	Dowling	Walker D	Ross	Penny	McKellar	Johnstone	Calderwood	Merrilees	Barker	F Hardisty
2	Whitton	Jeffrey	Dowling	Walker D	Kennedy A	Ross	McKellar	Johnstone	Cowan	Merrilees	Barker	M O'Hara
3	Whitton	Jeffrey	Dowling	Walker D	Kennedy A	Ross	McKellar	Johnstone	Dempsey	McKenzie	Barker	F Hardisty
4	Whitton	Jeffrey	Dowling	Walker D	Kennedy A	Ross	McKellar	Patten	Dempsey	McKenzie	Calderwood	Mr Cowen
5	Whitton	Jeffrey	Dowling	Walker D	Ross	Patten	Mackie	Patten	Dempsey (abs)	McKenzie	Calderwood	Mr Howcroft
6	Whitton	Graham A	Dowling	Walker D	Kennedy A	Ross	Mackie	Patten	Dempsey (abs)	McKenzie	Calderwood	Mr Stacey
7	Whitton	Jeffrey	Dowling	Graham A	Byrne	McCann J	Patten	Hardman	McCann E	McKenzie	Calderwood	Mr Grundy
8	Whitton	Jeffrey	Dowling	Fitzgerald	Byrne	McCann J	Patten	Gillespie	Dixon	McCann E	Calderwood	Mr Jamieson
9	Whitton	Jeffrey	Dowling	Fitzgerald	Kennedy A	McCann J	Patten	Gillespie	Byrne	McCann E	Calderwood	Mr Hardisty
10	Ryder W	Dowling	Taylor	Ryder J	Byrne	McCann J	Patten	McCrory	McLucas	McCann E	Calderwood	J Allan
11	Ryder W	Jeffrey	Dowling	Ryder J	Byrne	McCann J	Patten	McCrory	McLucas	McCann E	Calderwood	Mr Coleman
12	Ryder W	Jeffrey	Dowling	Wardropper Jos	Byrne	McCann J	Patten	McCrory	McCann E	McCann E	Calderwood	Mr Grundy
13	Ryder W	Jeffrey	Dowling	Ryder J	Byrne	McCann J	Patten	McCrory	McCann E	Calderwood	Heslop	
14	Ryder W	Jeffrey	Dowling	Ryder J	Byrne	McCann J	Patten	McCrory	Wood	McCann E	Calderwood	
1q	Whitton	Jeffrey	Taylor	Walker D	Ross	Graham A	McKellar	Patten	Dempsey	McKenzie	Calderwood	A H White
2q	Whitton	Jeffrey	Dowling	Walker D	Ross	Graham A	Patten	Kennedy A	Dempsey	McKenzie	Calderwood	Dr Wilson
3c	Whitton	Jeffrey	Dowling	Walker D	Ross	Graham A	Patten	Kennedy A	Dempsey	McKenzie	Calderwood	F Hardisty
1	Ryder W	Jeffrey	Dowling	Ryder J	Byrne	McCann J	Patten	McCrory	McCann E	Calderwood	Heslop	G Young
sf	Ryder W	Martin	Taylor	Thompson J/D	Walton	Ryder J	Halliday	Hardman	Cattell	Redpath	Heslop	
15	Whitton	Jeffrey	Dowling	Walker D	Ross	Kennedy A	McKellar	Calderwood	Dempsey	Merrilees	Barker	F Knott
16	Whitton	Jeffrey	Dowling	Walker D	Kennedy A	Ross	McKellar	Patten	Dempsey	Calderwood	Johnstone	T Wood
17	Whitton	Dowling	Taylor	Walker D	Ross	Fitzgerald	Hardman	Kennedy A	Dempsey	McKenzie	Calderwood	F Knott
18	Whitton	Jeffrey	Dowling	Walker D	Ross	McCann J	McKenzie	Patten	Dempsey	McKenzie	Calderwood	
19	Whitton	Jeffrey	Dowling	Byrne	Kennedy A	McCann J	Patten	McKenzie	Dempsey	Dempsey	Calderwood	F Knott
20	Whitton	Jeffrey	Dowling	Graham A	Byrne	McCann J	Dempsey	Graham A	McCann E	Dempsey	Calderwood	Mr Pratt
21	Jardine	Jeffrey	Dowling	Graham A	Byrne	McCann J	Patten	Calderwood	McCann E	Patten	McKenzie	
22	Whitton	Jeffrey	Dowling	Graham A	Byrne	McCann J	Patten	Newbery	McCann E	McKenzie	Calderwood	
23	Jardine	Jeffrey	Dowling	Graham A	Byrne	McCann J	Patten	Hardman	McCann E	McKenzie	Calderwood	G Young
24	Whitton	Jeffrey	Dowling	Graham A	Byrne	McCann J	Patten	Hardman	McLucas	McKenzie	Calderwood	M O'Hara
25	Whitton	Jeffrey	Dowling	Graham A	Byrne	McCann J	Patten	Hardman	McLucas	McKenzie	Calderwood	F Knott
26	Whitton	Jeffrey	Dowling	Fitzgerald	Byrne	McCann J	Patten	Gillespie	McLucas	McKenzie	Calderwood	
27	Jardine	Jeffrey	Dowling	Raylstone	Byrne	McCann J	Patten	Gillespie	McLucas	McKenzie	Calderwood	C L Glover
28	Whitton	Jeffrey	Dowling	Raylstone	Byrne	McCann J	Gillespie	Gillespie	McLucas	McCann E	Calderwood	Mr Grey
29	Whitton	Jeffrey	Dowling	Raylstone	Byrne	McCann J	Patten	Newbery	McLucas	McCann E	Calderwood	M Knott
30	Whitton	Dowling	Taylor	Raylstone	Byrne	McCann J	Gillespie	Newbery	McLucas	McCann E	Calderwood	F Wills
31	Whitton	Jeffrey	Dowling	Fitzgerald	Byrne	McCann J	Patten	Gillespie	McLucas	McCann E	Calderwood	Mr Grundy
32	Whitton	Dowling	Dowling	Raylstone	Byrne	McCann J	Gillespie	Gillespie	McLucas	Calderwood	Heslop	Mr Pratt
33	Whitton	Jeffrey	Dowling	Wardropper Jos	Byrne	McCann J	Patten	McCrory	McCann E	Calderwood	Heslop	W Tiffin
34	Whitton	Jeffrey	Taylor	Wardropper Jos	Byrne	McCann J	Matheson	McCrory	McCann E	Calderwood	Jeffrey	Mr Henderson
35	Ryder W	Jeffrey	Dowling	Byrne	Byrne	McCann J	Patten	McCrory	McCann E	McCann E	Calderwood	A H White
36	Ryder W	Jeffrey	Dowling	Byrne	Byrne	Wood	McCrory	Wood	Wood	McCann E	Calderwood	Mr Grey
37	Ryder W	Jeffrey	Dowling	Byrne	Byrne	Wood	McCrory	Wood	Wood	McCann E	Heslop	Dr Wilson
38	Ryder W	Jeffrey	Dowling	Byrne	Byrne	Wood	Patten	Collins	Wood	McCann E	McInnes	A H White
39	Whitton	Jeffrey	Dowling	Ryder J	McIntyre R	McCann J	Patten	McCrory	Kirkpatrick	Calderwood	Heslop	W Tiffin

Northern League Table

	P	W	D	L	F	A	Pts
Middlesbrough Ironopolis	14	9	2	3	37	24	20
Middlesbrough	14	8	3	3	33	17	19
Sunderland Albion	14	7	3	4	33	16	17
Stockton	14	7	3	4	38	19	17
Darlington	14	7	0	7	25	25	14
Newcastle East End	14	6	2	6	25	29	14
Newcastle West End	14	4	4	6	21	38	12
Darlington St Augustine's	14	0	3	11	14	44	3

Matches 3,9,21,27,34 : WE finished the game with 10 men due to injuries and illness

Northern League
Match 3 : Late in the first-half the referee called the players together and warned them about the rough play being displayed
Match 6 : Dempsey missed the train, so WE played with 10-men throughout the match
Match 30 : WE played with 10 men when Jeffrey refused to play at half-back

FA Cup
Round 3c : WE lodged a complaint after the game that Albion had played an ineligible player, but the FA rejected the complaint

Northumberland & Tyne Charity Shield
sf : Played at Heaton Junction

Other matches
Matches 22, 28, 32 : Arranged as Northern League fixtures, but played as friendlies because of the weather and poor condition of the pitch

1891-92
DECLINE & FALL

Season 1891-92 was to be a defining campaign for the West Enders on and off the field. They began in terrible fashion, losing 8-1 at St James' Park to Sunderland in what was to be the grand opening of the new season. Then three days later, as the Northern League started, the club fell heavily once more on home turf, 5-0 to champions Ironopolis. West End looked to have recovered when they recorded nine victories up to winter setting in. South Bank and Darlington were defeated in the Northern League as West End's forwards found their touch, netting 12 goals and even briefly topped the table. But during October supporters became increasingly dejected as for the second year running East End began recording humbling defeats.

First up, was a 2-0 Northern League reverse followed quickly by a 3-0 defeat in the FA Cup at St James' Park – two of five hidings in which they conceded 19 goals to their closest rivals. A crowd of 6,000 – although some reports stated the gate reached 8,000 – witnessed the cup meeting in October and showed again supporters would gather in numbers to watch big games.

There had been more changes in management and another clear out of players. West End brought in experienced heads from the Heaton Junction Ground in James Collins and James Connolly, while Tom Nicholson returned after a short period away, and Joe Wardropper was joined by his brother James from Rendel. As usual, a line of new Scots entered St James' Park; McFarlane, McLeod, Ferguson, Gilmour and Tom Hutchinson included. Paddy Dowling, one of last year's imports, along with Geordie warrior, Harry Jeffrey, and Tyneside-Irishman Mick McCrory, were a select few to perform well.

As the year turned, 1892 was to be the club's last. The second-half of the season saw East End continue to show their dominance by winning 7-1, and West End suffered by the same scoreline at the hands of Sunderland Albion too. Much worse though was the 10-0 ignominy at Stockton, this only days after losing 7-0 on a rare trip out of the North East to face Blackburn Rovers. That heavy defeat on Teesside was a game played by West End under protest. Scheduled to be a Northern League fixture but due to the poor condition of the pitch, it was later classed as a friendly. Bizarrely, that was the second such league match with Stockton in a little over a year which ended in a big scoreline to be declared a friendly. The Northern League concluded with West End finishing next to bottom once more, an ill-fated decline after being top of the table earlier in the campaign.

Support, not surprisingly dwindled. The club played out the season with a string of games over the Easter period. They defeated Irish visitors Derry, as well as Lincoln City, both by 3-1, before losing to Shankhouse. The final match of the programme – and West End's very last fixture – was the re-arranged Northern League meeting at the Victoria Ground to face Stockton on 23rd April 1892. They lost by a single goal, the final line-up was:

Whitton; Dowling, Bell; McCrory, Wardropper (Jos), Ryder (J); Wardropper (Jas), Nicholson, Connolly, Collins, Heslop.

The North Eastern Railway Company arranged trips to West End's last fixture at Stockton.

While football was mediocre at best, events off the field were in a mess. The club's management, now led by William Nesham and John Black, was juggling with financial ruin. It was to be the end for Newcastle West End.

- Turnstiles were used at St James' Park for the first time against Sunderland Albion in November.
- The only bright spot in the season was West End's amateur reserve side lifting the Senior Cup with a predominately young and locally produced team. During March they defeated Rendel by 2-1.
- Before West End's final match at Stockton, the team was cordially welcomed at the North Riding Hotel, run by a local well-known sculler JR Hyme.
- By a quirk of fate, as West End folded in May, it was just a few days before Newcastle East End applied to join the Football League. That bid was unsuccessful, but a year later they tried again and reached the game's elite.

Captain: Harry Jeffrey, Joe Wardropper.
Northern League: P16 W4 D0 L12 F21 A56 Pts 8.
Position: 8th (Champions: Ironopolis).
FA Cup: R2q (Winners: West Bromwich Albion).
Senior Cup: Winners.
Ground: St James' Park.
Average Home Attendance: 2,295, top crowd 6,000 (20/27 games).

Appearances: Collins J 39, Dowling P 36, McFarlane W 34, Wardropper JosW 33, McCrory M 31, Ferguson John 29, Jeffrey H 29, Whitton DR 25, Gilmour J 24, Hutchinson T 15, Wardropper JasR 15, Ryder W 14, Shaw T 14, Connolly J 11, Bell TW 10, Nicholson T 10, Ryder J 10, Simm W 7, Grierson JR 6, Fitzgerald JE 4, Heslop J 4, McKellar D 4, McLeod R 4, McNichol T/J 4, Swinburne W 4, Taylor J 3, Atteridge RX 2, Dixon H 2, Knox W 2, Ryder IJ 2, Sullivan M 2, Barker J 1, Baxter A 1, Baxter W 1, Cattell C 1, Dodds T 1, Gow J 1, Merrilees HF 1, McCurdie AH 1, Thompson J/D 1, Wilde GM 1, Willis RHB 1.
Goals: Collins J 14, Gilmour J 10, Connolly J 6, Hutchinson T 5, McFarlane W 5, Wardropper JasR 5, McCrory M 4, Shaw T 4, Nicholson T 2, Simm W 2, Wardropper JosW 2, Cattell C 1, Grierson JR 1, Heslop J 1, Jeffrey H 1, (scrimmage 2), (unknown 2).

Season 1891-92

Northern League — match details

Match	Date	Ven	Opponent	Att	Posn	Result	Scorers
1	05 Sep	H	Middlesbrough Ironopolis	2000	5	L 0-5 (0-2)	
2	12 Sep	A	Darlington	1200	5	W 4-2 (2-2)	Gilmour 2, Hutchinson 2
3	16 Sep	A	Sunderland Albion	800		L 1-5 (1-3)	Hutchinson
4	19 Sep	H	South Bank	2000	1	W 6-0 (2-0)	McCrory 2, Collins, Gilmour 3
5	26 Sep	A	Middlesbrough	2000	4	L 1-6 (1-2)	McCrory
6	10 Oct	H	Newcastle East End	5000	4	L 0-2 (0-1)	
7	31 Oct	H	Darlington	2000	5	W 2-1 (2-0)	Collins 2
8	07 Nov	A	Middlesbrough Ironopolis	3500	6	L 0-6 (0-2)	
9	19 Dec	A	Sheffield United	3000	6	L 1-5 (1-1)	Wardropper Jos
10	06 Feb	A	Newcastle East End	3000	6	L 1-5 (0-2)	Gilmour
11	27 Feb	A	South Bank	1000	6	L 0-2 (0-1)	
12	12 Mar	H	Sunderland Albion	3000	6	L 1-7 (1-3)	Nicholson
13	19 Mar	H	Stockton	1000		L 0-0 (0-0)	
14	26 Mar	H	Sheffield United	1200		W 4-3 (1-2)	McFarlane, Grierson, Collins, Simm
15	09 Apr	H	Middlesbrough	800		L 0-1 (0-1)	
16	23 Apr	A	Stockton	2000	8	L 0-1 (0-1)	

FA Cup

Round	Date	Ven	Opponent	Att	Result	Scorers
1q			bye			
2q	24 Oct	H	Newcastle East End	6000	L 0-3 (0-1)	

Northumberland FA Senior Cup

Round	Date	Ven	Opponent	Att	Result	Scorers
f	05 Mar	N	Rendel	1500	W 2-0	Cattell, Grierson

Other matches

Match	Date	Ven	Opponent	Att	Scorers
17	02 Sep	H	Sunderland	3000	Hutchinson
18	03 Oct	H	Kilbirnie	3000	Collins, Gilmour, McFarlane, McCrory
19	17 Oct	H	Accrington	4000	McFarlane, unknown (scrimmage), Gilmour 2
20	14 Nov	A	South Bank	2000	unknown 2
21	18 Nov	H	Newcastle Wednesday	2000	unknown (scrimmage)
22	21 Nov	H	Sunderland Albion	2000	Collins, Hutchinson
23	28 Nov	A	Darlington	800	Jeffrey, McFarlane
24	05 Dec	H	South Bank	1000	Wardropper Jas 2, Shaw
25	12 Dec	H	Gainsborough Trinity	1000	Collins 2, Shaw
26	25 Dec	H	Canadians XI	2000	Shaw, Wardropper Jas 2, Collins, Gilmour
27	26 Dec	H	Canadians XI	2000	Collins
28	01 Jan	H	Airdrieonians	2000	Collins 2, Wardropper Jos
29	02 Jan	H	Linthouse	1500	
30	09 Jan	A	Blackburn Rovers	1000	Collins, McFarlane, Shaw, Connolly, Simm
31	23 Jan	A	Stockton	4000	Connolly 2
32	20 Feb	H	Middlesbrough		Nicholson
33	05 Mar	H	Burton Wanderers		
34	30 Mar	A	Newcastle East End	1300	Collins, McFarlane, Shaw, Connolly, Simm
35	02 Apr	H	Bishop Auckland	600	Nicholson
36	13 Apr	A	Shankhouse		
37	16 Apr	H	County Derry		Connolly 2, Collins
38	18 Apr	H	Lincoln City		Heslop, Wardropper Jas, Connolly
39	19 Apr	H	Shankhouse		Cattell

Team line-ups and referees

Match	1	2	3	4	5	6	7	8	9	10	11	Referee
1	Ryder W	Jeffrey	Dowling	McLeod R	Ferguson Jn	Ryder J	McNichol	Collins	Hutchinson	Heslop	Merrilees	Mr Nolli
2	Ryder W	Jeffrey	Taylor	McLeod R	Ferguson Jn	Ryder J	McNichol	Collins	Hutchinson	McFarlane W	Gilmour	S Kemp
3	Ryder W	Jeffrey	Taylor	McLeod R	Ferguson Jn	Ryder J	McNichol	Collins	Hutchinson	McFarlane W	Gilmour	F Hardisty
4	Ryder W	Jeffrey	Dowling	Swinburne	Ferguson Jn	Wardropper Jos	McCrory	Collins	Hutchinson	McFarlane W	Gilmour	W Tiffin
5	Ryder W	Jeffrey	Dowling	Swinburne	Ferguson Jn	Wardropper Jos	McCrory	Collins	Hutchinson	McFarlane W	Gilmour	F Hardisty
6	Ryder W	Jeffrey	Dowling	Swinburne	Ferguson Jn	Wardropper Jos	McCrory	McKellar	Hutchinson	McFarlane W	Barker	S Kemp
7	Ryder W	Jeffrey	Dowling	Sullivan	Ferguson Jn	Wardropper Jos	Collins	McKellar	Hutchinson	McFarlane W	Gilmour	
8	Whitton	Jeffrey	Dowling	Sullivan	Ferguson Jn	Wardropper Jos	Collins	Collins	Hutchinson	McFarlane W	Gilmour	WE Clegg
9	Whitton	Jeffrey	Wardropper Jos	McCrory	Ferguson Jn	Wardropper Jos	Willis	Nicholson	Connolly	McFarlane W	Collins	
10	Whitton	Knox	Wardropper Jos	McCrory	Wardropper Jos	Wardropper Jos	McCurdie	McFarlane W	Connolly	Simm W	Collins	
11	Whitton	Jeffrey	Dowling	McCrory	Ferguson Jn	Wardropper Jos	Simm W	Simm W	Nicholson	McFarlane W	Collins	F Hardisty
12	Whitton	Dowling	Bell	McCrory	Ferguson Jn	Wardropper Jos	Nicholson	Nicholson	Nicholson	McFarlane W	Collins	AH White
13	Whitton	Dowling	Bell	Fitzgerald	Atteridge	Atteridge	Grierson	Simm W	Connolly	McFarlane W	Collins	CS Craven
14	Whitton	Dowling	Bell	McCrory	Atteridge	Wardropper Jos	Grierson	Simm W	Grierson	McFarlane W	Collins	JR Douglas
15	Whitton	Dowling	Bell	McCrory	Wardropper Jos	Ryder J	Grierson	Nicholson	Nicholson	McFarlane W	Heslop	Mr Boldison
16	Whitton	Dowling	Bell	McCrory	Wardropper Jos	Ryder J	Wardropper Jos	Nicholson	Connolly	Collins	Heslop	
2q	Ryder W	Jeffrey	Dowling	McCrory	Ferguson Jn	Wardropper Jos	Collins	McKellar	Hutchinson	McFarlane W	Gilmour	F Hardisty
f	Ward	Queen	Bell	Fitzgerald	Wilde	Atteridge	Cattell	Grierson	Dixon	Simm W	Dodds	R Campbell
17	Gow	Jeffrey	Dowling	McLeod R	Ferguson Jn	Ryder J	McNichol	Collins	Hutchinson	Gilmour	McFarlane W	F Knott
18	Ryder W	Jeffrey	Dowling	Knox	Ferguson Jn	Wardropper Jos	Collins	McCrory	Hutchinson	McFarlane W	Gilmour	W Tiffin
19	Ryder W	Jeffrey	Taylor	McCrory	Ferguson Jn	Wardropper Jos	Collins	McKellar	Hutchinson	McFarlane W	Gilmour	F Knott
20	Ryder W	Jeffrey	Dowling	McCrory	Baxter W	Thompson J/D	Collins	McFarlane W	Ryder J	Baxter A	Baxter A	
21	Whitton	Jeffrey	Dowling	McCrory	Ferguson Jn	Wardropper Jos	Shaw T	McFarlane W	McFarlane W	Hutchinson	Hutchinson	JW Johnstone
22	Whitton	Jeffrey	Dowling	McCrory	Ferguson Jn	Wardropper Jos	Shaw T	Collins	Dixon	McFarlane W	Gilmour	F Knott
23	Whitton	Jeffrey	Dowling	McCrory	Ferguson Jn	Wardropper Jos	Collins	Collins	Dixon	McFarlane W	Gilmour	
24	Whitton	Jeffrey	Dowling	McCrory	Ferguson Jn	Wardropper Jos	Shaw T	Collins	Wardropper Jas	McFarlane W	Gilmour	AH White
25	Whitton	Jeffrey	Dowling	McCrory	Ferguson Jn	Wardropper Jos	Shaw T	Collins	Wardropper Jas	McFarlane W	Gilmour	AH White
26	Whitton	Jeffrey	Dowling	McCrory	Ferguson Jn	Wardropper Jos	Collins	Wardropper Jas	Gilmour	McFarlane W	Collins	W Tiffin
27	Whitton	Jeffrey	Dowling	McCrory	Ferguson Jn	Wardropper Jos	Shaw T	Wardropper Jas	Gilmour	McFarlane W	Collins	F Knott
28	Whitton	Jeffrey	Dowling	McCrory	Ferguson Jn	Wardropper Jos	Shaw T	Wardropper Jas	Gilmour	McFarlane W	Collins	W Tiffin
29	Whitton	Jeffrey	Dowling	McCrory	Ferguson Jn	Wardropper Jos	Shaw T	Wardropper Jas	Gilmour	McFarlane W	Collins	F Knott
30	Whitton	Jeffrey	Dowling	McCrory	Ferguson Jn	Wardropper Jos	Shaw T	Wardropper Jas	Gilmour	McFarlane W	Collins	
31	Whitton	Dowling	Bell	Fitzgerald	Wardropper Jos	Fitzgerald	Shaw T	Simm W	Connolly	McFarlane W	Collins	Mr Beardshaw
32	Whitton	Dowling	Bell	McCrory	Wardropper Jos	Ryder J	Grierson	Wardropper Jas	Nicholson	McFarlane W	Collins	AH White
33	Whitton	Dowling	Bell	McCrory	Wardropper Jos	Ryder J	Shaw T	Wardropper Jas	Connolly	McFarlane W	Collins	F Knott
34	Whitton	Dowling	Bell	McCrory	Swinburne	Wardropper Jos	Wardropper Jas	Connolly	Connolly	McFarlane W	Collins	G Young
35	Whitton	Dowling	Bell	McCrory	Wardropper Jos	Ryder J	Grierson	Simm W	Connolly	Nicholson	Collins	F Knott
36	Whitton	Dowling	Bell	McCrory	Wardropper Jos	Ryder J	Grierson	Nicholson	Connolly	Collins	Heslop	
37	Whitton	Dowling	Bell	McCrory	Wardropper Jos	Wardropper Jos	Wardropper Jas	Nicholson	Connolly	Heslop	Collins	F Knott
38	Whitton	Dowling	Bell	McCrory	Ryder J	Nicholson	Nicholson	Nicholson	Connolly	Simm W	Simm W	AH White
39	Ryder W	Dowling	Bell	Fitzgerald	Wilde	Ryder J	Cattell	Grierson	Dixon	Simm W	Dodds	F Knott

Northern League Table

	P	W	D	L	F	A	Pts
Middlesbrough Ironopolis	16	14	1	1	49	13	29
Middlesbrough	16	13	0	3	33	13	26
Sheffield United	16	10	2	4	49	21	22
Newcastle East End	16	9	2	5	37	20	20
Stockton	16	6	2	8	31	34	14
Sunderland Albion	16	5	0	11	36	38	10
South Bank	16	3	2	11	21	50	8
Newcastle West End	16	4	0	12	21	56	8
Darlington	16	2	3	11	17	49	7

Northern League
Match 14 - No nets were used and Sheffield complained that for one of WE's goals the ball had gone past the post
Match 16 - Final WE match before the club went into liquidation

Northumberland FA Senior Cup
f: Reserve team XI, played at Heaton Junction

Other matches
Match 21 : WE described as a scratch team although they fielded 7 first-team regulars
Match 31 : Scheduled as a league game, both teams lodged a complaint before ko because of the state of the ground and the match was classed as a friendly and the league fixture rescheduled
Match 32 : Scheduled as a league game, WE lodged a complaint because of 6 inches of snow on the ground and the match was classed as a friendly and the league fixture rescheduled
Match 34 : Played in aid of the labourers who had been thrown out of work by the Tyneside Engineers strike

THE WEST ENDERS: DEMISE

The mood in the West End camp as the 1891-92 programme closed towards the end of April was anything but good following a second miserable campaign. Finances collapsed as income fell and expenditure increased. Support at St James' Park dwindled as fans stayed away. During 1889-90 an average crowd of around 3,400 watched home games, while for 1891-92 that average had dropped to 2,300.

Reasons for West End's rapid deterioration are not recorded in any detail, but it is not difficult to relate a mix of issues. Over the past four or five seasons West End had anything but stability on and off the pitch. There was a constant turnover in players and the policy of heading to Scotland and seemingly grab any footballer keen to cross the border did not work. Admittedly several Scots that arrived were decent players, including of course one or two Scottish internationals, notably Bob Kelso, however the majority did not perform adequately in a red-and-black shirt. Several appeared to be there just for the money. One correspondent wrote that in the last two seasons imports had "not been good enough". From a footballing and monetary view, the plan had failed.

During the 1930s a rare team group was published in the local press of West End during their last season of 1891-92. The players were all named. Back row, left to right: Bennett (secretary), Shaw, Whitton, Dowling, Ferguson, Foreman (linesman), Kennedy (trainer). Second row; McCrory, Jeffrey, Joe Wardropper. Front; James Wardropper, Gilmore, McFarlane, Collins.

Another strategy which proved unsuccessful was the approval of financial guarantees to bring clubs to St James' Park in the hope that better-quality opponents would generate more interest and produce larger attendances and with it, income through the gate. Certain clubs did that such as Aston Villa and West Bromwich Albion, but pledging cash to sides which were far from appealing proved an economic disaster. Only 1,000 watched Blackpool Olympic and a mere 400 London Caledonians.

Crucially perhaps, the club's management appeared to be unable to decide on an organisation which worked. From the mid-1880s there were constant changes and disputes behind the scenes brought disharmony (see Management, page 117). Prominent individuals came and went and while the one steadying influence seemed to be William I'Anson, he departed in 1890 as the club became a limited company.

There were also suggestions in the Tyneside press that West End should amalgamate with Newcastle East End, seemingly, although not prosperous by any means, in a much healthier state than the St James' Park outfit. However, both clubs were against such a move.

West End's management made a great effort to rectify results on the pitch and the finances off it, but nothing seemed to work and they eventually gave up the struggle for survival.

Newspapers of the day reported the demise of West End during the middle of May 1892:

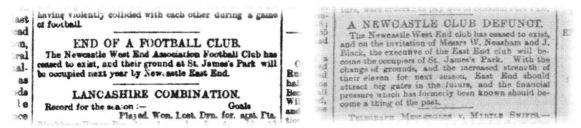

Northern Daily Telegraph 11 May 1892.   Sunderland Daily Echo 10 May 1892.

END OF A FOOTBALL CLUB.

The Newcastle West End Association Football Club has ceased to exist, and their ground at St. James's Park will be occupied next year by Newcastle East End.

LANCASHIRE COMBINATION.

Record for the season:—

A NEWCASTLE CLUB DEFUNCT.

The Newcastle West End club has ceased to exist, and on the invitation of Messrs W. Neasham and J. Black, the executive of the East End club will become the occupiers of St. James' Park. With the change of grounds, and the increased strength of their eleven for next season, East End should attract big gates in the future, and the financial pressure which has formerly been known should become a thing of the past.

NEWCASTLE AND MIDDLESBRO' GOSSIP.

[BY T. T. MAC.]

As stated by me in Monday's "Referee," rumours have been current for some time past as to the future of the Newcastle West-End Football Club. For the last two seasons it has had anything but a prosperous career, and has resulted in a heavy financial loss to the management. Messrs Neasham and Black, who have had the control of affairs, have done everything in their power for the success of the venture, but have had the worst of luck, and last week announced their intention of severing their connection with the club, but in a sportsman-like manner made known their intentions to the executive of the East-End Club, and offered them the use of their field for the remainder of the lease, some eleven or twelve years of which have still to run.

The secretary of the East End club informs me that this offer was considered at a meeting of his directors on Monday night, and accepted. We therefore regretfully bid farewell to West End, and next season shall only have the East End as our representative club for Newcastle.

The East-enders therefore take possession of St. James Park. Their team is of the strongest possible description, and we look forward to an eventful season. The field is in a most central position, and the gates are bound to be very large.

Scottish Referee 13 May 1892.

SHOOTING.

MATCH NEAR NORTH BIDDICK.—A great shooting match was decided yesterday morning between "Tavern" of North Biddick and "Scamp" of Washington, who shot at a 4-inch ring, 40 yards off, single guns, 1¼oz. shot, for a tenner. Result:— Tavern, 6 marks; Scamp, 5.

FOOTBALL.

ASSOCIATION.

GOODBYE TO WEST END.—We are informed that the Newcastle West End Club has now ceased to exist, and on the invitation of Messrs W Neasham and J Black, the executive of the East End club will become the occupiers of St. James' Park. With the change of grounds, and the increased strength of their eleven for next season, East End should attract big gates in the future, and the financial pressure which has formerly been known should become a thing of the past.

ATHLETICS.

FIVE MILES WALKING MATCH AT MIDDLESBROUGH.—Yesterday

Newcastle Daily Journal 10 May 1892.

Newcastle upon Tyne at that time could not support two ambitious and developing football clubs. There was a hardcore of support for both West End and East End, and when the two rivals met, crowds were good. In the latter seasons, recorded attendances reached 6,000 at St James' Park and 4,000 at the Heaton Junction Ground. But there was only room for one team. And that single outfit could harness the joint support of around 10,000 as a basis to progress into a football club on a national stage.

The North East also saw the demise of another prominent football club at the end of the 1891-92 season. On Wearside, Sunderland Albion followed West End into the annals of history. Both Tyne and Wear communities now only had one major club to support. It was a defining moment in North East sporting history. The Darwinian theory of evolution and now famous words of 'survival of the fittest' applied to football too.

The Aftermath

In the wake of Newcastle West End's sorry passing, the game on Tyneside rapidly developed. West End's everlasting legacy in football's history is that they played a significant part in the evolution of Newcastle East End into Newcastle United. At that time William Nesham and John Black were West End's most fervent officials. On the club's collapse they approached their counterparts from the other side of the city at East End. A now famed meeting took place at Joseph Bell's house on Rothbury Terrace in Heaton, where Nesham and Black explained the dire position of the West End club and offered their assets, including the lease of St James' Park – a much more favourable ground than East End's Chillingham Road base.

There was no formal merger of the two clubs as the West Enders disbanded and had financially collapsed. But East End's management were open to relocation and taking any beneficial goods. They were also keen on adding West End's successful reserve eleven to their playing ranks. Soon an agreement between officials was reached. Most important of all in the accord between the two past rivals was that Newcastle East End would move to St James' Park. As a result of that decision, a chain of events was set-in motion which saw the club retitled *Newcastle United*.

May 1892: *West End fold and are disbanded.*
May 1892: *Officials of West End approach the directors of Newcastle East End and offer the club's assets to their rivals, including the lease of St James' Park. East End arrange to move from Heaton to West End's ground.*
Sept 1892: *East End play their first game at St James' Park, against Celtic.*
Dec 1892: *Newcastle East End change their name to Newcastle United.*
May 1893: *Newcastle United elected to the Football League.*

Note: Some years later during the 1930s another Newcastle West End FC was formed, playing local football in the city. They were based near Fenham Hall Drive, likely at the Hunter's Moor ground. This club had no connection to the original West Enders apart from their title.

RESERVE & OTHER TEAMS

From very early years Newcastle West End fielded more than one senior line-up. Along with other clubs in the region, at times the club had several teams competing in the area. During 1883-84 they fielded a West End 2nd XI for the first time and even a West End 3rd XI outfit was occasionally noted. The Northumberland Football Association introduced a "Second Team Competition" and "Junior Challenge Cup" to give lower-ranking sides competitive football with appropriate trophies. The Temperance Festival football tournament also had prizes on offer for reserve and junior sides, West End reaching the final of the Seconds during 1886.

Over the next few seasons, the Newcastle press reported on West End's secondary teams, at times maybe four or even five different sides, although it is suspected that certain combinations were mixed up with differing titles. But for season 1886-87, the club's official Rule Book notes four teams played in their colours: "1st Team", "Swifts", "2nd Team" and "Juniors". The term Swifts was used by several clubs, usually the leading reserve line-up.

White Rose Juniors, also from the Westgate district, amalgamated with the club at the start of August 1887 giving West End a new batch of young players. But that arrangement only lasted a year before Rose reformed. West End's subsidiary teams fielded many local players up to then, but by the time they had started to become a professional outfit and used players from Scotland, several experienced footballers played for the second-string on a regular basis, occasionally even the odd Scottish international.

During season 1889-90, the club appears to have streamlined operations but still fielded two reserve sides, noted as a "reserve team" and a "2nd team". They went on to win the NFA's Second Team Competition, initially defeating Elswick Rangers 3-1, but having to replay the final due to a successful protest. They won again, this time by 6-2.

As season 1891-92 began, the Northumberland Football Association decided to make their flagship Senior Cup tournament an amateur only competition. So West End turned out a side composed of young, amateur footballers from the district. And they started well in the opening round, defeating Science & Art 3-0, a game played in heavy snow. Prior to the kick-off, Science & Art had lodged a protest against the contest being played and this was later sustained. The tie had to be replayed a couple of weeks later in front of a crowd estimated at 500 to 700, a match that ended with the same result and West End progressing.

The referee for that tie was the renowned Newcastle East End stalwart, Alec White. He also officiated at the next game against the cup holders, Shankhouse, a fixture that attracted a very healthy crowd of 1,500. Underdogs West End won again by 2-1, with goals by Wilde and Dodds. Another good crowd turned up for the semi-final, played on the neutral ground of Rendel in Benwell. The West Enders progressed to the final, this time by virtue of a 3-1 triumph against Newcastle Albion. Two goals by Grierson plus a scrambled affair did the trick.

The club's reserve combination were just about the strongest amateur side in the North East by this time. So much so that the Northumberland County side that defeated Cleveland 6-3 in an inter-county game at the end of February 1892 included no fewer than four West End players; Bell, Fitzgerald, Atteridge and Dixon.

West End Reserves (wearing red jerseys) faced Rendel in the Senior Cup final that year and the tie was staged at East End's Heaton Junction Ground attracting a 1,500 crowd. Captained by John Fitzgerald, the West Enders secured the trophy thanks to two first-half goals by Charlie Cattell and Joe Grierson. Rendel pulled a goal back through Price in the second period but could not force an equaliser. So West End lifted silverware. Or did they? Rendel were not content and they submitted a protest on the grounds that two of the West End players, Cattell and Dodds, were professional runners in contravention of the Northumberland FA's amateur status. The objection was over-ruled so West End lifted the trophy, the club's last. They went out of existence on a high.

Although by the summer months Newcastle West End no longer existed as a club, a meeting was held of their reserve team hierarchy during mid-June 1892 when it was unanimously decided to combine the whole side with Newcastle East End who had disbanded their own reserve line-up, East End Amateurs. West End's second-eleven became the Newcastle East End 'A' team, and by December, Newcastle United 'A'.

West End Reserves showing off the Northumberland Senior Cup after defeating Rendel just before the club folded in 1892. They are likely pictured when the team migrated to join Newcastle East End, and wearing black & white stripes, occasionally worn by the East Enders as an alternative to their normal red shirts.
Back row, left to right: Dixon JW (secretary), Redding, Queen, Ward, Bell, Nesham (director), Black (director), Pears (trainer).
Middle row; Cattell, Anderson, Fitzgerald, Wilde, Atteridge, Dodds,
On ground: Grierson, Dixon H, Simm.

Over West End's decade, the club's reserve line-ups usually played on the ground of the first-team, although it was detailed that they also used the pitch of Percy Iron Works FC on Leazes. Attendances for these games were at times good, notably for clashes with prominent rivals. During 1889 and 1890 over 1,000 watched games against Sunderland Reserves and Ironopolis Reserves, with even better crowds peaking at 2,000 for a home match against South Bank 2nd XI a few months earlier which West End won 9-0.

GROUNDS

Football grounds during the 1880s were very basic, at first simply a marked-out pitch, a set of posts, and perhaps the playing area roped off. There was little in the way of facilities, there were no stands or dressing areas, players arriving ready changed or walking from a nearby building, usually a popular public-house. From the mid-years of the decade as clubs developed and found suitable locations, small stadiums took shape – comparable to old-style non-league grounds of later years. Rudimentary dressing-rooms were built as well as a small grandstand. Railings were erected at pitch level, a fence around the ground and gates with turnstiles for spectators.

West End had a home base at three locations during their ten years in the game.

Town Moor/Leazes

West End used the vast green area of the Town Moor to play the game at first, no doubt close to, or at the same place as the club's cricketers. They formed a pitch on the Moor known as "Newcastle Leazes", near to Leazes Park and St James' Park, the home of Newcastle Rangers until 1882. The *Northern Athlete* newspaper during 1884 described the pitch as "situated on Leazes at the North side of the Park". As a young boy playing for Larkspur, the great Colin Veitch of Newcastle United and England, remembered that the site was off Richardson Road and opposite where the Royal Victoria Infirmary stands, "just below the path which now leads from the [Leazes] Park to Spital Tongues".

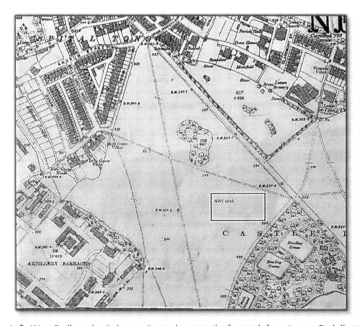

Left: West End's early pitch was situated next to the footpath from Leazes Park (bottom right) to Spital Tongues (top left). The Royal Victoria Infirmary was later extended onto land opposite the Bowling Green. St James' Park is located to the south of the park. Right: A view at the turn of the century of the park's boating lake in front of Leazes Terrace; its other symmetrical elevation overlooks St James' Park.

By early 1885 newspaper reports indicate West End also played some games at Jesmond. This may have been as a result of a somewhat controversial issue which developed in the city. As the 1885-86 season began, West End faced a major setback, along with several other clubs that played their football on the Town Moor. The Freemen and Corporation decided that football should be banned from the wide expanses of the Moor. In September, the Town Clerk issued a notice, reported as "prohibiting the putting of posts on the Town Moor or Leazes".

There had been complaints to the authorities earlier in the year that "six or seven" football clubs had left holes on the Leazes and Town Moor after erecting goal-posts. The reports did not name the teams, but no doubt Newcastle West End was one of them. It was noted that these clubs had "destroyed the herbage" while grazing animals could be injured as the holes had not been filled in. Although a 35-acre site had been allocated by the Freemen for sporting and recreational activity which was allowed by their charter – likely the area of the

Temperance Festival – teams arranged games elsewhere on the Moor without, seemingly, gaining formal permission.

When Brunswick and West End met for the opening game of the season on 12th September, the secretary of the Brunswick club proceeded to erect posts into ground. A policeman was in attendance and took his name, being in breach of the Town Clerk's order. It is not known if the match was stopped, although there is no record of the actual result. No doubt consequences would follow for the Brunswick official.

Several clubs were far from happy and made a challenge to the order, backed by the Northumberland FA. Following a meeting in the Crown & Thistle Hotel a few days later, it was decided to test the legality of clubs playing football on the Moor and a "test case" would be brought before Newcastle magistrates. No such challenge could be traced in contemporary newspapers so the outcome isn't known. It is recorded matches were still played on the Moor, but it certainly appears that the ban likely remained in force through 1885 and 1886, the Temperance Festival excluded.

As a result, West End frantically began a search for a new pitch and towards the end of 1885 agreed to share facilities with Newcastle FA, taking over the ground of the recently disbanded Jesmond club.

Brandling

West End's new base was located on the edge of the Town Moor, just off the primary North Road, one of three pitches close to each other. Described as "on the first field north of Brandling Park" and often referred to as "Moor Edge", it was next to Abbotsford Terrace and the bowling green, a short walk to Tyne's ground at Warwick Place. On New Year's Day 1886 they played there, against visitors from Middlesbrough, the Melbourne club.

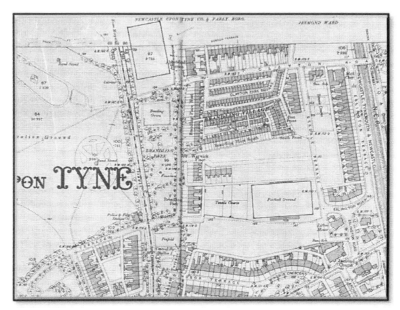

Brandling in Jesmond was the location of three football venues. Tyne's Warwick Place is shown at the bottom, West End's pitch is adjacent the main route north at Abbotsfield Terrace. Another field was just to the north, opposite the Orphanage.

West End's stay in Jesmond was a short one. By the end of that 1885-86 season they were offered the lease of the old Rangers ground, St James' Park at Leazes, part of the Town Moor but which had prior permission for recreational purposes – including football when Rangers played there in the early Eighties. A wealthy merchant, William Nesham had control of the 5.25-acre plot of Castle Leazes. West End agreed a lease of initially four years, extended during 1890 to another 14 years at a ground rent of £10 2s 6d (£10 13p) per acre.

St James' Park

Before moving to a new home, West End had to overcome the ban of football which seemingly was still in place. Secretary Tom Watson led a deputation to discuss the matter with the Freemen and Corporation. He managed to reach an agreement and permission was granted for football to again be played at St James' Park. Having been unused for four years the ground needed care and attention, while the playing surface was described as a "boundless prairie"! West End retained the old name and the St James' Park pitch had a quick makeover. West End spent an estimated £200 as the field was levelled and the site was enclosed by "high paling" at eight feet high to give the arena a distinct boundary. It was noted that there was a "rather deep gradient towards the bottom goal". That Leazes to Gallowgate slope is still evident even almost 140 years later, although not nearly as pronounced as it would have been during 1886.

West End's first game at St James' Park took place on 2nd October 1886, against Newcastle East End. The Sheriff of Newcastle, Thomas Bell, formally opened the new ground by kicking the ball to start the match. A crowd of around 2,000 were present and receipts were recorded of 7s 11d (40p). It was noted that the only lady present was "Mrs Watson, wife of Tom Watson, secretary of West End". A celebration event took place after the game at the Northumberland Restaurant on Clayton Street.

The Tyneside press gave directions to potential spectators: "The West End ground is situated between Leazes Terrace and Gallowgate and can be entered from either side – in the first case from the back of St James' Street, in the other, over Leazes from Gallowgate. After the game the large gate at the foot of the field will be opened to facilitate the exit." It was added: "The game will be played in any weather, the ground near the goals and where it is slippery having been covered with spent bark."

Early West End and East End footballer, William Findlay, recalled the early St James' Park in an account for the *Chronicle Football & Cricket Edition* during 1930. He nicknamed the area "The Tub" and described that just past the corner flag, there was a "big water tub, partly sunk, for the liquification of cows and sheep grazing in the field". He remembered that off Barrack Road, "a wicket gate gave admittance". There was, "a small enclosure" called "the Croquet" with an entrance from Leazes Terrace, and banking at the Gallowgate, "a mountain to the bottom goal". Findlay added that after the game fans made "a dash down the mountain to the Strawberry hospice". Towards Leazes Park, he described that there was a "grassy hill" and "to the top of the goal, a few yards from railings, cows, sheep and a few horses chewed the hollow herbage".

Another rare picture of the arena was compiled by a West End supporter of the era. He noted around 1890: "From the Strawberry you stepped across the narrow road to some 'stobs' which guarded the entrance, on to a cinder path which led past the top of Bulmer Street to a gate leading to a gate to the Gallowgate road. The ground at that time was bordered by a low stone wall, low enough for us lads to 'loup' over instead of using the gate."

When West End moved in, Newcastle Corporation wouldn't give permission for a substantial grandstand to be constructed, but it was noted that during the later years of the 1880s, the club erected a "well sheltered stand" or "Pavilion", which must have been small, but at least it served the wealthier supporters and officials of the club. And what was described as an "oblong contraption which seated three or four reporters" was erected on the Leazes Terrace side of the ground. At the time the gents of the press were not too happy, one commenting: "Why those in authority over these football fields should not give reporters a decent place to sit I cannot make out." Footboards were laid on the grass for supporters.

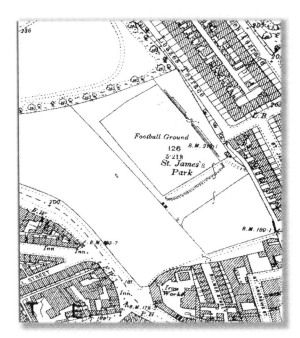
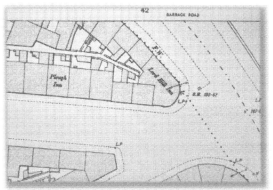

St James' Park as located on the 1890s OS plan, showing banking at the Gallowgate and very small enclosures along the Leazes Terrace touchline. The Lord Hill public-house is marked to the left, on the corner noted "Inn", and shown, right, at the junction of Barrack Road and Pitt Street. John Black's pub was often used as West End's HQ.

West End made modest improvements to St James' Park over their six years as tenants of the ground. During the close-season of 1891 the pitch was greatly improved, moved 40-yards north and returfed, described in the *Newcastle Daily Chronicle* as "now in capital order". More timber boards were also laid for supporters to stand on the touchline.

Not possessing any meeting rooms or office at St James' Park, the headquarters of the club was located away from the ground. During the mid-1880s it was often noted that officials congregated at "Mrs Halls, North Road", although it hasn't been discovered what 'Mrs Halls' actually was. By 1889, the "Clock Restaurant" on Clayton Street East was extensively used for official and social gatherings. The owner, William Liddle was described as "mine host of the Clock Restaurant, the home of footballers". He was an avid enthusiast and welcomed several clubs to his establishment. Liddle later was connected to the Newcastle Wednesday team. John Black's Lord Hill public-house on Barrack Road became a favoured location too, also used as a dressing-room into the 1890s. On certain occasions West End changed at the Lord Hill, and visitors at the Clock Restaurant, both sides walking in full kit to the ground.

Attendances

During the early seasons of West End, the local press hardly ever published attendance figures for matches, usually describing crowds as "small" or "modest". At the outset only a handful of spectators would have watched the club on their initial Town Moor pitch. Gradually though enthusiasts gathered and fixtures had around 500, then 1,000 at games yelling the popular cry back then of "Play Up West End".

By 1886 crowds were now being recorded, albeit estimates by journalists present, which of course varied from newspaper to newspaper. The first average attendance when West End moved to St James' Park for season 1886-87 has been assessed at around 1,450. Crowds would increase in size and local meetings against Newcastle East End and their foes from Wearside, both Sunderland and Sunderland Albion, were well attended as all four clubs developed rapidly after the mid-1880s.

When West End arranged visits from top sides in England and Scotland, attendances were also good. Tyneside's footballing public revelled in seeing the best clubs and some of the finest players at St James' Park. Crowds of up to 6,000 gathered at St James' Park to see these contests. But usually, they only reached 2,000 at best for other games.

At the top end of the scale, it did show that the West Enders could maintain a viable club if they ever reached that level on a consistent basis. Of course, that never happened, although it did for their rivals from Heaton. Admission to games was sometimes reported. As West End occupied St James' Park, admission prices were "Gentlemen 6d (3p), Reserve 6d (3p) extra, Ladies free". And season-tickets were available, during 1887-88 they were priced at 4s (20p) each

Average home attendances, 1886-87 to 1891-92
1886-87: *1,442 (12 of 19 games traced).*
1887-88: *2,689 (9/21).*
1888-89: *2,667 (18/27).*
1889-90: *3.375 (16/27).*
1890-91: *2,745 (22/31).*
1891-92: *2,295 (20/27).*
Overall average/season: 2,575 (97/152).

Top gates for Newcastle 'derby' games at St James' Park
6,000 v Newcastle East End, 25 Dec 1890 (Fr).
6,000 v Newcastle East End, 24 Oct 1891 (FAC).
5,000 v Newcastle East End, 25 Dec 1888 (Fr).
5,000 v Newcastle East End, 25 Dec 1889 (Fr).
5,000 v Newcastle East End, 10 Oct 1891 (NL).
5,000 v Newcastle East End, 25 Dec 1891 (Fr).

Top gates for Tyne v Wear 'derby' games at St James' Park
6,000 v Sunderland, 28 April 1888 (ICC).
6,000 v Sunderland, 26 April 1890 (Fr).
5,000 v Sunderland, 20 April 1891 (Fr).
4,000 v Sunderland Albion, 10 Nov 1888 (FAC).
4,000 v Sunderland, 13 Nov 1886 (FAC).

Top gates for other visitors to St James' Park
6,000 v West Bromwich Albion (FAC winners 1888), 3 April 1888 (Fr).
6,000 v Aston Villa, 4 April 1890 (Fr).
6,000 v Stockton, 8 Feb 1890 (NL).

Top gate for other fixtures at St James' Park
7,000 Shankhouse v Aston Villa, 17 Dec 1887 (FAC).

By the late 1880s West End's home of St James' Park rivalled East End's Heaton Junction enclosure as the regular neutral venue for the region; hosting inter-county games, Newcastle & District matches and Senior Cup finals. Also staged there was one of the biggest fixtures of the era, a FA Cup tie between Shankhouse and Aston Villa at the end of 1887, switched to St James' Park due to a huge interest for the visit of trophy holders Villa. The largest crowd for a game of football in the district up to then, of 7,000 (or even 8,000 in certain reports), saw Villa put on a show and win 9-0. Gate receipts were an exceptional £120.

By the time West End had passed the lease of the ground to their rivals in 1892, St James' Park was regarded as the top venue. Attendances for representative games didn't reach the level of that FA Cup meeting, but were generally decent. A gate of 2,000 watched Northumberland play a Lancashire eleven during 1887 and it was reported that the players "were both on the ground in good time, and some time was occupied in the process of photographing each team". The photograph of the Northumberland XI survives, kept by West End's Jack Barker. Another marvellous team group at St James' Park from the Barker archive show what is very likely to be an 'England XI' in May 1890 when they met a 'Scotland XI' to raise funds for the Northumberland FA Minor Cup. Both line-ups were selected from locally based players.

Left: Northumberland line-up in front of Leazes Terrace at St James' Park during February 1887 before meeting Lancashire. Although individual players are not captioned, included in the county team were seven footballers who played for West End at one time or another; Robert Oldham, James Duns, Joe Wardropper, Jack Beattie, Willie Thompson, James Raylstone and Jack Barker. The Northumberland side wearing their black & white striped shirts won 4-1.

Right: With a group of tartan clad Scots in the background, the 'England XI' pose for a pre-match photograph for the contest against a 'Scotland XI'. Eight West End connected players were in the side; Harry Jeffrey, Joe Wardropper, Alec White, Frank Carnelley, Willie Thompson, Harry Dixon, Joseph Jefferson and Jack Barker. Unfortunately, again the photo is not captioned, but as White skippered the team, he could be the player with the ball in the centre of the front row. Almost certainly Thompson and Barker are to his left and right. Joe Wardropper is standing in the back row, third from the right. England played in the county colours of black & white stripes and won 3-0.

KIT & COLOURS

Little information is recorded in contemporary newspapers regarding West End's colours, but the short-lived *Northern Athlete* sports paper produced football club directories from the mid-1880s which gave valuable information on kit and colours. So did a surviving Northumberland FA handbook and rare team groups showing the kit. Piecing together evidence traced, West End sported kit as follows:

1884-85: *All-blue shirts.*
1885-86: *"Red & Black jerseys & hose with white knickers".*
1886-87: *"Red & Black jerseys".*
1890-91: *"Maroon & light blue vertical stripes with blue knickers".*
1891-92: *Red & Black halved shirts, dark shorts.*

The earliest report of West End's colours reveals the team wearing blue shirts, but during most of their playing time the club pulled on kit of red & black, either halved or hooped jerseys. For season 1890-91, it was detailed that for the game with Preston North End at the start of September, they appeared in "new uniforms, the jerseys being maroon and light blue vertical stripes with blue knickers".

A unique West End team group kept by Jack Barker shows the team wearing attire of *hooped shirts, white shorts and hooped stockings* with one player wearing a club badge 'WEFC'. Footballers also often sported Northumberland caps in front of the camera. Another group, indicates a halved shirt. The colours are likely red and black.

Change colours have been recorded as having kit of *all white*. West End Reserves were described as the "Blues" during the mid-1880s, wearing *blue shirts* before changing to *red*. After the reserve side lifted the Northumberland Senior Cup at the end of the 1891-92 season, they were pictured with the trophy in striped shirts and dark shorts, probably black & white stripes as occasionally worn by their new parent club, Newcastle East End.

A West End group from the late 1880s in their hooped shirts, likely at St James' Park. Note the footballer pictured in the front row, far left, is wearing a jersey with large initials "WEFC" across the chest. Unfortunately, the players are not named in this rare photograph, part of Jack Barker's mementoes.

PART 2

WHO'S WHO

Introduction & Notes

All first-team players traced to represent Newcastle West End are featured in the biographical history. Club officials are also included. In addition, the reserve team players who lifted the Northumberland Senior Cup in 1892 are also included, although all bar two had already featured in first-team action.

Information relating to footballers during this period moved from being scant at the start of the 1880s decade, to what could be termed as adequate, but at times ambiguous as the 1890s opened. Football's authorities were in their infancy and official player registration and transfer documentation did not begin until the latter part of the period as the 1890s created a more regulated approach to the game. No original record books exist for West End FC and formal documentation is extremely limited, although Scottish FA Minutes of Meetings contain references to West End players when they crossed the border and were suspended for professionalism, a useful source.

Consequently, biographies are at times the result of cross referencing, piecing together a jig-saw of data, and using detective-like assessment. Footballers at that time did not reside far from the football club they were attached to. There was no lengthy travelling to play football, and most worked locally. Decisions are sometimes based upon the 'balance of probability' or 'beyond reasonable doubt'; that such and such an individual who is recorded in census documents living near to West End's heartland is more than likely the footballer.

These judgments have been made at times, such as the identity of two men named 'R Davison'. In census records, one lived in Whitley Bay, the other in Elswick, both of a similar age which could fit as being the footballer. However, it is unlikely that someone from Whitley Bay would travel to play for West End on a regular basis, so the conclusion reached that it's highly probable the player was Davison of Elswick. As it turned out, this was confirmed by a much later press report of his golden wedding anniversary. Such family history data has been invaluable tracking many of West End's players

Correspondents of the various newspaper titles were not too accurate with players' names. Christian names were rarely given, while initials and spelling vary. Many individuals had their names shown in differing ways. Even official records such as census returns, birth and death registers, also reveal inconsistencies. And as West End fielded four Waggotts, as well several other identical names like Mather and Scott at the same time, these all proved a headache. And when the many Scottish footballers arrived, players such as McKay and McDonald seemed to be playing everywhere! This all has been problematic to unravel.

Before the use of formal and strict player contracts and a full professional set-up, footballers were in many ways free to appear for any club, and several moved around between teams. Some appeared in only the odd game, and a few on a trial outing. West End fielded players who were attached to other clubs, but assisted the side as "guests" to bolster the West Enders' line-up, at times, against stronger opponents. Occasionally, the number of guests in the side became ridiculous. Against Everton in May 1890, West End played with six guests including five from Sunderland Albion. And facing Albion Rovers during January 1887, they included five Dumbarton Athletic players. There were also close relationships between West End and other neighbouring sides, such as Elswick Rangers and Gateshead Association, and several players often appeared for each line-up.

As a multitude of footballers began to land on Tyneside from Scotland, a number arrived from the same parts of north of the border, especially from the West of Scotland, in particular Dunbartonshire. And many played together for the same clubs at one time or another, team-mates and friends, heading to England in search of pots of gold. Groups landed in England from clubs such as Renton, Vale of Leven, Dumbarton and, in Glasgow, from Northern and Partick Thistle. During September 1888 against Halliwell, it was reported that West End's line-up included six "Rentonians".

Biographies

Player profiles follow the format of *name/role/birth/death/career/honours.*

Birth and death details at times refer to the official records and show quarterly periods, eg *1861 (Q2)* being 1861 during April to June.

Totals for appearances and goals cover first-team matches only. It should be noted that as match details are incomplete for the early seasons, totals are for those games which have been traced. Players in the era were versatile in several positions; where this is the case their West End roles are shown.

Where footballers assisted a club when they were generally attached to another side, this is notated as *guest* in their career movement. And if they also played occasionally or supplementary football with clubs, especially in local midweek Wednesday fixtures, these are added at the end of the career section, eg *Also appeared for Newcastle Wed, Corinthians.*

The *Honours* section at the end of certain biographies show only first-class achievements, such as international caps, title wins or national cup finals. Years noted are the second part of the season, ie *1887* indicates the 1886-87 season. Where players have made less than 10 appearances in title winning seasons, the number of games registered is shown. District representative appearances and local finals, such as playing for Northumberland or reaching the Northumberland Senior Cup final are not included, but are generally mentioned in the biographical text.

If an individual is family related to another in the who's who, this is cross-referenced by *(qv)*.

Where judgements are not totally precise and confirmed, information quoted is shown in *[square brackets]*.

PLAYERS

Notable West Enders

International Players

Aitken RA: Scotland 1886-88, 2 caps.
Arnott W: Scotland 1883-93, 14 caps.
Calderwood R: Scotland 1885, 3 caps.
Hannah J: Scotland 1889, 1 cap.
Kelso RR: Scotland 1885-98, 7 caps.
Sawers W: Scotland 1895, 1 cap.

Football League Title Winners

Brady A (Everton), Hannah J (Sunderland x3), Kelso RR (Preston North End).

Scottish League Title Winners

Byrne F (Celtic x2), Galbraith J (Dumbarton x2), McCann E (Celtic), McCann J (Celtic).

FA Cup Winners

Brady A (Sheff Wed), McInnes TFM (Nottm Forest).

Scottish Cup Winners

Arnott W (Queen's Park x3), Brady A (Celtic), Hannah J (Third Lanark), Kelso RR (Renton x2), McKechnie D (Renton x2).

Most Appearances for West End: Top 5

1 Harry Jeffrey 157 app.
2 Jack Barker 156 app.
3 William Swinburne 131 app.
4 Jock Taylor 122 app.
5 Donald McColl & Dave Whitton 98 app.

Most Goals for West End: Top 5

1 Tom Nicholson 54 goals.
2 Jack Barker 44 goals.
3 Jock McDonald 43 goals.
4 Jack Angus 35 goals.
5 Donald McColl 32 goals.

Longest Serving Player in First XI

Ned Waggott, 6 years 11 months.
Tom Minnikin, 6 years 10 months.

Also appeared for Newcastle United in Football League or FA Cup

Collins J, Jeffrey H, McCurdie AH, McDermid R, McInnes TFM, Raylstone JB, Ryder IJ, Ryder J, Sawers A, Scott D, Simm W, Thompson WP, White AH, Whitton DR, Wilson WA.

A

AITKEN Ralph Allan

1886-1887 Outside-left
b. Kilbarchan, Renfrewshire, 16 February 1863/d. Dumbarton, 10 January 1928
Career: Dumbarton 1883/**WEST END** Sept 1886/Dumbarton Jan 1887 (**WEST END** guest Sept 1887)/Alloa Ath Oct 1889/Our Boys (Dundee) Aug 1890/Southampton Naval Works 1890-91.
Described as Newcastle's first footballing idol, Ralph Aitken was the first international footballer to appear for any club on Tyneside. Along with fellow Scot, Bob Kelso, he placed the name of West End on the football map during those early years. Aitken knew something of the North East having spent part of his childhood in Hartlepool when his father was working in a shipyard. He was offered a good deal by West End's management to relocate to their new St James' Park HQ, perhaps as a professional, although as Aitken recorded, he was a "pure amateur". That was at the time when a debate raged in Scotland over players turning professional in England. There was a huge outcry in his native town and Ralph considered it necessary to pen a letter to the local Lennox Herald newspaper maintaining he was not taking money from West End but moved to Newcastle "having been offered a good job". That was confirmed later by West End's secretary at the time Tom Watson when recalling his career, noting that Aitken "came for nothing except a weekly wage at his trade". Whether he was paid for playing is open to judgement, West End certainly found him a shipyard role as a plater, maybe at enhanced renumeration? Ralph had come to prominence with Dumbarton during the previous season, playing for Dunbartonshire and being capped only six months before landing on Tyneside. A sturdy and diminutive winger full of tricks, the Glasgow Evening Post noted that he is "quick on the ball, and, for his size, very speedy" and added that he "dribbles well, and is altogether a first-class player". Aitken made his debut for West End against Morpeth Harriers and stole the show, hitting two goals in a 4-1 victory at Almonds Field. During his five months in the North East, he was selected by Northumberland as well as the Newcastle & District XI. At turn of the year in January 1887 though, Aitken headed back to Dumbarton, offered a better paid position on Clydeside, apparently more than the 39s 0d (£1.95) per week at the Newcastle yard. While he showed his talent in attack on several occasions, local reporter 'Custos' remarked in the press when he departed: "I don't think that his absence will be much of

a loss to the West End club. Either he was demoralising their team, or their team was demoralising him, so in either case he is better away." Aitken did return to St James' Park, during September 1887 he arrived to assist the West Enders along with Bob Kelso against Scottish Cup holders Hibernian. But the Edinburgh club called off the fixture at the last moment and the international pair appeared in what was described as a "scratch" contest before a sizable crowd. After another stint in England, on the south coast at Southampton, Ralph returned to Dumbarton and continued to work in the shipyards. His son, William Aitken, appeared for the Dumbarton club too, later becoming a director at Boghead Park.
App & Goals: 10 app 4 gls.
Honours: 2 Scot caps 1886-88/SC final 1887.

AMORY J

1884-1887 Goalkeeper, Full-back, Half-back
Career: WEST END 1884 to c1887.
The club's regular second-choice 'keeper over three seasons during the mid-1880s. Amory managed six senior outings at full-back or half-back in 1884-85 and then deputised between the posts for Robert Oldham as West End faced Gainsborough Trinity in a big FA Cup meeting during November 1886. Family history information show very few men with this surname who could be the footballer, but a Newcastle-born John Thomas Amory (or Amery), a joiner, aged around 23 when he would have played for West End, was living in Gateshead during the early 1880s.
App & Goals: 7 app 0 gls.

ANGUS John William

1886-1888 & 1889 Forward
b. Glasgow, 1 December 1868/d. London, 4 January 1933
Career: Glasgow & Liverpool local football/**WEST END** March 1886/Pollokshields Ath cs 1888/Kelvinside Ath by Sept 1888/Third Lanark 1888 briefly/Everton Dec 1888/Gainsborough Trinity cs 1889/**WEST END** Aug 1889 to Nov 1889/Gorton Villa Dec 1889/Halliwell March 1890/West Manchester Aug 1890/Ardwick March 1892/Stockport Co Jan 1893/Southampton St Mary's May 1893 (Partick Thistle guest Sept 1893) to late 1896/Fulham Nov 1899 briefly.
Known as 'Jack', the Scot joined West End towards the end of the 1885-86 season although where he came from is unconfirmed. Census information show his family moved from Glasgow to Liverpool but as a teenager he ended up in Newcastle. Angus soon made an impression, scoring on a regular basis before moving back to his native Glasgow and with Kelvinside Athletic showed up well and was good enough to join Third Lanark. He was quickly spotted by Everton, having a successful trial at the end of 1888. He joined the Merseyside club and was in and out of their Football League line-up (5 app) for half-a-season before returning to Tyneside in the close-season of 1889. During that summer he signed transfer forms for two clubs at the same time – Gainsborough and once more for West End – being handed a suspension by the FA. Angus was prominent during those two spells on Tyneside, especially in seasons 1886-87

and 1887-88 when he scored over 30 goals. He was a dangerous attacker, grabbing the goal which defeated Sunderland in the FA Cup during November 1886 while Jack once hit the net on four occasions as West End registered their record victory of 15-0 over North Eastern in February 1888. Angus was twice a runner-up in the Northumberland Senior Cup final, then scored as the trophy was secured against Shankhouse during 1888. He was good enough to represent Northumberland and the Newcastle & District sides.

After his stint at St. James' Park, Angus became something of a wanderer around England, having short periods with a number of teams including at West Manchester where he played alongside former team-mate on Tyneside, Tom Nicholson. When based on the south coast with St Mary's, he enjoyed a good spell totalling 40 games (25 goals) for the early Saints, noted in the Hampshire Advertiser that "when at his best Jack Angus was a brilliant forward". It was also reported in the southern press that after the 1894-95 season he intended to join the crew of a "well-known yacht" but played on for another year. Angus obviously had a liking for the sea, as soon it was confirmed that he was due to set sail for China by the end of 1896. The Scot returned to London and signed briefly for Fulham where he appears to have worked on the capital's Tower Bridge project. After leaving Fulham around the start of 1900, information on Angus is contradictory. Southampton's Player Archive website notes that he stayed in the Canton district of China and died there during 1903. However official court documents from 1906 relating to his divorce, raised by his wife Charlotte of Southampton, reveal that solicitors acting for Mrs Angus traced Jack "living at Newcastle upon Tyne". The documents also confirm he was a mechanical engineer and at the time of his marriage during 1898 was in London. Subsequent documents reveal he remarried, to a Newcastle lady, continuing to work as an engineer around the country. He settled in London and died there during January 1933.
App & Goals: 63 app 35 gls.
(Note: During the same period there was also goalkeeper, John Alexander Angus of King's Park, Sunderland Albion & Everton, their careers being often tangled.)

ARNOTT Walter

1887 Full-back
b. Glasgow, 12 May 1861/d. Glasgow, 18 May 1931
Career: Pollokshields Ath 1880/Queen's Park May 1882/Pollokshields Ath Jan 1884/Queen's Park Jan 1885 (Blackburn Rovers guest April 1886)(**WEST END** guest Dec 1887)/Ballina (Ireland) 1889/Third Lanark Oct 1892/Edinburgh St Bernard's March 1893/Notts Co Feb to March 1895/Mossknow Rovers (Dumfries) 1896 to 1898.
Also appeared for Corinthians/London Caledonians.

W Arnott, Queen's Park.

One of Scotland's foremost players in the amateur era, perhaps the best-known footballer north of the border at the time. 'Watty' Arnott was captain of Queen's Park and Scotland, at 5'9" tall, he was considered the finest defender in Victorian times, capped on 14 occasions for his country, winning the Scottish Cup on three occasions – as well as reaching two FA Cup finals with the Glasgow club in England. Sound and solid, he displayed an artistic, classy style and as a staunch amateur he appeared for several clubs around the country over nearly two decades. His link to West End occurred during December 1887 when club officials heard that the famous defender was to be in the city on business. They quickly acted and met Watty at the Central Station asking him if he would like to play. Arnott accepted and ran out in West End colours against Shankhouse at St James' Park but had to leave the game 20 minutes into the second period to catch a train back north. Even though Arnott only played that single game for West End – and at that, only around an hour – the Tynesiders could boast they had fielded the game's two finest full-backs in Arnott and Bob Kelso. Residing most of his life in Glasgow, he was also a noted bowls, cricket and tennis player as well as a keen curler and yachtsman. Arnott became a popular writer and after-dinner speaker.
App & Goals: 1 app 0 gls.
Honours: 14 Scot caps 1883-93/FAC final 1884, 1885/SC winner 1884, 1886, 1890.
(Note: Arnott was scheduled to play as a guest for Celtic in 1895, but he failed to appear for the match. Certain sources have Watty appearing for Linfield, that was his brother William Arnott.)

ATKINSON F [Frank Octavius]

1882-1883 & 1887-1889 Half-back
b. [Newcastle upon Tyne, 1864 (Q3)/d. [Whitley Bay, 11 January 1908]
Career: **WEST END** 1882/Elswick Leather Works 1883/**WEST END** cs 1887/Elswick Rangers Jan 1889.
A member of the West End cricket eleven in 1883, he is likely the footballer who was selected once for the football side against Newcastle FA during that year. After joining the Elswick Leather Works team in 1883 it appears Atkinson returned to the West End squad during the summer of 1887 and became a regular reserve player. From census information, the probable individual is Frank Atkinson, one of two brothers residing in the Elswick and Westgate area, being around 18 years of age when he first appeared for the West Enders. Frank became an electrical engineer and after the turn of the century resided in Whitley Bay. During the same period a F Atkinson played the oval game for North Elswick as well as cricket with Elswick Leather Works and Benwell, this could be the same individual.
App & Goals: 2 app 0 gls.

ATTERIDGE Richard Xavier

1890-1892 Half-back
b. Newcastle upon Tyne, 1869 (Q3)/d. Transvaal, South Africa
Career: Telegraph FC (Newcastle) by Feb 1888/**WEST END** 1890-91/Newcastle East End-Newcastle Utd cs 1892 to 1894/Also Trafalgar 1892-93/Telegraph FC (Newcastle) 1893-94.
Also appeared for Newcastle Wed/Newcastle Wand.

At the height of his career, 'Rick' Atteridge was selected for the Northumberland County team during February 1892. He was then elevated from the youthful West End reserve side to the club's senior eleven in Northern League action while Atteridge was part of the half-back line when the second-string lifted the Northumberland Senior Cup during March 1892. He was a leading player in that side and on West End's demise a couple of months later, was a member of the squad which moved en bloc to Newcastle East End. The Tynesider eventually turned out for the Newcastle United 'A' team and reached his second Senior Cup final in 1894, this time losing to Shankhouse. Like many footballers of that era, Atteridge was a decent cricketer with the Bath Lane CC and reached trial matches for Northumberland County in 1887. He lived on Stanhope Street near St James' Park when he was with the West Enders, and away from his sporting prowess, Rick trained to be a telegraphist,

successfully passing exams in technical telegraphy at the Durham College of Science. With an expertise in setting up communication systems he moved to Pretoria in South Africa just as the second Boer War erupted and between 1899 and 1902 was reported as a "civilian employed in Army – telegraphist".

App & Goals: 2 app 0 gls.

B

BARKER John

1884-1891 Forward, Secretary, Committee
b. Brampton, Norfolk, 1868/d. Newcastle upon Tyne, December 1933
Career: Drysdale (Newcastle) 1884/**WEST END** Dec 1884, becoming secretary 1884-86, committee 1886-89 (Newcastle East End guest Dec 1886, Jan & Dec 1887, May 1889)/Newcastle East End-Newcastle Utd Dec 1891/Trafalgar Sept 1893/Shankhouse later 1893 briefly/Trafalgar Oct 1893 to 1896.

One of the most prominent of Tyneside's pioneer footballers, 'Jack', as he liked to be known, served both Newcastle clubs, West End and East End during their formative years on Victorian Tyneside. Only Harry Jeffrey appeared more for the West Enders than Barker's 156 matches – and that by a single appearance. He was also a goal-getter, hitting 44 over his eight seasons in the first-eleven, including 12 when they finished as runners-up in the Northern League for 1889-90. Jack also sat on West End's committee and acted as club secretary. At 5'9" tall, he was an effective forward over a long period, on the field for the West Enders opening FA Cup fixture in 1886, and he took part in their first FA Cup proper tie against Grimsby Town during season 1889-90 as well as the club's debut in Northern League football. Barker also reached three Northumberland Senior Cup finals (1886, 1887 and 1888 as a winner) and when he switched allegiance to Newcastle United's embryo club, took part in their first season at West End's old home of St James' Park during 1892-93, appearing once in a Northern League fixture with Middlesbrough. John is also recorded as being the first player sent-off in a competitive match

for the West Enders, during a feisty local derby and very first match in the Northern League with East End during September 1889 when he received his marching orders along with East End's James Miller. During his teens Barker joined West End and soon became an established footballer, a regular for the Northumberland County XI as well as representing the Newcastle & District side. In 1891 the Newcastle Daily Chronicle noted that Jack had been "one of the most clever and popular players in the North". Information from Barker's descendants on Tyneside noted he was born in the south of England and later lived in Benwell; census records show one John Barker born in Norfolk, the family relocating to Newcastle before 1881 and settling in Elswick. After retiring he managed several pubs, The Turks Head and Albion Hotel included, Barker was also employed at a local factory and lost an eye in a work accident. A popular character on Tyneside, he has the distinction of being awarded a benefit match when with West End, staged at St James' Park against Sunderland during April 1891; a huge crowd for the day of between 5,000 and 6,000 turned up. Barker was also a noted cyclist, a popular sport during his era, appearing for the Clarion Bicycle Club, while he played cricket for the Bath Lane, White Rose and West End clubs. He died at the end of 1933 when living in Benwell, and the Newcastle Evening Chronicle wrote that Barker had been "always a great credit to football by reason of his ability and his clean tactics".

App & Goals: 156 app 44 gls.

BAXTER A

1891 Outside-left
Career: Willington Ath 1891 (**WEST END** guest Nov 1891) to c1898.
With two players by the surname of Baxter linked to West End in season 1891-92, and three altogether, it has been a challenge identifying which played in the club's senior matches. From a report in the Jarrow Express for the game against South Bank during November 1891, it confirms that West End tried Willington Athletic's half-back "A Baxter" in the line-up. Baxter served Willington for several seasons during the 1890s.
App & Goals: 1 app 0 gls.

BAXTER John

1889 Outside-left
b. Lesmahagow, Lanarkshire, 30 December 1863/d. Newcastle upon Tyne, 6 September 1927
Career: Partick Thistle 1885/Northern (Glasgow)/Elswick Rangers by Feb 1887 (**WEST END** guest April 1889) to 1892.
Known as 'Jock' Baxter, he was a well-respected footballer on Tyneside, serving Elswick Rangers with distinction for almost five years. Born in the village of Lesmahagow near Lanark, he settled in the Anderston district of Glasgow working as a brass finisher. Having been largely a reserve player with Partick Thistle, Baxter was one of a batch of Scots from established clubs to join the Elswick team as they began to be stern rivals to both West End and East End in Newcastle. Jock was one of the many short-term guest players for West End, appearing

and scoring against Derby Junction during April 1889, playing alongside his forward colleague from Rangers, James Nugent. A Northumberland Senior Cup runner-up with the Mill Lane club in 1889, Baxter was also capped by Northumberland. He remained in Newcastle once his footballing days were over, employed as an iron-turner at the Armstrong ordnance factory like many of Newcastle's footballers of the era. He resided in Benwell to his demise.

App & Goals: 1 app 1 gl.

BAXTER W

1889-1892 Half-back

To be seen in West End's reserve ranks usually as a forward from 1889 to 1892 when the club folded, Baxter is likely to be the player who stepped in at half-back to appear against Newcastle Wednesday during November 1891. Little has been traced of the individual.

App & Goals: 1 app 0 gls.

BEATTIE John William

1886 Half-back

b. Glasgow, 27 August 1859/d. Burnley, 25 March 1933

Career: Partick Thistle c1877/Burnley Dec 1884/Elswick Rangers Sept 1886 (**WEST END** guest Nov 1886)(Gateshead Ass guest 1886-87)/Union Star (Burnley) Oct 1887 to cs 1891 when he retired.

Also appeared for Newcastle Wed/Victoria Wed.

Born and raised in Partick, 'Jack' Beattie is recognised as one of the pioneer footballers of Partick Thistle. Starting with Thistle as a teenager, he was captain and highly regarded at their old Muir Park ground, noted in one report as being "a splendid half-back for years". He represented the Glasgow XI and appeared almost 70 times for Thistle before moving to Lancashire and turning professional. Described as an excellent tackler, and very judicious in placing the ball to his forwards, Beattie was outlawed by the Scottish FA in December 1884 when he joined Burnley along with several other footballers who had crossed the border. Jack joined the Elswick Rangers club for their debut season of 1886-87, being one of numerous Scottish footballers in Newcastle then. Appearing in their first match, Beattie was a sterling player for his one season with Elswick. Selected for Northumberland and the Newcastle & District XI when on Tyneside, he assisted West End during November of that campaign against Sunderland. For that game, the Sunderland Echo reported that West

End's special guest "is considered equal to an international player" while Jack's wages were also reported, a salary "of £2 10 shillings (£2 50p) per week". Afterwards Beattie returned to Burnley and joined the Union Star club for a period. He married a local girl there and later worked as a "beamer" at Grey's Mill for around 30 years.

App & Goals: 1 app 0 gls.

BELL Thomas William

1892 Full-back

b. Newcastle upon Tyne, 1872 (Q1)

Career: Benwell Adelaide/Armstrong Jnrs/Benwell Hill (all Newcastle)/Newcastle East End 1891-92/**WEST END** by March 1892/Newcastle East End-Newcastle Utd cs 1892/Rendel later 1892 to c1896/Heaton Rovers by Nov 1896.

Also appeared for Newcastle Wed.

One of several young West End players to be elevated to the first-eleven as the club struggled through their final season of 1891-92, a regular in defence during March and April. Growing up in Scotswood, he was employed as a turner, Bell took part in the club's very last fixture against Stockton and was in the reserve line-up which secured the Northumberland Senior Cup at the end of that fateful season. He served Rendel with merit, becoming skipper at their Benwell ground and was twice runner-up in the Senior Cup competition. With Newcastle East End for a short period during the 1891-92 season, Bell made a friendly appearance against the local Wednesday League side, Victoria Wednesday but was largely a reserve in the Heatonites second-string, then known as East End Amateurs. Bell was recognised as a good footballer and represented Northumberland County during and after his days with West End.

App & Goals: 10 app 0 gls.

(Note: Somewhat remarkably another Tynesider by the name of Thomas William Bell was also involved in football at that time. No relation to the West End player, this TW Bell was born in 1865 and hailed from Heaton, a player with Brunswick then becoming a distinguished local referee and administrator until the 1940s. He was with the Northumberland FA as secretary as well as acting for the Northern Combination League, Tyneside Football Alliance, North Eastern League and at North Shields FC too. He is also likely to be the Bell who lived on Heaton Road and purchased shares in Newcastle United.)

BENNETT William

1887-1889 Outside-right
Career: White Rose Jnrs 1884/**WEST END** Aug 1887 to
c1889/[Elswick Rangers by 1891].
Also appeared for Science & Art/Newcastle Wed.
When West End took over White Rose Juniors at the end of the summer of 1887, a whole team of young local players joined the ranks, included was William Bennett. Initially with West End Swifts, he turned out once in their first-team, during January 1888 against Motherwell when the Scottish club was on a New Year trip to the North East. Football columns in the press reveal Bennett had departed to London for a period at the start of 1891, but he may have returned and appeared with Elswick Rangers during March.
App & Goals: 1 app 0 gls.

BEST Andrew

1882-1888 Full-back, Half-back, Forward, Secretary, Committee
b. Newcastle upon Tyne, 1864 (Q2)
Career: **WEST END** Aug 1882, becoming secretary 1883-84, 1884-85 & committee 1886-87, 1887-88.
The son of the Registrar of Births & Deaths in the city and born in Elswick, as a teenager Andrew Best began working as a clerk for a gas company. He was a football enthusiast and with Billy Tiffin, the Mathers and Waggotts, was an important member of the club as they began and developed. Best played for the West Enders in the opening fixtures during the autumn of 1882 and was on the field as the side was paired with Tyne Association for the very first competitive match a year later. The Northern Athlete football directory of 1883 and 1884 records Best as "West End Secretary" living at the family home in Camden Street near Ellison Place. Andrew took part in senior matches over four campaigns, selected on a regular basis during 1883-84 and 1884-85. By 1886 he was noted as "second team captain" while Best also sat on the club's cricket committee the following year. During the mid-1890s, Andrew followed his father becoming Deputy Registrar of Births & Deaths in the All Saints district of Newcastle and by the time of the 1901 census, had moved from Tyneside, employed in Manchester as a county council clerk.
App & Goals: 40 app 0 gls.

BEWLEY William Henry

1889-1891 Full-back
b. Newcastle upon Tyne, 29 August 1868
Career: Newcastle FA 1886/Elswick Rangers 1887-88/**WEST END** by Sept 1889/Rendel 1891-92 (Gateshead NER trial Oct 1892)/Gateshead NER Jan 1893 to c1895.
Also appeared for Science & Art.
Billy Bewley became a well-known personality in Newcastle during the 1890s and into the new century. Brought up in the All Saints area of Newcastle, he was an athlete with Newcastle Harriers for a time and started playing football, joining West End for the 1889-90 season. Elevated from the second-string for the visit of Dumfries to St James' Park during November 1889, he had an easy outing in defence as West End won 11-1. That was his only senior game recorded for West End,

but later Billy did well with Rendel, taking part in the Northumberland Senior Cup final of 1892, a runner-up against the West Enders. Once his playing years were over, during 1896 Bewley successfully passed referee exams and was registered by the Northumberland & Durham Referees' Association, officiating at local matches, a long serving official up to World War One. He challenged Billy Tiffin for the Northumberland FA secretary position during 1904, but while Bewley lost the vote he later gained a seat on the governing council. Much involved with the local game, Billy was also a Vice-President of the Northern Combination League by 1909. Residing in Newcastle all his life, he was employed as a railway clerk, becoming a prominent union man with the Railway Clerks' Association before and after the Great War. Bewley was later a top-class bowls player, for many years with the Forest Hall club and received a Northumberland County "Champion of Champions" award during 1939, by then residing in that district. When he played for Gateshead NER, Bill appeared alongside brothers John and Thomas Bewley.
App & Goals: 1 app 0 gls.

BOSWELL William

1887 Forward
b. Winsford, Cheshire, December 1864/d. Gateshead, 1951 (Q2)
Career: Gateshead Ass 1886 (Newcastle East End guest Feb 1887)/**WEST END** April to July 1887/Gateshead Ass cs 1887/Gateshead NER 1889 to 1891.
A noted player with the Gateshead Association outfit, William Boswell appeared for both West End and East End during 1886-87. He featured wearing the red-and-black shirt over the spring and summer of 1887, appearing on five occasions including an attractive exhibition friendly against Edinburgh St Bernard's. Born in Cheshire, he settled in Gateshead during the early 1880s and William was described as a bricklayer's apprentice then afterwards as a locomotive fire-man. By then, Boswell worked at the giant North Eastern Railway Company alongside the Tyne, later becoming an engine-driver. Playing football with his younger brother Joseph for Gateshead, he was a decent forward, good enough to represent the Durham County XI during 1886-87 and 1887-88. The two brothers were both residents of Hexham and employed as engine drivers by the time of the 1911 census.
App & Goals: 5 app 3 gls.

BOUCKLEY J

1885 Half-back
Recorded playing one outing in a brief report in the Newcastle Journal, J Bouckley was part of the line-up for a low-key meeting against Ovingham during November 1885. That was a fixture arranged at short notice after games against the Cathedral club, then Morpeth Harriers, were both cancelled. Nothing can be traced about this footballer during the decade. Perhaps his name was a newspaper miss-print, conceivably the player was reserve team captain J Bayley who filled in, at West End during the same time.
App & Goals: 1 app 0 gls.

59

BRADY Alexander

1888 Inside-forward
b. Glasgow, 9 February 1870/d. Renton, 19 October 1913
Career: Renton Star/Renton Thistle/**WEST END** Jan 1888/Sunderland Aug 1888/Gainsborough Trinity Nov 1888/Burnley Dec 1888/Sunderland Feb 1889/Sunderland Albion April 1889/Everton Aug 1889 (& Burnley Aug 1889, agreeing two contacts)/Celtic Aug 1891/Sheffield Wed Sept 1892/Clydebank Aug 1899/Renton Aug 1901.

Brought up in the Cathcart area of Glasgow, Brady was one of many talented footballers to cross the border to chase money as professionals. Known as 'Alick' or 'Alec', he joined plenty of his fellow Scots in the North East on Tyneside and Wearside at the time. Brought to St James' Park after being on the fringes of the Renton XI, he quickly made an impact for West End, scoring almost a goal a game over his short burst with the club before joining Sunderland for the new season of 1888-89. Afterwards Brady moved around England, even joining two or even three clubs at the same time. Firstly, arriving to play for Gainsborough Trinity he was poached by Burnley officials as soon as he arrived to the anger of the locals and at the railway station was pelted with eggs and tomatoes! He also ran into trouble when at Everton, when he was claimed by both Burnley and Sunderland Albion being subsequently suspended for three months. A "little'un" at 5'5" tall, Brady was once described as a "wee barrel of a man" and possessed pace and knew where the goal was. To many judges Alec was considered unlucky not to play for his country, one of the best uncapped forwards around. He did especially well on Merseyside, at Celtic and with Sheffield Wednesday in a long career. Wearing Everton's colours he scored a hat-trick in the club's record 11-2 victory over Derby County and became a title winner when they played their football at Anfield (rather than Goodison Park).

Then back in Glasgow, he was prominent as Celtic lifted the Scottish Cup for the first time, netting six goals in five ties. At Hillsborough, Brady totalled 178 league and cup games (39 goals) appearing for the Owls debut in the Football League and lifting the FA Cup – for years one of only a handful of players to hold English and Scottish Cup winners' medals. Away from the game he supplemented his income with a variety of jobs; working at an engine works in Gainsborough while in Burnley as a window-cleaner. After his football days, Brady returned to Renton and worked in the Clyde shipyards. His brother Joe Brady also played for Renton, St Bernard's and later Sheffield United.

App & Goals: 8 app 7 gls.
Honours: FL champs 1891/FAC winner 1896/SC winner 1892.
(Note: Brady's birthdate varies, but a new gravestone erected during April 2016 in Renton shows 9 February 1870. There were quite a few players by the name of Brady in the same era, their careers being something of a jig-saw to solve. Apart from A Brady and W Brady of West End, Sunderland had another Brady – Alec, a goalkeeper – and Newcastle East End featured James Brady. Burnley also selected Arthur Brady.)

BRADY William

1889-1890 Outside-left
b. Dundee or Ireland
Career: Johnstone Ath Aug 1884/Dundee Harp Dec 1885 (occasionally with Johnstone Ath 1886)/Burnley Aug 1888/Sunderland Feb 1889/**WEST END** Aug 1889/Lincoln City cs 1890/Dundee Harp cs 1891/Newton Heath Feb 1893.
Another footballer of the Brady clan who also appeared for West End, Sunderland and Burnley. A 5'11" tall forward, he came from Dundee football and spent a season on Tyneside. He had an excellent campaign with West End during 1889-90 as the club experienced regular competitive football for the first time in the newly formed Northern League. Brady took part in the opening game against Newcastle East End and was prominent as they made a bid for the title. The winger once scored four goals against Elswick Rangers while he was also eye-catching in the club's FA Cup run to the First Round proper. Brady scored 13 goals in his 28 outings and not surprisingly was selected to appear for the Northumberland XI as well as for the Newcastle & District representative side. He was described when he joined Burnley as "a tall, athletic, young Irishman from Scotland", which indicates either he was born across the Irish Sea or almost certainly had Irish parents that settled in Dundee. When with Burnley he played alongside Alec Brady, also to join West End and was known as "Young Brady" to distinguish the pair.
App & Goals: 28 app 13 gls.

BROWN

1882-1883 Half-back
With West End during their opening campaign of action in 1882-83, Brown took part in the club's third fixture against Tyne Association Juniors during November. He also played a part in the summer's regular Temperance

Festival football tournament on the Town Moor against Hebburn. Nothing has been traced as to his career or life in Newcastle.
App & Goals: 2 app 0 gls.

BROWN William E

1885-1889 Forward
Career: White Rose Jnrs/Elswick Leather Works/**WEST END** 1885/[Gateshead NER cs 1889 to c1891].
A member of West End's junior ranks, Billy Brown made his debut for the seniors during 1885-86 then became a regular with the Swifts XI during season 1887-88. The forward enjoyed an extended run in the first-team the following campaign, registering 10 games. He did well in front of the posts as well, netting five goals. The Morpeth Herald reported that for one of the Swifts line-ups, included was a "EW Brown"; a William E Brown (b. Newcastle c1864) is registered in the 1881 census as living in Jesmond as a 17-year-old servant to ship owner Frederick Springburn. This may be the West End footballer.
App & Goals: 13 app 5 gls.
(Note: There were several players named W Brown in the North East during the mid-to-late 1880s, with Rendel, Elswick Leather Works, Morpeth Harriers, Gateshead NER as well as West End. The Rendel footballer wasn't linked to West End, but he may have been the Gateshead player.)

BRYMER Robert

1882-1883 Goalkeeper
b. Sunderland, October 1864/d. Portsmouth, June 1904
Career: Elswick Leather Works/**WEST END** 1882/Elswick Leather Works cs 1883.
Two footballing brothers named Brymer appeared in the same Elswick Leather Works team during season 1882-83; Robert and John. During West End's first year they faced the Works Junior side and Robert turned out for the West Enders, maybe on trial, or if the club arrived a man short. That was his only appearance for West End. Census records for 1881 show that the brothers were born on Wearside and had moved to the Westgate area of Newcastle at an early age, residing in Elswick at De Grey Street. He was an apprentice engineer-fitter and later moved to the far south by the next census of 1891, living in Portsea near Portsmouth. Robert passed away at a relatively young age in his late thirties. His brother also died young, in Newcastle during 1903.
App & Goals: 1 app 0 gls.

BYRNE (O'BYRNE) Fergus

1890-1891 Half-back
b. Gavieside, West Calder, 19 August 1871/d. Ottawa, Canada, 19 January 1950
Career: Broxburn Shamrock/**WEST END** Dec 1890/Broxburn Shamrock Aug 1891 (Celtic loan Jan 1892)/Celtic May 1893/Broxburn Shamrock Feb 1894 to 1896.
Referred also as Fergus O'Byrne, he grew up at West Calder in Central Scotland and was a team-mate of the McCann brothers at Broxburn as well as Newcastle East End forward Michael Mulvey. And like the McCanns he

landed with West End to play football. During 1890-91, 'Fergie' as he was known, was an effective midfield player, a regular selection in red-and-black colours all season. When with Celtic, Byrne appeared in Old Firm derby games; a Glasgow Cup semi-final during 1893 and the 1894 New Year's Day clash. He also played a small part in the Celts first two Scottish League title victories. Like his friend of many years, Ned McCann, after football he worked as a shale miner in West Lothian, living in Uphall.

Fergus later emigrated to Nova Scotia, Canada where he became a newspaper correspondent for the Sydney Post and Sydney Record on Cape Breton Island during the Twenties and Thirties. As was described, he also "promoted a successful provincial newspaper", the New Waterford Times in the Canadian province.
App & Goals: 29 app 1 gl.
Honours: SL champs 1893 (1 app), 1894 (5 app).

C

CALDERWOOD Robert

1890-1891 Forward
b. Busby, Lanarkshire, 4 October 1862/d. Busby, Lanarkshire, 13 May 1939
Career: Cartvale 1879/Paisley Ath 1882/Cartvale 1883/Cowlairs cs 1886/Bootle Aug to Sept 1887/Cowlairs Feb 1889/**WEST END** Aug 1890/Thistle (Glasgow) cs 1891/Cartvale 1892 to c1900, becoming secretary.

Raised in Busby not far from Glasgow, Bobby Calderwood made a name for himself with early Scottish club Cartvale being quickly elevated to the national stage. Capped in 1884-85, he scored two goals in his three games for Scotland during March of that season. Often outside-left or centre-forward, Bobby became one of the numerous footballers to be charged and

61

suspended by the Scottish FA for professionalism when he answered an advert for players at Bootle. Calderwood joined the Merseyside club and although he remained there only around two weeks, had taken money and was banned for two years, a severe punishment. He became another star arrival for West End after Aitken and Kelso, appointed captain but soon relinquished the role although continued to play an important part in his only season of 1890-91, appearing in 41 of the 46 matches. And Bobby was ever-dangerous in attack scoring 20 goals. When in Newcastle, the 1891 census captured him residing at Wellington Street near to St James' Park and recorded as a "general labourer", footballers rarely confirming their professional football status then. Calderwood later operated as a referee in Scotland and lived in his home town of Busby at the turn of the century, retaining the "labourer" tag as his occupation.
App & Goals: 41 app 20 gls.
Honours: 3 Scot caps 1885.

CAMERON J/W

1886-1887 Goalkeeper
Career: Elswick Ordnance Works 1884/Elswick Leather Works 1885/**WEST END** 1886-87.
Having been with the two early Elswick football clubs, he was reported in the Tyneside press as either J or W Cameron. He guarded West End's posts once as a deputy to customary 'keeper Robert Oldham, his single outing being against the Newcastle FA side at their ground in Jesmond.
App & Goals: 1 app 0 gls.

CAMPBELL A

1886-1887 Half-back, Forward
Career: Rosehill/**WEST END** 1886 to 1887.
Not much is known about Campbell who turned out at half-back or inside-forward during season 1886-87 when he registered 17 games. Campbell has the distinction of scoring West End's first landmark goal in the FA Cup competition against Sunderland during October 1886, a bad-tempered match which ended in the tie being replayed after protest. He then took part in the next round, a match with Gainsborough Trinity. At the time the Newcastle Daily Chronicle reported that Campbell had arrived from the Rosehill club, classing him as a "foreign" player, ie from out with the area. That appears to be a strange comment, Rosehill being just about part of Newcastle at Willington on Tyne. Likely, Campbell hailed from another Rosehill or the newspaper correspondent made an error. There was a Tom Campbell regularly in the Tyneside-based Rosehill line-up during 1884 and 1885 and later with Boundary, Newcastle East End by 1887 then Rendel. But he was still appearing with Rosehill when West End's Campbell was at St James' Park.
App & Goals: 17 app 2 gls.

CARNELLEY Frank

1889-1890 Half-back
b. Nottingham, 4 October 1871/d. Nottingham, 29 May 1913

Career: St James's (Nottingham) by 1886/Nottingham Forest/**WEST END** Aug 1889 to cs 1890.
Described in newspaper columns variously as Carnelli, Carnellie, Carnelly or Carnelley, official documentation confirms Carnelley, as signed on the 1911 census papers by his brother Albert. Frank's elder brother was also a footballer, and a decent forward turning out at the top level for a string of clubs including Notts County, Forest, Leicester Fosse and especially with Loughborough. Carnelley junior arrived at St James' Park at the start of the 1889-90 season along with two other Forest reserves, Marshall and Danks; all three though do not appear to have played for Forest's first-team. Maybe the trio were fringe footballers at Forest, or even only local players in the Nottingham area. Frank operated in the left-half role on a number of occasions for West End and made the eleven that lifted the Northumberland Senior Cup during April. It is likely when he left Tyneside, he returned to his roots in Nottingham as Frank is recorded as a member of the volunteer part-time Robin Hood Rifles battalion during the 1890s. The 1911 census records Carnelley living in Nottingham working as a boot repairer.
App & Goals: 13 app 1 gl.

CATTELL Charles

1890-1892 Forward
b. Birmingham, 1863 (Q4)/d. [Birmingham, 1944]
Career: Newcastle Garrison 1880s to 1890s/**WEST END** 1890 & Rendel occasionally 1891/Newcastle East End-Newcastle Utd cs 1892 to c1894.
Also appeared for Newcastle Wed, and as a committee member.

Born in the Aston district of Birmingham, by the 1880s Charlie Cattell was living in Newcastle's Elswick district, described as a soldier, a bombardier with the Royal Artillery. He had enlisted when around 20 years of age during the early 1880s and was stationed on Tyneside at the Newcastle garrison on Barrack Road. The army unit boasted a decent football team and he impressed in local games joining the West Enders as the new decade opened. Cattell was more often seen in the club's reserve side during 1890-91 and 1891-92, including the victorious Northumberland Senior Cup final against Rendel during March 1892 when he scored in the 2-1 success. For that match the local press reported that West End included two "professional athletes" in their line-up, Cattell and Tom Dodds. Apart from prowess on the football pitch, Charles took part in athletic meetings

around Tyneside. He is on record as registering the West Enders' last ever goal before their demise, against Shankhouse on 19th April 1892. At the same time as playing for West End, Cattell was also a keen footballer with the Newcastle Wednesday club which had close links to West End, the outfit also based at St James' Park. By the time of the 1901 census, Charles had left the army and was a bootmaker and shop-keeper into the 1920s and 1930s based on Wingrove Road in Newcastle's western suburbs.

App & Goals: 2 app 1 gl.

CHALMERS J

1886-1887 Half-back
b. Scotland
Career: Dundee football/**WEST END** Sept 1886 to cDec 1887.

A regular choice for West End during 1886-87 at half-back, or occasionally in a full-back role, Chalmers also played in the side which reached the Northumberland Senior Cup final. Frustratingly there is little trace in contemporary newspapers of this player joining the West Enders at the start of that season, a strange anomaly as almost all new arrivals during that period to make an impression are noted. As there seems to be no footballer of that name to play locally over that time, it is likely he arrived on Tyneside from another region, maybe – and probably – one of the many Scots to land in the North East as indicated by the Newcastle Daily Chronicle when they noted he was a former Dundee player. Apart from collecting a Senior Cup medal, Chalmers was also involved in what were high-profile FA Cup games against Sunderland and Gainsborough Trinity. Losing his place for the following season, he made a last appearance for West End during November 1887, then vanished, perhaps returning north of the border.

App & Goals: 28 app 0 gls.

COLLIER G/J

1887 Goalkeeper
Career: **WEST END** 1887/Newcastle Rangers 1888.
Just before a new goalkeeper Thomas Fyfe arrived from Scotland, Collier was a stand-in between the posts on a single occasion for West End, against Redcar in October 1887. Reports note the goalkeeper as either G or J Collier and he played briefly for the Newcastle Rangers second-eleven, a new club formed by January 1888 with the title of the defunct pioneering side.

App & Goals: 1 app 0 gls.

COLLINS James

1891-1892 Forward
b. Dalmuir, near Dumbarton, 1872/d. Rochester, Kent, 2 January 1900
Career: Dalmuir Thistle 1887/[Shawfield Ath]/Dumbarton Rangers/Dumbarton/Newcastle East End Aug 1888 (**WEST END** guest April 1891)/**WEST END** cs 1891/Newcastle East End-Newcastle Utd May 1892/Nottingham Forest July 1893/Newcastle Utd Aug 1895 £20/Sheppey Utd Aug 1897/Chatham Utd May 1899 to death.

James Collins was a mobile and dangerous forward on the football field who assisted West End, firstly as a guest when a prominent East End player. Collins moved to Tyneside from Dumbarton, as the Lennox Herald noted, after "English agents have been prowling about Dumbarton for the last week" and resulted in a "Vigilante Committee" being set-up to watch out for more incursions. He was described as a player who "dribbles brilliantly, runs speedily and shoots strongly". Although heading to England as a footballing professional, like many Scots he also had a trade, as a riveter, and Collins worked in the Tyne shipyards too.

He was a versatile footballer appearing in both inside positions and on the wing, one of the best of East End's early finds from Scotland, described in the local press as invariably giving "splendid expositions of the game". At 5'9" tall, James recorded over 100 matches in all fixtures for East End and later, Newcastle United during their early Football League days. He assisted West End in April 1891 as a guest, then switched camps from Heaton to St James' Park for a season when he netted 14 goals, the West Enders' last in football before re-joining East End. Well-known and admired in the region, James was gentlemanly off the park, yet could be an aggressive individual on it. The Scot had a decent spell with Forest after leaving Tyneside, playing on 44 occasions at the top level, scoring four goals on his debut against Wolves during 1893. Sadly, Collins died of tetanus after being injured when turning out for Kent club Chatham in a Southern League match against New Brompton (Gillingham) on Boxing Day 1899. He fell on a piece of flint and contracted lock-jaw. An obituary noted: "He was a quiet, inoffensive man, and many will miss him." James was part of East End's line-up for their debut home fixture at St James' Park against Celtic during September 1892, while he also represented Northumberland during his stay in the North East. Collins also tried his hand at baseball on Victorian Tyneside, a popular sport for a fleeting period, being a 'catcher' for the Brunswick club during 1890.

App & Goals: 40 app 14 gls.

CONNOLLY James

1892 Forward
b. Scotland
Career: [Queensferry Hibs 1888]/Hibernians 1890-91/Stockton April 1891/Newcastle East End Aug

1891/**WEST END** Jan 1892/Fairfield (Lancs) June 1892/Rotherham Town 1892/Burnley Feb 1893/Walsall Town Swifts Aug 1893/Ryhope Villa Sept 1893/Trafalgar Aug 1894/Seaham Harbour Aug 1895/Ryhope CW Dec 1895/Ryhope Villa.

Arriving in Newcastle from Stockton, firstly playing for the East End club at the start of the 1891-92 season, Connolly operated across the forward-line and only appeared in a handful of pre-season fixtures. Yet he did register four goals during a friendly against Queen of the South Wanderers, before causing much controversy on Tyneside. His career with East End was short and colourful, being sent-off in the opening Northern League fixture against Darlington for striking an opponent. Leading the attack, Connolly had an altercation with an opponent and lost his cool, ordered from the field for hitting Waites the Quakers' defender. He was afterwards told by East End officials he would never play for the club again. As a result, James was suspended for a lengthy period and soon moved across the city to St James' Park during January 1892 joining rivals West End. But after some good displays he found the club in a perilous financial state and didn't stay long. Connolly then moved on and courted more controversy, sacked at Rotherham after passing team information to opponents Burnley who afterwards signed him. On the field at his best, the Scot was described as a "fast, sturdy, energetic little player".

App & Goals: 11 app 6 gls.

COWAN Robert

1890 Centre-forward
b. Scotland
Career: 5th KRV (Kirkcudbright Rifle Volunteers) 1887/Mid-Annandale Sept 1889/**WEST END** July to cDec 1890 when he returned to Scotland.

Cowan stood out in football around Dumfries, appearing for the 5th KRV as well as the Mid-Annandale club based in Lockerbie. He was given an opportunity to join West End for season 1890-91 and quickly was elevated to the first-eleven, stepping in for Scottish international Bobby Calderwood during September for a challenge with Northern League champions Ironopolis on Teesside. Strangely, although three newspaper reports show Calderwood appeared, the Scottish international actually played for the reserve side that day in the reverse fixture on Tyneside – and he scored a hat-trick against the Ironopolis second-string. Cowan only turned out for West End's reserve team afterwards and had departed before 1891 began.

App & Goals: 1 app 0 gls.

D

DAVIDSON Robert

1883, 1887-1888 Half-back, Forward
Career: WEST END 1883/Science & Art cs 1883, also secretary 1884/Elswick Leather Works 1886/**WEST END** 1887/Elswick Rangers 1888.

Robert Davidson appears to have enjoyed two spells with the West Enders, as a reserve during their opening season of 1882-83 then later during 1887-88 and 1888-89. In between he played with college side Science & Art in Newcastle and with Elswick Leather Works. For a period, he was in the ranks alongside close namesake William Davison for both West End and the Leather Works in 1887 and later for Elswick Rangers. During the early years of the decade, he also played cricket for West End CC.

App & Goals: 14 app 2 gls.

(Note: Press reports inconsistently label the player as Davidson and Davison, but the majority show Davidson. Data indicates he is not related to William Davison.)

DAVISON William

1885-1887 Full-back
b. Gateshead, c1867
Career: Elswick Leather Works 1882/**WEST END** 1885/Elswick Leather Works 1887/Gateshead Ass cs 1887/Gateshead NER/Elswick Rangers 1888/Trafalgar cs 1889.
Also appeared for Newcastle Wand.

Having been captain of the Elswick Leather Works outfit, William Davison joined West End's squad during 1885 and made his debut for the club as a defender in a clash with Sunderland during March 1886. He was selected once more the following year and was described as a "very sound back". During April 1888 when playing for Elswick Rangers, he took part in an inventive early floodlit match against the Palmershill club of Sunderland at the Ashfield Ground on Wearside. William was employed for over 30 years at the Richardson Leather Works factory, then for 15 years at Redheugh Gas Works in Gateshead. By 1937 he was residing close to Redheugh Park football ground. Davison also played cricket for West End during the early 1880s.

App & Goals: 2 app 0 gls.

(Note: Contemporary reports variously use Davison and Davidson, but a feature on William's golden wedding anniversary in the Newcastle Evening Chronicle confirms his surname as Davison as does census information.)

DEMPSEY William

1890-1891 Forward
b. Kilsyth, 8 December 1863/d. Glasgow, 2 April 1924
Career: Campsie 1888/Cowlairs Sept 1889 briefly/Glasgow Hibs Sept 1889/Hibernians Jan 1890/Cowlairs Aug 1890/**WEST END** Sept 1890/Campsie June 1891 to c1892/Campsie Minerva committee 1920s.

William Dempsey crossed the border in a double-deal with Alex Kennedy from the Cowlairs club in Glasgow. The pair appeared in West End's eleven together and Dempsey did well, hitting eight goals in his 13 outings. The Scot was skipper at St James' Park for a short period during 1890-91, his only season on Tyneside. Just before joining West End, he took part at the start of the Scottish League's first programme of action during 1890-91 with Cowlairs. He later settled around Campsie and worked as a printer, also being a committee member of his local Co-operative Society.

App & Goals: 13 app 8 gls.

DEWAR John

1887 Half-back
b. Dumbarton, 30 March 1865
Career: Dumbarton Ath 1884 (**WEST END** guest Jan 1887)/Leith Ath Nov 1887 to cs 1892.
One of no fewer than five Dumbarton Athletic players to display West End colours for a game during January 1887 with Albion Rovers, the Scottish Cup runners-up. The Athletic team had just faced the West Enders in a holiday fixture on New Year's Day and remained in the city. John Dewar was the older brother of George 'Geordie' Dewar who also played for the Dumbarton club and who went onto become a celebrated international footballer, notably for the senior Dumbarton FC eleven and then for Blackburn Rovers. John was a decent player too, a regular forward for Dumbarton Athletic and selected by Dunbartonshire, then later when at Leith, by the East of Scotland XI. He served the Leith team at Lochend with distinction, being skipper for a period, and was part of their reserve line-up which won the Second XI Cup during February 1892. Employed as a plumber, Dewar remained in the Edinburgh district into the 1930s. His death is untraced but possibly in the capital during 1931 (3 December 1931).
App & Goals: 1 app 0 gls.

DEWAR William

1888-1889 Half-back
b. Scotland
Career: [Clydebank]/Northern (Glasgow)/**WEST END** Dec 1888/Pollokshaws Aug 1889/[Cathcart (Glasgow) Sept 1889].
With the strong Northern outfit in the Springburn area of Glasgow, William Dewar moved south out of reach of the Scottish FA's amateur-only legislation at the end of 1888 and joined West End. He made the first of only three games for the club in the Tyne derby with Birtley at St James' Park, a 2-1 victory. Suspended for professionalism the following year, he was unable to play again in Scotland until reinstatement took place for the new season of 1889-90. It was reported that he joined Glasgow's Pollokshaws club although one newspaper has a William Dewar appearing for a neighbouring new side, Cathcart FC in the same month. During 1891 and 1892 a footballer, W Dewar, turned out for Glasgow Wanderers and briefly in Manchester with Ardwick, this could be the same player.
App & Goals: 3 app 1 gl.

DIXON Henry

1887-1888, 1889-1892 Forward
b. Newcastle upon Tyne, 16 October 1869/d. Darlington, 17 December 1945
Career: White Rose Jnrs 1884/**WEST END** Aug 1887/White Rose Jnrs Aug 1888/**WEST END** Sept 1889/Newcastle East End-Newcastle Utd cs 1892 to c1893.
Also appeared for Science & Art.
Henry Dixon originally was vice-captain of White Rose, joining the St James' Park set-up when they took over the club later returning to them as they reformed. Dixon then arrived back with West End during the 1889-90

season. The brother of club official John Dixon (qv), as described in news columns, Henry was "a more than average good player".

He was in West End's reserve ranks for most of his four seasons and made a bow in first-team action during 1889-90 when he went on to total five outings. Selected for Northumberland, just before West End folded, Dixon was part of the side which lifted the Northumberland Senior Cup then was bonded to the East End club on the demise of West End during the summer of 1892. Not a regular with East End either, Henry afterwards assisted the Science & Art College eleven. As a cricketer, Dixon appeared, and was treasurer, for White Rose, later renamed as Bath Lane Cricket Club. Residing in Westgate, as a youngster he worked as a railway clerk on Tyneside with the NER company based in Elswick before moving to a new post at Darlington sometime after the Great War.
App & Goals: 8 app 2 gls.

DOBSON Thomas Kell

1886 Outside-right
b. Whitburn, 3 September 1865/d. Wetheral, near Brampton, 23 December 1921
Career: Whitburn c1884 (Rosehill guest Dec 1885)/North Eastern by April 1886/**WEST END** Oct 1886/Whitburn Dec 1886/Sunderland Jan 1891/Whitburn by cs 1892.
Only briefly wearing the West End shirt during the autumn of 1886-87, Thomas Kell Dobson was a celebrated sportsman from the County Durham coast. Although a very good footballer, appearing for the Durham side, as well as for the Newcastle & District line-up when with North Eastern, he was more prominent on the cricket field. Tom starred for the Whitburn club and for Durham County on 21 occasions between 1886 and 1896. A dashing batsman, in one match he scored an unbeaten 117 against Yorkshire. Dobson had a long career in the summer game not retiring until just before World War One. He was also involved in the earliest days of the County club and attended the meeting during 1882 which created the County side. On the football field at St James' Park, Tom boosted the attack for a few weeks and figured in important FA Cup ties against Sunderland and Gainsborough Trinity. But he returned to

his first love, to Whitburn, after only four games. Dobson had a period in Sunderland's reserve 'A' team during the early Nineties when the Wearsiders lifted the Football League title in 1891-92. Born and bred at Whitburn and from a family of footballers and cricketers, his son, TK Dobson (junior) also played cricket for Durham, captain of the County and who appeared 100 times from 1922 to 1936. A railway audit clerk, Tom became deputy accountant to the NER company but met a tragic end just before Christmas 1921. He was found dead on the railway line near Brampton having fallen from the Carlisle to Newcastle train.

App & Goals: 4 app 1 gl.

DODDS Thomas

1890-1892 Outside-left
Career: White Rose Jnrs/**WEST END** 1890/Newcastle East End-Newcastle Utd cs 1892/Trafalgar cs 1893 to c1896.
Also appeared for Newcastle Wed/Graingerville.

Like several of West End's locally based footballers, Tom Dodds began with White Rose, the second incarnation of that club. He was described as a "professional athlete" when Tom was selected to appear in West End's reserve eleven for the prestigious Northumberland Senior Cup final during March 1892. That was a trophy winning afternoon for Dodds and he went on to progress into the first-eleven once before the club folded, the penultimate fixture in April against Shankhouse. After joining up with East End's set-up, he won a Northumberland County cap.

App & Goals: 1 app 0 gls.

DOUGLAS John Robert

1884-1886 Goalkeeper, Half-back, Forward
b. Newcastle upon Tyne, 1863
Career: Newcastle Rangers 1880, and committee/**WEST END** Nov 1884 to late 1886, also Jesmond 1884-85 & Gateshead Ass 1885 to 1887, later becoming President/also, Durham FA Member of the Council 1885,

Treasurer 1899 to May 1901/Northern Alliance League President by 1900.

John Douglas was a young school-teacher living in Gateshead when he began as one of Tyneside's early footballers with the Newcastle Rangers club. He was selected as goalkeeper for Northumberland's first inter-county fixture during November 1883 against Cleveland, while John played in the inaugural Northumberland Senior Cup final against Tyne the following year. It looks as if he turned out for West End, Jesmond and Gateshead through the mid-seasons of the 1880s, hopping from game to game at all clubs. His best return for the West Enders was 10 appearances in 1885-86 when he played mainly at full-back, but also once between the posts. Douglas was an ever-present in the side's five-match run to meet Shankhouse in the Senior Cup final. Skipper of Gateshead, by the late 1880s, John had started refereeing fixtures in the North East continuing into the early years of the new century and was a founding member of the Newcastle & Durham Referees' Association when it was created during 1896. He became associated with the Durham FA for a lengthy period until he left the region during May 1901 moving to Whitehaven having received promotion at his business, by then in insurance. Douglas was later based in the Edgbaston district of Birmingham for a period.

App & Goals: 14 app 0 gls.

DOWLING Patrick

1890-1892 Full-back
b. Greenock, 15 August 1864/d. Greenock, 16 July 1931
Career: Port Glasgow Ath by Jan 1886 (Thornliebank guest Aug 1887)/Celtic Jan 1889/(Port Glasgow Ath occasional guest Jan-June 1889)/Alloa Ath Dec 1889 briefly/Third Lanark Dec 1889/**WEST END** Aug 1890/Middlesbrough July 1892 briefly/Shankhouse Sept 1892/Blyth Feb 1893.

Newcastle West End had a massive clear out of players during the close-season of 1891 and Dowling was one of only two senior men retained – along with Harry Jeffrey. Known as 'Paddy', and a past full-back with Celtic, he joined the Tynesiders after a few months with Third Lanark. Having represented Renfrewshire during his early years playing in the West of Scotland, at St James' Park he was one of the club's most consistent performers in a frequently changing line-up during 1890-91 and 1891-92 – almost an ever-present in defence. When the club collapsed, Dowling was all set to play for Boro, but changed his mind and stayed around Tyneside appearing for Shankhouse and Blyth. Paddy took part in a

memorable FA Cup game for Shankhouse when they met Notts County at Trent Bridge as 1893 began. By March 1900, Dowling had joined the army, a gunner serving in South Africa with the Royal Artillery. Paddy wrote a letter back to his brother in Greenock noting that he had been "bombing the Boers" and "had a very narrow shave a few days ago from a bullet". He was based near Kimberley with Lord Methuen's column and added that it was "very hot out here – 101 degrees in the shade". Dowling grew up on a farm near Greenock, while on Tyneside he was recorded as being employed as an engine-fitter, then later when back on Clydeside as a riveter in the shipyards.
App & Goals: 77 app 0 gls.

DOWNES John

1889 Forward
b. Scotland
Career: Northern (Glasgow) 1888/**WEST END** Feb 1889/Darwen Aug 1889/Newton Heath Jan 1890/Northern (Glasgow) cs 1890.
When John Downes signed for West End, he was described by Scottish Referee newspaper as a "crack winger" and "one of the smartest in Glasgow". Playing for the Northern club in Springburn, Downes was a touch fiery on the field and he brought his quick temper to England. In one match for the West Enders facing Sunderland Albion on Wearside during March 1889, he clashed with an opponent and the pair were ordered off after a set-to over a throw-in when Downes "threw the ball into the face of Richardson" and a fight erupted. He then argued with the officials and initially refused to leave the pitch, but eventually did so "amidst the hooting of the spectators". The Scot was reported to the FA for violent conduct and handed a lengthy suspension. He spent half-a-season at St James' Park alongside several of his countrymen before moving to Darwen, later joining Newton Heath (the early Manchester United) but didn't play a senior game.
App & Goals: 11 app 3 gls.
(Note: Newspaper reports generally use Downes, while the Scottish FA official handwritten Minutes of Meetings note Downs.)

DUNS James

1886-1887 Full-back
b. Milfield (or Ford), Northumberland, 9 January 1862/d. Alnwick, 23 May 1941
Career: Alnwick Town 1881/**WEST END** Oct 1886 (Alnwick Working Men's Club guest Dec 1887)/Alnwick Town by March 1888 to 1890, also assisting Alnwick Working Men's Club.
Jimmy Duns was a steadfast footballer of the early game in Alnwick, skipper of the local club during the 1880s. He was often praised, late in 1883 Northern Athlete remarked "he is a powerful kick and has good tackling powers" while another newspaper once described him as being "regarded as one of the finest backs in all England", quite an accolade if rather exaggerated. Jimmy was a top player in the region, moving to Newcastle for just over a year and took over as West End captain half-way through the 1886-87 season. Capped
by Northumberland on several occasions, he also represented the Newcastle & District XI and made a huge impression when facing the star-studded Corinthians. He played alongside his older brother William Duns for Alnwick Town. Jimmy began to officiate at matches in Northumberland during the late 1880s and 1890s while he also played cricket for Alnwick, and for West End CC when in Newcastle. Duns resided in Alnwick's historic town centre at Ballifgate and ran a cabinet-maker and fishing-rod business.
App & Goals: 29 app 0 gls.

F

FAWCETT Thomas

1882-1885 Goalkeeper, Half-back, Forward, Committee
b. Newcastle upon Tyne, c1864
Career: **WEST END** Aug 1882, committee 1883 to 1885/Brunswick (Newcastle) 1885 to 1886/Wellington Rovers (Newcastle).
One of West End's group of early footballers to assist in the formation of the club during 1882, Tom Fawcett took part in their earliest fixtures. He was a reliable player during the first three seasons as West End became established in Newcastle, like many then, he appeared in a number of roles. Also part of the management set-up, Tom was a native of the Westgate district and the son of Selby Fawcett (qv), a club Vice-President and a celebrated local police detective.
App & Goals: 38 app 0 gls.

FERGUSON J

1886 Full-back
Career: North Eastern Oct 1884/Tyne Association 1885 (Newcastle East End guest April 1885)/**WEST END** Sept 1886/Newcastle East End Nov 1886 to 1887.
Ferguson featured with pioneers Tyne Association just before they folded in the autumn of 1886 and then appeared for both West End and East End before settling with the Heatonites. He was selected twice for the Newcastle & District XI and was also included on several occasions for the Northumberland County side between 1884-85 and 1886-87. Ferguson played a bit of rugby on Tyneside as well and was an unyielding defender, Athletic News made the comment that "he can play a capital game". Ferguson only turned out once for West End, during October 1886 against Elswick Rangers, while he was in the Heaton club's line-up against Darlington for the 1885 Northumberland & Durham Inter County Challenge final.
App & Goals: 1 app 0 gls.

FERGUSON John

1891-1892 Half-back
b. Alexandria, Dunbartonshire, [18 August 1864]/d. Alexandria, Dunbartonshire, [c1932]
Career: FC Alexandria/Vale of Leven Wanderers by 1886/**WEST END** Aug 1891 to cs 1892.
Captain of the Wanderers side in Alexandria when he decided to move to England, Ferguson represented

Dunbartonshire in Scotland. Known as Johnnie, he was an experienced footballer who battled through the final season with the West Enders in 1891-92.

Normally operating in the centre-half role – a midfield position back then – Ferguson was one of the mainstays of that closing struggle. Returning to Dunbartonshire, John was well-known in the district north of the Clyde and was employed at the giant Alexandria textile works. He was later a rower of note, a member of the Loch Lomond Isobel Crew which won several local prizes.
App & Goals: 29 app 0 gls.

FIGURES William H [Henry] (Wheeler J)

1886 Outside-right
b. Birmingham, [15 April 1866]/d. [Birmingham, 6 April 1949]
Career: St John's Utd/St Andrew's Rovers/Small Heath Alliance April 1885/**WEST END** Sept 1886/Small Heath Alliance Oct 1886/Great Bridge Unity Dec 1887/Cradley Heath Welfare.
Identifying West End's new arrival at St James' Park during September 1886 has been something of a challenge and needed detective-like scrutiny, typical of what was at times a mysterious and secretive nature of football transfers in an era when switching clubs led to sanctions. For the fixture with Newcastle FA at the start of the 1886-87 season, reports note the club fielded a player named as "Wheeler" at outside-right. Yet no trace of any footballer by this name can be traced. It is very likely that was a pseudonym for an established forward from Small Heath Alliance (later Birmingham City). The respected Athletic News wrote rather cryptically at the time that West End had signed "Wheeler or Figures, who played last year for Small Heath Alliance". It was also reported in the local columns that "Figures of Small Heath Alliance" would appear against Morpeth Harriers, but never did, while the Northumberland FA, in their trial match, selected "J Wheeler", he again did not appear. It seems that Figures was all set to join West End, but returned to continue his football in the Midlands with Small Heath Alliance, back in action for them during October. Maybe he didn't quite fancy the deal offered by the West Enders after his single appearance as 'Wheeler'? Remarkably somewhat, during early December of the same year, the Newcastle Daily Chronicle noted that "Wheeler of Small Heath Alliance" was due to join Gateshead – once more the move never materialised. What is certain is that Billy Figures enjoyed a couple of excellent seasons playing for the future Birmingham City. He reached the FA Cup semi-final

during March 1886 when his side lost to rivals West Bromwich Albion. He was an important part of a good forward-line appearing at inside-forward or on the wing. Having played his early football in the Sparkbrook district of Birmingham, during the 1900s Figures remained living in that district, connected to the Eadie Works, still being there by 1939, described as a commercial traveller. It appears Billy spent time in New South Wales, Australia during the 1890s.
App & Goals: 1 app 0 gls.
(Note: Although some biographies note a full name of William Horace Figures, the probable individual is William Henry Figures.)

FINDLAY James

1887-1888 Full-back
Career: Newcastle Harp player-secretary/**WEST END** 1887-88.
Also appeared for Newcastle Wed/Victoria Wed.
At St James' Park during 1887-88, Findlay stepped up to the first-eleven during November and January, deputising for regular defenders Jock Taylor and Bob McDermid. Beginning his football with the Harp club, previously St Mary's & St James's FC, like several of West End's footballers he took part in Tyneside's popular Wednesday circuit.
App & Goals: 2 app 0 gls.

FINDLAY William Stanley

1883-1884 Forward
b. Aberdeen, 1 April 1864/d. Newcastle upon Tyne, 16 March 1957
Career: Stanley-Newcastle East End Nov 1881, becoming secretary to c1883/**WEST END** by Dec 1883 to 1884/St Peter's 1886-87.
Also appeared for Science & Art/Newcastle Wed.
The Findlay family moved from Aberdeen to settle on Tyneside, brothers Billy and Robert Findlay becoming leading figures in the birth of Newcastle United in South Byker as Stanley FC during November 1881. Like many of United's early footballers, Billy was only a teenager as the club was formed. He was part of the club's pioneer line-up and was appointed the first secretary of the new organisation. Also Stanley's cricket secretary, he was a regular in that original football season for the fledgling outfit, appearing in eight matches, including the historic first outing when he was a goalscorer. Billy became Stanley captain during 1882 when they changed title to Newcastle East End and took part in the club's first competitive fixture. Then a clerk living at Belvedere Street in Byker, a decade later Findlay was still a resident of the district, in Hotspur Street, working as a Brewer's agent. Soon after Stanley's birth, Billy switched to West End where he had a brief stay, selected once in senior action against Rendel as December began during 1883. Findlay also played cricket for several other clubs; Guild of St John, Armstrong, St Luke's, Woodbine and for West End. During 1927, he was featured in the Newcastle Weekly Chronicle as a fervent Newcastle United supporter due to travel to the Corinthians FA Cup tie in London. He was also a club shareholder having purchased equity in East End during July 1895. By the

time of the 1939 National Register, William was the owner of a wine and spirit shop in Newcastle. He died when living in Fenham.
App & Goals: 1 app 0 gls.
(Note: Birth & death records note the family surname as Findlay rather than Finlay.)

FISH Alex

1883-1887 Inside-forward
A reserve forward for the West End outfit over four seasons during the mid-years of the 1880s first wearing their colours in 1883. Fish was appointed vice-captain of the second-eleven for season 1884-85 and was elevated to first-team action during November 1884 when West End faced Lemington Rangers. He remained at the club until the end of 1886-87.
App & Goals: 1 app 0 gls.

FITZGERALD John Edward

1887-1892 Half-back
b. Newcastle upon Tyne, 24 February 1868/d. Newcastle upon Tyne, 1942 (Q3)
Career: White Rose Jnrs/**WEST END** Aug 1887 (Gateshead Ass guest 1888-89)/Newcastle East End-Newcastle Utd cs 1892 to c1894.
Also appeared for Newcastle Wed.

One of a group of young footballers who joined Newcastle West End's expanded set-up when White Rose were amalgamated into the St James' Park club during the summer of 1887. John Fitzgerald stayed with the West Enders to their collapse, mainly operating with the reserve side, captain of the Swifts eleven and at times the reserves too. He was skipper of the team which lifted the Northumberland Senior Cup during March 1892 against Rendel just before the red-and-blacks folded. Fitzgerald was awarded a Northumberland County cap, and the half-back made a senior debut in November 1888 at Birtley, then filled in for absent regulars on five occasions during 1890-91 and four times the following campaign. Census information records John as being employed as a steam-engine turner residing in the St Andrew's district, then by 1901 in Byker.
App & Goals: 10 app 0 gls.

FORSTER

1886 Full-back
When Newcastle West End travelled to South East Northumberland and faced Sleekburn Wanderers during

March 1886, they were two men short and one of the home side's reserve players, Forster, filled in as a guest. The Blyth News reported he was "a good substitute at the back" and "played a good game throughout" as West End fielded only ten men.
App & Goals: 1 app 0 gls.

FORSTER Robert

1887 Goalkeeper
Career: Rendel 1883-84 (**WEST END** guest Jan 1887) to 1894.
Also appeared for Newcastle Wed.
Known as Bob and Rendel's first choice goalkeeper over nearly 10 seasons at their Benwell ground, Forster was a top custodian and well-respected during the era. He took part in the club's four unsuccessful Northumberland Senior Cup finals against West End (1890 and 1892) as well as Shankhouse (1891 and 1893). Bob assisted West End once for a prominent contest, a New Year's Day holiday clash with Dumbarton Athletic when the Scots toured the North East. He then quickly represented the Newcastle & District XI against the Corinthians in the same month when the celebrated Arthur Wharton couldn't get to the fixture in time to play. After serving Rendel with distinction, West End's Billy Jardine eventually replaced him.
App & Goals: 1 app 0 gls.

FOTHERINGHAM John

1887 Half-back
b. Scotland, c1868
Career: Dumbarton Ath 1884 (**WEST END** guest Jan 1887)(Leith Ath guest April-May 1889)/[Willington Ath 1891 to cs 1893].
Visiting the North East with Dumbarton Athletic, Fotheringham assisted West End against Albion Rovers over the festive holiday programme of matches during 1886-87. He was one of no fewer than five Dumbarton players to guest for West End on New Year's Day. A first choice for Athletic, normally at full-back, he was good enough to turn out for the strong Dunbartonshire XI. It is likely that he returned to Tyneside, possibly finding work in the many industries, as a J Fotheringham was prominent with Willington Athletic during the early 1890s. Playing with the club during 1891-92 and 1892-93 alongside other Scots, including West End's Robert McLucas, he was captain at times. It was reported during September 1893 that Fotheringham had "returned to his native hills"...otherwise, Scotland. The 1891 census shows a John Fotheringham living in Jarrow across the river from Willington, a lodger from north of the border, working as an engine-fitter.
App & Goals: 1 app 0 gls.

FOWLER George

1889 Full-back
b. Scotland
Career: Cowlairs 1887/Glasgow University 1888/**WEST END** Feb 1889/Northern (Glasgow) Aug 1889/Cowlairs cs 1890/Vale of Leven 1891-92.
George Fowler was one of two young players (with W McDonald) who joined West End's ranks from Glasgow

University's football club during season 1888-89. Fowler claimed only a single outing when on Tyneside, maybe as a guest player when staying in Newcastle as a student or an employee. That match was a significant clash during February with rivals East End at the Heaton Junction Ground. Back then, as they still do, Glasgow University fielded a strong combination and in Victorian times competed with all of Scotland's top sides of the era. Back in Glasgow, Fowler took part in the Scottish League's inaugural season with Cowlairs.
App & Goals: 1 app 0 gls.

FRAZER James William

1884 Outside-left
b. Gateshead, 1868 (Q1)/d. Newcastle upon Tyne, 16 April 1936
Career: Newcastle Rangers 1881 (**WEST END** guest Oct 1884)/Gateshead Ass Dec 1884 to c1886.
An early pioneer footballer with Newcastle Rangers, captain of their junior team during 1881-82 when the club were the very first tenants of St. James' Park. Known as 'Jack', he later guested once for West End when they faced his Rangers club during October 1884, likely being a stand-in at outside-left when the West Enders perhaps were a man short. At the time he was still a teenager, around 17 years of age. He played alongside his elder brother John E Frazer for both Rangers and for Gateshead Association when they were formed in the aftermath of the collapse of Rangers at the end of 1884. And when Jack pulled on West End's colours his brother was in the Rangers' line-up. Born in Gateshead from a well-to-do family, Frazer lived in Tynemouth when he was a youngster for a time, the census of 1871 showing the household having four servants. Frazer trained to become an architect and by the 1890s ran a business on Grey Street in Newcastle. He later resided in Low Fell, during 1898 unsuccessfully contesting the local elections as a candidate for the council. Records show Jack moved to New Brunswick in Canada for a period but by the time of his death in 1936 had returned to Tyneside, living in Jesmond.
App & Goals: 1 app 0 gls.

FYFE Thomas

1887-1888 Goalkeeper
b. Dumbarton, c1875
Career: Dumbarton/Clyde by 1887/**WEST END** Oct 1887/Bootle cs 1888/Derby Co Feb 1890/Stockton March 1891/South Bank Sept 1891/Cowlairs by Jan 1893/Edinburgh St Bernard's June 1893 to cs 1894.
Thomas Fyfe joined West End to replace Robert Oldham when the regular 'keeper had too many business commitments to continue playing. The Scot became an automatic choice between the posts for the West Enders during that 1887-88 season and was custodian as they lifted the Northumberland Senior Cup in March 1888 against Shankhouse. At the end of that campaign Fyfe moved on, joining the Bootle club on Merseyside, then Everton's main rivals and aiming to join the newly formed Football League. He then stepped up another level when he linked up with First Division Derby County but only claimed two games at the very top stage. Fyfe

once vacated his West End goalkeeper's role to join the side's forward line as the red-and-blacks trounced North Eastern in a record 15-0 victory.
App & Goals: 34 app 0 gls.
(Note: Contemporary reports also note his surname as Fyffe, but official documents confirm Fyfe.)

G

GALBRAITH James

1887 Outside-left
b. Scotland
Career: Dumbarton Ath (**WEST END** guest Jan 1887)(Newcastle East End guest April 1888)/Dumbarton cs 1889 (Celtic guest May 1890)/Middlesbrough cs 1892 briefly.

As an amateur Dumbarton Athletic footballer, James Galbraith faced Newcastle West End twice in exhibition friendly matches on Tyneside at New Year 1887 and 1888. During January 1887, the Scottish visitors remained in Newcastle for a few days and Galbraith guested for the West Enders against Albion Rovers and as was noted, "distinguished himself" in a red-and-black shirt. He must have enjoyed Tyneside life as he was back again the following year, spending a period in the North East. This was at a time when, as the Dumbarton club history notes, "approaches by English clubs stepped up", agents attracting Scots with professional contracts south of the border. Noted as possessing a brilliant left foot and "full of tricks" on the field, he was given an opportunity in Newcastle East End's line-up against Elswick Rangers during April and reports noted the Scot showed up well. However, he did not remain with the Chillingham Road club and Galbraith returned to the west of Scotland joining the stronger Dumbarton FC outfit. He became a prominent member of that side which lifted the title north of the border (shared with Rangers) in the very first season of the Scottish League, 1890-91. James also reached the Scottish Cup final that year as runner-up to Hearts. Galbraith, who appeared for the Dunbartonshire eleven, made a move back to England as a professional with Middlesbrough during the summer of 1892. But his stay in Cleveland was short, appearing only once in senior action for Boro, for the opening game of the 1892-93 Northern League programme. He was sent-off and did not to play again on Teesside.
App & Goals: 1 app 0 gls.
Honours: SL champs 1891, 1892 (7 app)/SC final 1891.

GALL J

1886 Outside-left
b. Scotland
It was reported in local newspapers that for the fixture with Elswick Rangers during December 1886 "West End tried a new player up front, Gall". Added was the comment, "however it was his first game in two years". Arriving on Tyneside from Scotland's capital Edinburgh, it seems his appearance wasn't deemed a success. The only footballer traced at that time in the Firth of Forth area was a J Gall turning out for Burntisland Thistle.
App & Goals: 1 app 0 gls.

GARDINER S

1886-1888 Forward
Career: White Rose Jnrs/**WEST END** 1886/Gateshead Ass 1888-89.
Gardiner was a forward who recorded his debut for West End on the wing during December 1886 against the Newcastle FA line-up, a successful 2-0 victory. Over three seasons at St James' Park, he stepped up occasionally before moving to appear for the Gateshead club.
App & Goals: 4 app 1 gl.

GILLESPIE John Scott

1890-1891 Forward
b. Greenock, 6 November 1866/d. Durban, South Africa, 10 September 1947
Career: Renton/Greenock Morton 1889/Sunderland April 1890/**WEST END** Dec 1890 to cs 1891.
When John Gillespie joined the St James' Park staff mid-way through the 1890-91 season, he was described as a "Sunderland amateur". An ex-Morton forward, he left the Wearside club as very much a reserve player although he did appear twice in Sunderland's very first Football League season before moving to Tyneside – scoring on his debut against Wolves. Gillespie played his football at the same time as working as a marine draughtsman and after his six months with West End he left the football scene and continued his career, moving to South Africa.
App & Goals: 10 app 0 gls.
(Note: Until recently the careers of three Scottish players by the name of Gillespie with Sunderland during the same era have been intermingled. It was suspected this Gillespie may have been the later Scottish international James Gillespie but he is not. The three on Wearside were; John Scott Gillespie (b Greenock), John Gillespie (b Glasgow) and James Gillespie (b Glasgow).)

GILMOUR James

1891-1892 Forward
b. Scotland
Career: Benburb (Glasgow)/**WEST END** Sept 1891/Blyth Aug 1892/Shankhouse cs 1893.
Newcastle West End officials tried countless Scottish footballers during their latter seasons, many were failures, but James Gilmour proved to be one of the successes, albeit for a short period. He scored 10 goals in 24 outings after arriving from Glasgow as the 1891-92 season was due to start. Often on the wing or at centre-forward, he began with an impact during September, hitting five goals, including a hat-trick against South Bank at St James' Park.

However, as the side's form deteriorated during the spring of 1892, the goals dried up and he played few games. On the club's collapse, James moved up the coast to join Blyth and Gilmour continued scoring plenty of goals, described as making "demon runs" for his new club. He was one of two professionals with the Blyth club for that 1892-93 season.
App & Goals: 24 app 10 gls.
(Note: A Clyde player by the name of Gilmour joined Stockton during June 1890, he may be the same footballer to end up in Newcastle the following season.)

GOW John

1891 Goalkeeper
b. Scotland, c1868
Career: Vale of Leven 1888/Renton cs 1889/Blackburn Rovers Oct 1890/Vale of Leven Aug 1891/Clyde Aug 1891 briefly/**WEST END** Sept 1891 briefly/later Northwich Victoria June 1892/West Manchester cs 1893 to c1895.
John Gow was described as a "famous goalkeeper" when he arrived at St James' Park to replace the injured David Whitton and the experienced Scot played in the first game of the new season. That was an attractive challenge against Sunderland on Tyneside, a club to be Football League champions by the end of that campaign, and the West Enders lost by all of 8-1. West End's new custodian did not have a good afternoon and he wasn't seen again, one journalist making the comment, "the Novocastrians professed to be much disappointed with the performance of Gow between the sticks". Before that however, John did show he was a top-rated 'keeper, firstly for Renton until the club was embroiled in a professionalism scandal, then making 19 appearances for Blackburn, a regular for their Football League programme during 1890-91. And at Ewood Park he took part in a FA Cup run to the final, but after playing in the early rounds as first choice, had a poor game and was replaced for the semi-final and ultimately for the final. Gow wasn't too happy and departed in the close-season.
App & Goals: 1 app 0 gls.

GRAHAM Alexander Thomas

1890-1891 Half-back, Inside-forward
b. Tarbert, Dunbartonshire, 1873
Career: Renton Thistle/Renton 1888/**WEST END** Sept 1890/Bootle cs 1891/Liverpool Caledonians cs

1892/Barrow Jan 1893/Renton by 1894/Reading Aug 1895 to 1896.

Known as 'Sandy' Graham and described in a lengthy profile in the Reading Standard during 1895 as "from the land of heather and has had a useful if not wonderfully brilliant career". The half-back or inside-forward headed to Tyneside from Renton's reserve line-up although he appeared on several occasions for the eminent first-eleven. Graham made a quick promotion from West End's second ranks after the seniors had lost 7-1 to city rivals East End, being drafted in for the FA Cup qualifying match with Elswick Rangers during early October. It was reported that Sandy did well and noted "he will prove a decided acquisition to the strength of the team". He remained in the West End side until 1891 opened, yet after playing in prestige matches against Rangers, Clyde and the famous Corinthians, appears to have vanished from action. He was next seen on Merseyside with Bootle and moved to enjoy a short but rewarding spell with Liverpool Caledonians, a side essentially made up of Scots. Graham then continued in the far south with Reading before returning to Dunbartonshire.

App & Goals: 16 app 0 gls.

GRAHAM G

1883 Half-back

With the West End club for their debut season, 1882-83, little has been traced of this early footballer. The Newcastle Journal noted him as "G Graham" when he made his single first-team appearance against St Cuthbert's during January 1883.

App & Goals: 1 app 0 gls.

GRANT James

1888 Half-back
b. Scotland
Career: Leith Ath/Edinburgh St Bernard's 1885/**WEST END** April 1888/Leith Ath Aug 1888/Edinburgh St Bernard's Sept 1888/Burnley 1888-89/Nottingham Forest Nov 1889 to May 1890/[Leith Ath 1891-92].

Jimmy Grant settled on Tyneside as a replacement for his fellow countryman James Raylstone towards the end of the 1887-88 season. The former Leith Athletic and St Bernard's player made an impression during April as he took part in a 4-1 victory at Darlington. He was then immediately drafted into West End's ranks for the significant Inter County Championship meeting with Sunderland at St James' Park, a game in which it was revealed that the Tynesiders kept secret the identity of a new Scottish player to face the Wearsiders, that being Grant. Following a handful of games for West End, Grant relocated, to join both Burnley and Nottingham Forest; registering a couple of outings in Forest's Football Alliance programme. Nicknamed "Puddin" when playing his football in Edinburgh and noted as having performed "yeoman service for the St Bernard's", he was rated highly and selected for the Edinburgh District XI. It is likely he returned to appear for Leith Athletic for season 1891-92.

App & Goals: 5 app 0 gls.

GREENER John William

1887-1889 Inside-forward
b. Newcastle upon Tyne, 21 October 1869/d. Whitley Bay, 7 June 1950
Career: St Cuthbert's (Newcastle)/White Rose Jnrs/**WEST END** Aug 1887 to 1889.
Also appeared for Science & Art/Newcastle Wand.

John Greener was the elder of two brothers from the Westgate district with Newcastle West End reserves during the mid-to-late 1880s. He stepped up for a solitary outing against Ashington during May 1889. Together with his brother Tom, the pair joined the St James' Park roll-call from White Rose when they were integrated with West End for season 1887-88 and played together in the Swifts line-up. By 1911, Greener resided in Jesmond and was employed as a solicitor's clerk in Newcastle with Ryott & Swan. He died in 1950 when visiting Whitley Bay.

App & Goals: 1 app 0 gls.

(Note: During the 1890s, a local man by the name of Greener was a regular match official in North East football involved in the formation of the Northumberland & Durham Referees' Association at Lockhart's Café in Newcastle and elected to the committee alongside Newcastle United's Jack Patten. Reports note this individual as mainly GW Greener, but occasionally JW Greener, the former later becoming Vice-President of the Northumberland FA.)

GRIERSON Joseph Robinson

1887-1888, 1892 Forward
b. Newcastle upon Tyne, 1 January 1871/d. Newcastle upon Tyne, 5 April 1944
Career: White Rose Jnrs 1884/**WEST END** Aug 1887/White Rose Jnrs cs 1888/**WEST END** 1891-92/Newcastle East End-Newcastle Utd cs 1892 to cs 1894.
Also appeared for Science & Art.

Joe Grierson was elevated to West End's first-team when the club struggled to survive at the end of the 1891-92 season. He was one of a handful of talented young players that were successful in the reserve line-up that season as the seniors toiled – lifting the Northumberland Senior Cup. Grierson netted in the 2-1 victory over Rendel to secure the trophy. On the West Enders extinction, he joined the East End set-up as they took over St James' Park and went onto appear for the Newcastle United 'A' side as well as for Northumberland. Like many players of the time, he also was a cricket enthusiast, appearing for White Rose CC and Bath Lane

CC, becoming club secretary. Grierson was brought up at the family home on Bath Lane Terrace, near the club ground, and later became a successful businessman running a printing firm with his brother, TM Grierson Ltd, which traded into the 1980s. Joseph resided at Tamworth Road near Nun's Moor, the family also became early shareholders in Newcastle United when they purchased a holding during 1895.

App & Goals: 6 app 1 gl.

GUILD George (Gunter)

1887 Half-back
b. Arbroath, 17 April 1864/d. Prestonpans, near Edinburgh, 7 February 1936
Career: Arbroath July 1879/Edinburgh St Bernard's 1884, becoming match-secretary for a period (**WEST END** guest April 1887)(Arbroath guest 1889-90) to 1891 when he retired.

Although Tyneside newspaper columns included reports that the St Bernard's guest player who pulled on West End's red-and-black shirt in April 1887 was named "Gunter", this was an error. It was confirmed by the Edinburgh Evening News and Edinburgh Evening Dispatch that St Bernard's George Guild was in fact the footballer, an established half-back who had been part of the Edinburgh club's squad to visit the North East and face West End a few days earlier. Guild helped the West Enders against Redcar along with his colleague Donald Sutherland, reports describing they "played in splendid style" and "materially assisted West End to win their match". Nicknamed 'Doddy' north of the border, Guild hailed from Arbroath and was well-known in that coastal town, a pioneer of the game at Gayfield Park. Appearing for the Edinburgh XI in district representative games, George was also a fine cricketer in the East of Scotland. Noted as a "left-handed batting star and top-notch fielder", he turned out for Arbroath United and Heriot's as well as Penicuik, all prominent cricket clubs and often for Forfarshire. A respected sportsman, during 1918 George was described as "a hero of a hundred and one football and cricket matches". Gaining a Master of Arts at the leading Heriot's School in Edinburgh, he became a teacher, being headmaster at Cockenzie for around 30 years. Guild was also a Justice of the Peace.

App & Goals: 1 app 0 gls.

H

HALLIDAY R

1890-1891 Outside-right
Career: White Rose Jnrs/**WEST END** 1890/Newcastle Albion by Nov 1891/Trafalgar by April 1893/Hebburn Argyle 1894.
Often turning out for West End's reserve line-up during the 1890-91 season, Halliday was handed an opportunity during May in the local Charity Shield tournament against Willington Athletic, his only senior game. On joining Newcastle Albion, he soon became skipper, playing alongside his former St James' Park colleague Joe Ryder – the pair also appearing for Northumberland together.

App & Goals: 1 app 0 gls.

HAMILTON T

1887-1888 Half-back
Another former White Rose youngster who teamed up with West End in August 1887 when his side joined up with the St James' Park club. Playing for the Swifts, it is likely Hamilton was a late stand-in for James Raylstone for a game at Gainsborough Trinity during November 1887. The senior Scot was all set to play but according to reports a telegram was waiting for club officials before kick-off advising them that Raylstone had been suspended for previous foul play. Furthermore, correspondents wrote that West End played with 10 men against Trinity, although another confirmed Hamilton made up the numbers.

App & Goals: 1 app 0 gls.

HANNAH James

1890 Outside-left
b. Glasgow, 17 March 1869/d. Sunderland, 1 December 1917
Career: Elmwood (Glasgow)/Third Lanark 1887 (Edinburgh St Bernard's guest April 1889)/Sunderland Albion Aug 1889 (**WEST END** guest May 1890)/Sunderland May 1891/Third Lanark May 1897/QPR Nov 1899/Retired 1900/Sunderland Royal Rovers trainer-coach Jan to May 1901.
Raised in the Hutchesontown district of Glasgow and nicknamed 'Blood' Hannah, he rapidly became a noted forward in Third Lanark's attack when a teenager. James had just turned 20 years of age when he was part of the side which lifted the Scottish Cup during 1889, soon after being selected for the national team against Wales. Hannah became hot property, eyed by English clubs plundering the Scottish game. Indeed, West End tried to lure him to Tyneside but he chose to link up with Sunderland Albion instead, appearing in the Football Alliance during 1889-90 and 1890-91. Jimmy was a big success claiming 39 goals in 50 league and cup matches and was selected for the Alliance XI. At that time, he assisted West End in a prestige end-of-season fixture with Everton during May 1890 along with four other Albion team-mates. A versatile forward, good with both feet, Hannah was a box of tricks, described as a "classic

dribbler" being rarely flurried with the ball. He stepped up another level joining Wearside's stronger club, Sunderland, for their Football League campaign in 1891-92. The Scot became an influential player over six seasons, totalling 171 games (76 goals) as they lifted the title on three occasions and became the country's very best side.

When on Wearside, Hannah combined football with being the landlord of the Aquatic Arms in Monkwearmouth and later worked for Reid & Co managing pubs in the area, notably the Mountain Daisy Hotel. James resided in Millfield where he died at a young age. His son wus an amateur with Sunderland during the Twenties. Neil Hannah (qv), the older brother of James, enjoyed a period with West End in 1888-89 while a cousin, JD Hannah was a Renton reserve player.

App & Goals: 1 app 0 gls.

Honours: 1 Scot cap 1889/FL champs 1892, 1893, 1895/SC winner 1889.

HANNAH Neil

1888-1889 Forward
b. Glasgow, 31 December 1866/d. Glasgow, 10 February 1936
Career: Third Lanark 1888/Clydesdale (Glasgow)/**WEST END** Nov 1888/Sunderland Albion Sept 1889/Thistle (Glasgow) 1889-90/Glasgow Wand 1891-92/Thistle (Glasgow) 1893-94/Also, Elmwood (Glasgow) Vice-President Aug 1892.

A young striker who grew up in Glasgow and the elder brother of future Scottish international James Hannah (qv) who guested for West End, Neil moved the 150 miles to Newcastle as the 1888-89 programme was underway. Hannah had just appeared for the Lanarkshire XI against Northumberland and must have made an impression to West End officials. Described in the Glasgow Evening Post as "a centre-forward of considerable merit", he proved to be a potent addition to the West End attack. Hannah scored seven goals in only 15 appearances but was soon poached by Wearside rivals, Sunderland Albion, who had just signed his brother. He didn't stay too long at the Blue House Field, heading back to Clydeside to continue his football. Neil was employed as an engine-fitter when in the North East, he later resided in the Govan area of Glasgow.

App & Goals: 15 app 7 gls.

HARDMAN Henry Girling (Herdman)

1888-1892 Forward
b. Newcastle upon Tyne, 1869 (Q2)/d. Newcastle upon Tyne, 16 November 1910
Career: White Rose Jnrs 1886/Elswick Leather Works cs 1886/**WEST END** by February 1888/Trafalgar cs 1892/Newcastle Utd Feb 1893/Trafalgar 1894 to 1895. Also appeared for Newcastle Wed.

During the period from 1887 to 1892 newspaper commentary frequently referred to a West End player by the differing surnames of 'Hardman' and 'Herdman'. This proved something of a conundrum to solve. The footballer could be two different players, or the same person, the press being inconsistent with spelling of surnames in general. The conclusion of extensive investigation is that the West End player is one individual, Harry Hardman. A key document from the 1891 census reveals the Hardman family residing at Jefferson Street in Westgate and lodgers were West End's recent arrivals from Scotland, John and Edward McCann along with Fergus Byrne. The Hardmans' sons are recorded as Henry, 22 years of age, Samuel, 20, and George 16. With this West End connection, the footballer at St James' Park is almost certainly Henry Hardman as his brother Sam was also with the club at the same time, a goalkeeper for the reserve side. Harry appeared in the red-and-black shirt over three seasons, totalling 16 games. Hardman lived all his life in the same district of Newcastle, employed as a fitter-turner.

App & Goals: 16 app 4 gls.

(Note: Newcastle's pioneer club Tyne fielded the family-related Nicholas Herdman and John Herdman, but records do not show any linkage to the Hardmans of Westgate. There was also a seemingly unrelated W Herdman/Hardman to appear for Boundary, West End reserves and Rendel during the same era, twice in the Northumberland Senior Cup final for the Rendelites. And there was a Harry Herdman to play with Newcastle United's reserves and Blyth during the late 1890s.)

HARRISON W

1883-1885 Half-back
Negligeable information has been discovered to identify W Harrison. The half-back was chosen for one fixture during October 1884 when opposing the Newcastle Rangers eleven. He was with West End's reserve squad for season 1883-84 and 1884-85.

App & Goals: 1 app 0 gls.

HAYES J

1886-1887 Half-back
Listed in a unique club Rule Book from 1886, J Hayes was noted as vice-captain of the West End Swifts XI. He was a regular for the reserve side and stepped up to participate in a senior game when the team was missing a handful of players for a meeting with Newcastle FA during December 1886. The footballer could be one of three individuals. One played the game around Bedlington and may have moved to Newcastle for a period, featuring for the Sleekburn Wanderers attack during the mid-1880s and facing East End in the final of the Northumberland Senior Cup in 1885. Selected to appear for a

Bedlingtonshire XI to face a Newcastle XI in the same year, it is likely he was John George Hayes who by the time of the 1891 census was an assistant to the parish clerk in the Northumberland town. Alternatively, two teenagers, James Hayes, residing in the Cowgate area of Newcastle's west end, as well as John Hayes of Elswick, both around 17 years of age at the time, could be the player.
App & Goals: 1 app 0 gls.

HENDERSON James

1882-1885 Goalkeeper, Half-back, Forward
Career: WEST END Aug 1882/Boundary (Newcastle) by March 1885/[Gateshead 1888].
James Henderson was one of the original group of enthusiastic players at the very start of the West End club in August 1882. He was on the pitch for their opening fixtures during October and also took part in the following season when he claimed 12 appearances. Henderson played in the club's maiden competitive match, a Northumberland Senior Cup tie against Tyne, which ended in a heavy 7-0 defeat. James also played cricket with the Elswick-based Gloucester CC.
App & Goals: 17 app 0 gls.

HENDRY Anthony

1887 Full-back
b. Scotland
Career: Dumbarton Ath 1885 (WEST END guest Jan 1887) to c1889.
In the football breeding ground that was Dunbartonshire during the 1880s, Hendry was a decent reserve player for the Dumbarton Athletic side at their Burnside Park ground, selected for the district's representative combination. Appearing on a handful of occasions for the first-eleven, he was part of the squad which travelled to the North East to take part in festive holiday games during 1886-87, and was invited with several of his colleagues to turn out for West End against Albion Rovers.
App & Goals: 1 app 0 gls.

HESLOP James

1890-1892 Forward
b. [Newcastle upon Tyne, c1873]/d. [Newcastle upon Tyne, 1939 (Q2)]
Career: WEST END 1890/Rendel cs 1892 (Newcastle Utd guest March 1894) to c1895.
Known as 'Jamie' and a reserve player at St James' Park during West End's final two seasons, he was a regular player at that level operating at inside or outside-left. During each season Heslop was given opportunities in the first-eleven; six games in 1890-91 and four in 1891-92 – figuring in the club's final match against Stockton during April. Moving to the Normount Road ground with Rendel when West End collapsed, Jamie was a popular footballer in Benwell, selected for Northumberland and reaching the Northumberland Senior Cup final. Heslop once faced the Newcastle United first-team in a practice fixture during 1894 when he assisted their 'A' team.
After playing football it is likely he resided in Benwell at

the time of the 1901 census, working as a furnaceman at a shell department of the Scotswood armament works.
App & Goals: 10 app 3 gls.

HUNT

1889-1890 Outside-left
With the West Enders during season 1890-91 as a reserve forward, Hunt was a late replacement when Donald McColl couldn't play in a Northern League derby clash with Newcastle East End during January 1890. At the Heaton Junction Ground, it was reported that he "did not have a bad game" in a close affair which East End won 2-1.
App & Goals: 1 app 0 gls.

HUNTER (Haig JS)

1888 Full-back
Mystery surrounds the identity of the player dubbed "Hunter" for what was an important Inter County Championship meeting with Sunderland during April 1888. In that prestige match which West End wanted badly to win, newspaper columns reveal that officials "went further afield to secure players" and apparently obtained a big star who arrived on the morning of the game, but kept the footballer's identity a secret! It was noted that the club's management "took great pains" not to reveal the player's identity. Match details in the press record "JS Haig" being in the line-up, written markedly in quote marks. But of course, this was West End's secretary at the time and obviously a pseudonym for the 'secret' footballer. Certain other journalists at the game cited the player as being "Hunter". Rumours went as far as to name the unknown star as Johnny Forbes, a famous Scottish international then with Vale of Leven, but it appears he did not play – or maybe he did? Forbes later defected from Scotland to England by joining Blackburn Rovers.
App & Goals: 1 app 0 gls.

HUTCHINSON Thomas

1891 Centre-forward
b. Glasgow, [20 June 1872]
Career: Whitefield (Glasgow) by 1887/WEST END Aug to Dec 1891/Darlington Sept 1892/Nelson Aug 1893/West Bromwich Albion July 1894/Celtic July 1896/Abercorn Nov 1896.
From the Govan area of Glasgow, Tom Hutchinson was described by the Scottish Referee sports newspaper as a "promising young player". He moved to Tyneside for West End's final campaign of 1891-92 and started well at St James' Park. The Newcastle Daily Chronicle reported that he is "the best centre West End has ever had" and Hutchinson looked the part during the first half of the season hitting five goals in 15 matches. However, by the end of the year he wasn't to be noted in press coverage and looks to have left Tyneside, next turning up with Darlington for 1892-93. The Glaswegian eventually found his way to the Midlands and became a more than decent striker for West Bromwich Albion, being "a good trier and hard worker", possessing "a good turn of speed" and "knows where the goal is". At The Hawthorns the Glaswegian was an important player as

the club reached the 1895 FA Cup final, scoring in the semi-final against Sheffield Wednesday.

He clocked up 58 league and cup appearances for Albion, scoring 21 goals. It was stated in one Baggies' history that Tom was released too soon following "several breaches of training rules".
App & Goals: 15 app 5 gls.
Honours: FAC final 1895.
(Note: A different T Hutchinson also appeared for Darlington during the 1880s and early 1890s while another player of the same name played with Stockton.)

I

IRWIN Thomas

1882-1886 Goalkeeper, Forward
b. Newcastle upon Tyne, 13 November 1866/d.
Longhorsley, Northumberland, 6 May 1942
Career: WEST END by Nov 1882 to c1886/White Rose Jnrs 1886-87/Strawberry Cabinet Works (Newcastle).

Raised on Bath Lane, in the shadows of what would become Newcastle United's modern HQ at St James' Park, Thomas Irwin spent most of his life around the football ground. He started a cabinet workshop on Strawberry Lane nearby and developed a successful business there, Thomas Irwin & Sons which became well-known as a shop-fitting company in the North East. On the football field, Irwin assisted West End during the club's infancy for three seasons when they played the game on the Town Moor and before moving to St James' Park. Also a cricketer for West End, Tom later was an accomplished artist, exhibiting paintings at the Laing Art Gallery in Newcastle during the Twenties and Thirties. His younger brother James Irwin was also with West End in the mid-1880s as a reserve player. Retiring to

Longhorsley, Irwin died in that Northumberland village during 1942.
App & Goals: 6 app 0 gls.
(Note: Another footballer with a similar name, John T Orwin, was with West End Juniors in season 1887-88.)

J

JARDINE William

1888-1891 Goalkeeper
b. Alexandria, Dunbartonshire, 27 June 1866/d.
Newcastle upon Tyne, 1952 (Q2)
Career: Renton 1887-88/WEST END cs 1888/Rendel cs 1891 to cs 1896.

Billy Jardine was reserve goalkeeper with the celebrated Renton line-up, appearing in a few games for their senior eleven as the club were a major force in Scotland. Jardine took over the West End custodian's role from Tom Fyfe when he moved to Merseyside – also a Dunbartonshire lad, the pair no doubt knowing each other. By the time he had established himself at St James' Park, Jardine was described as "one of the safest goalkeepers in the north of England". Just before he joined the West Enders, Jardine featured for Renton at Sunderland in April 1888, a day the Scottish Cup trophy was brought to Wearside. Appearing for Northumberland, he only missed one fixture during the 1888-89 programme, once playing at half-back against Bishop Auckland Church Institute. But for some reason another Scot, Dave Whitton took over between the posts and Jardine became second choice. He moved on, a couple of miles along the West Road to join the Rendel club at their Normount Road ground. He was a fine servant to the Benwell side, captain from 1892 to 1896 and skipper when they reached the Northumberland Senior Cup final of 1895. Billy once faced Newcastle United in the FA Cup with the Rendelites during the same year, then described as being "a tower of strength to his club". Also on the Newcastle cricket circuit during the summer months, he turned out for Newcastle Wednesday CC and Newcastle Working Men's Club. Jardine settled in the Benwell district of the city, employed as an ordnance machine-man, likely at the Armstrong factory alongside other West End personalities.
App & Goals: 44 app 0 gls.
(Note: Another Scottish goalkeeper with the surname of Jardine appeared during the same period; David Jardine of Bootle and Everton.)

JEFFERSON Joseph

1889 Centre-forward
b. Alnmouth, 1 March 1868/d. Newcastle upon Tyne, 1946 (Q4)
Career: Alnwick Hotspur Rangers 1887-88/Ashington 1888-89 (Morpeth Harriers guest March 1889)(**WEST END** guest April 1889)/Alnwick Working Men's Club cs 1889/Rendel Sept 1889 (Alnwick Town guest May 1890) to c1891.

Born and bred in the Northumberland coastal town of Alnmouth and the son of a local fisherman, Joe Jefferson made a name for himself on the football field with Ashington, being selected for the Northumberland line-up. He boosted West End's attack for the Easter exhibition contest with FA Cup runners-up Wolves during April 1889, yet was on the end of a heavy 9-2 defeat. Only two days before, Jefferson had represented the Newcastle & District XI against a strong Corinthians line-up – another big holiday attraction on Tyneside. When Joe teamed up with Rendel he was described as a player who had "distinguished himself last season". Jefferson did well for Rendel too and was in their team when they lost the Northumberland Senior Cup final to a rampant West End. The Northumbrian settled in Newcastle's western suburbs at Newburn, working as a joiner. He later resided in Benwell and was associated with Rendel for some years.
App & Goals: 1 app 0 gls.
(Note: A discrepancy exists with the year of his birth, certain records show 1869, but his birth certificate notes 1868.)

JEFFREY Harry

1885-1892 Full-back
b. Newcastle upon Tyne, March 1867/d. Newcastle upon Tyne, 16 February 1930
Career: Drysdale (Newcastle) by 1884/**WEST END** March 1885 (Sunderland guest 1890)(Third Lanark guest 1890)/Newcastle East End-Newcastle Utd April 1892/Retired due to injury 1895/South Shields June 1897.
Also appeared for Boundary/Drysdale/Newcastle Wed occasionally (all when with West End).

One of the club's earliest personalities, Harry Jeffrey was a regular for Newcastle West End, and on joining East End during the summer of 1892, took part in his new club's debut at St James' Park against Celtic. He went on to be good player for Newcastle United, totalling 55 senior appearances all told, including the Magpies' debut in the Football League at Arsenal. Strong-tackling, Jeffrey was something of a controversial character at both West End and East End, once refusing to play against Ironopolis during 1891 because he was chosen at right-half. In addition, he was suspended for two weeks for being, as the East End club's Minutes of Meetings note, "a non trier", while he also received a ban for playing in the close-season without permission. Then it was reported in September 1894 that, due to a fracas, he "will not be seen upon the team again". In West End colours, Harry won silverware when the club secured the Northumberland Senior Cup during 1888, then was almost an ever-present as they entered the Northern

League to finish as runners-up. Starting with the club's junior eleven and with the side over eight seasons, he can be recognised as one of West End's most prominent players, totalling 157 appearances – no other footballer has turned out more in a West End shirt. Jeffrey sustained a bad leg injury during January 1895 when sporting the black-and-white stripes, serious enough to force him to quit the top-class scene; against Sunderland he was carried from the field with a knee-cap injury and dislocated ankle. It was noted that Harry was "very ill" for a lengthy period and that serious mishap kept him out of action for over two years, ultimately forcing him to play at a lower level in the Northern Alliance.

At 5'9" tall, he was noted by one biography of the day as a, "stylish and scientific exponent of the game". Jeffrey captained Northumberland, as well as West End, and played cricket for the Drysdale, Boundary and Bath Lane clubs. During his later years he resided at Stanhope Street near to St James' Park. When Harry died in 1930, the Newcastle Evening Chronicle obituary penned that his footballing motto was, "the game, and nothing but the game".
App & Goals: 157 app 5 gls.
(Note: It was indicated in the Bootle Times that Jeffrey had joined the Bootle club during July 1889, but it appears he never appeared for the Mersey club.)

JOHNSTONE Robert Thomson

1890 Forward
b. Stirling, 9 September 1866/d. Stirling, 3 February 1940
Career: King's Park 1888/Northern (Glasgow) Sept 1889/Preston North End Dec 1889/**WEST END** Aug to cOct 1890/King's Park May 1891.

Robert Johnstone – nicknamed 'Dabber' Johnstone to all north of the border – arrived at St James' Park for the start of the 1890-91 season after having a spell at Preston. He was well-known in the Stirling district, and having learnt his football at Laurelhill Park, home of the King's Park club, became a popular player. Talented on the ball, during his early days one report described him as "paralysing his opponents in his passing and dodging". The Bridge of Allan Gazette though noted a failing in his style, Johnstone being at times "decidedly lazy", but he must have been quite a character, the local newspaper later writing that he was "as usual very active with his tongue when giving his feet a rest"! Following an opening burst of Scottish magic on the

pitch with West End, Johnstone quickly disappeared from the scene and later resurfaced back with King's Park. A blacksmith in his younger days, Robert worked also as a motor-mechanic and engine-fitter, later at the major ordnance depot at Forthside in Stirling.
App & Goals: 4 app 1 gl.
(Note: His surname is stated as both Johnstone and Johnston. It was reported West End also signed Tom Johnston, an ex-St Mirren centre-forward in 1888-89, but it appears he never played for the club – see 'Near Misses'.)

JONES Ben

1888 Centre-forward
The Northern Echo newspaper confirmed that Ben Jones was a very late addition to West End's side when they were a player down at Stockton during November 1888. It was stated that "West End came minus a centre-forward, but found a capital substitute in Ben Jones". He had appeared for the Stockton line-up during that 1888-89 season and was at the ground to act as a substitute. Ben continued to appear with Stockton into the early 1890s and was in their line-up facing West End for the Newcastle club's last fixture during April 1892.
App & Goals: 1 app 0 gls.

JONES J S

1885 Outside-left
Career: Jesmond 1883/Cathedral (Newcastle) 1884, also secretary (**WEST END** guest April 1885).
Also appeared for Newcastle Wand, and as secretary.
Appearing once for West End, the footballer is very likely to be a player called JS Jones. He turned out for the club in a low-key fixture against Tantobie during April 1885 and available records show no reserve outings at the time under that name. Probably his call-up was a one-off when he assisted West End. In the district then was a footballer, JS Jones, who assisted Jesmond and Cathedral in Newcastle, the Northern Athlete directory of football clubs record him as also being secretary of the Cathedral club. When playing for Jesmond he once represented a Northumberland XI which faced a combined Tyne & Rangers line-up during September 1883.
App & Goals: 1 app 0 gls.

K

KELSO Robert Robison

1887, 1888-1889 Full-back
b. Renton, 2 October 1865/d. Dumbarton, 19 November 1950
Career: Renton 1883 (**WEST END** guest Sept 1887)/**WEST END** May 1888 (Everton guest Jan 1889)(Preston North End guest March 1889)/Preston North End April 1889/Everton May 1891/Dundee May 1896/Bedminster May 1898 to 1899.
One of the most famous names of Victorian football and Newcastle West End's greatest player during their short existence, Bob Kelso was a defender of sure judgement

and one of the stars in the formidable Renton side of the era. He was once described by the Scottish Referee newspaper being "dour, gritty, determined with an unfathomable gift of resourceful energy". At 5'9" tall, Bob was vividly nicknamed the 'Renton Ruffian', he was a tough character and took part in the famous so-called Championship of the World meeting of Renton and West Bromwich Albion in 1888 when his side were crowned the very best after a 4-1 victory. When it was announced that Kelso was to join West End, many were disbelievers, one newspaper writing, "this statement was looked upon with distrust". But like many players in Scotland, especially in Dunbartonshire, he was tempted to turn professional and head to England.

Kelso in Scotland colours (top) and with Everton (below) as League champions, back row, second from left.

Like Ralph Aitken before him, the arrival of Kelso was a huge coup. The club's secretary John Haig recorded how he signed Kelso and had to endure the wrath of an ugly crowd, he wrote, "there were hundreds of men, women and children waiting to get on the track of the Englishmen who was after somebody near and dear to them...we were surrounded and had a bad time of it". Kelso had pulled on West End colours once before, during September 1887 when he was due to guest for the club against Scottish Cup holders Hibernian. The Edinburgh side though had to cancel the fixture at a late juncture and he played in a "scratch" game at St James' Park in front of a good crowd. Bob remained with West End for a whole season, and during 1888-89 became hugely popular on Tyneside, appearing for Northumberland during his time in the city. When the Scot departed for Preston – to become the top side in the country – he was presented with a gold watch and silver-mounted walking stick as tokens of appreciation. Kelso went onto lift the title at Deepdale before switching to Merseyside and Everton where he totalled 103 games, including reaching the 1893 FA Cup final. He first appeared for Scotland as a 19-year-old and later captained his country. His younger brother James was also with Renton, and recorded one game for Liverpool, while a nephew, Tom Kelso, was later with Dundee and Manchester City, capped for Scotland too. Bob settled back in Dunbartonshire, employed as a ship plater.

App & Goals: 31 app 3 gls.

Honours: 7 Scot caps 1885-98/FL champs 1890/FAC final 1893/SC winner 1885, 1888/SC final 1886.

(Note: Some biographies state Kelso's death in 1942, but that is not correct.)

KENNEDY Alexander

1890-1891 Half-back, Forward
b. Campsie [or Lennoxtown], Stirlingshire, 31 January 1864/d. Mossley, Lancashire, 25 [or 26th] February 1940
Career: Campsie 1883/Falkirk cs 1889/Campsie 1890-91/Cowlairs cs 1890/**WEST END** Sept 1890/Lennoxtown 1891/Campsie 1892-93/King's Park 1893-94.

Arriving at St James' Park during September 1890 and known as 'Sandy', he played most of his football around Stirlingshire and Dunbartonshire. Travelling to have a stint with West End along with William Dempsey from Cowlairs, the new Scottish imports made their debuts in a high-profile opener for the new season against Preston North End – Football League champions and the finest team in the country. Like many Scots who landed on Tyneside at that time, he remained with the red-and-blacks only for a few months, leaving in the spring of 1891 as the club went through a high turnover of footballers. Once reinstated as a player by the Scottish FA north of the border, he resumed playing in his native area, for Lennoxtown, Campsie and King's Park in Stirling. Kennedy looks to have been a decent cricketer as well, appearing for his local clubs in the summer. Sandy later settled in Ashton, then Mossley near Manchester, the 1939 National Register recording him as an "engraver's polisher".

App & Goals: 12 app 3 gls.

KENNEDY Donald Cameron (Dan)

1888-1890, 1891-1892 Forward, Trainer
b. Renton, c1863/d. Newcastle upon Tyne, 24 November 1926
Career: Vale Heatherbell/Vale of Leven 1881/Burnley Jan 1886/Vale of Leven Wand Sept 1886/**WEST END** Oct 1888/Sunderland asst-trainer & groundsman Nov 1890/**WEST END** trainer 1891-92/Rendel trainer Sept 1892/Newcastle Utd asst-trainer Aug 1894/Swalwell Axwell Rovers (Gateshead) trainer/Swindon Town trainer Aug 1905 briefly.
Also appeared for Science & Art.

An eminent character in Dunbartonshire football before moving south, he quickly became a noted personality on Tyneside as well. Although christened Donald, he was known as 'Dan' and began his football as an outside-left developing into a top player with the strong Vale of Leven side during the 1880s. During five years with the Vale, he appeared for the district team and reached two Scottish Cup finals – and would have played in a third but his club declined to take part in the final against Queen's Park during 1884. Dan tried a stint in Lancashire with Burnley, then Kennedy was a danger up front for West End during season 1888-89, scoring 13 goals in 16 games. He was an effective forward over two seasons at St James' Park and was capped for Northumberland described as a "capital player" and "a great favourite amongst the football public". As 1890 was coming to a close, Kennedy took a position with Sunderland – combining coaching with the groundsman's role at their Newcastle Road base – and helped develop the line-up which secured club's first Football League title victory of 1891-92.

Kennedy moved back to West End then onto Rendel when the club folded. Afterwards, the Scot also had a brief stay training the Newcastle United 'A' line-up while during 1891-92 he assisted England as trainer for the international against Wales on Wearside. Since joining West End, Kennedy lived in Newcastle, a resident of Benwell and during 1925 old stars regrouped at Boldon to feature in his benefit match. A football enthusiast to the end, during April 1926, just before he died, Dan sent a Rabbie Burns-like poem to Willie Maley who oversaw the Home Scots XI which faced the Anglo Scots at St James' Park – it was published in the Sunday Post.

App & Goals: 26 app 15 gls.

Honours: SC final 1883, 1885.

KIRKHAM Fred

1889 Half-back
b. Preston, December 1865/d. Fairhaven, near Lytham St Annes, 17 October 1936
Career: Preston Wand/Preston North End 1885-86/Newton Heath 1888-89/**WEST END** July 1889/Sunderland Albion Nov 1889 to 1890/Became a football referee 1890s/Tottenham Hotspur secretary-manager April 1907 to July 1908, then returned to refereeing until 1913.

Fred Kirkham had an interesting and rather unique career in football becoming a footballer, top referee then club manager. Joining the West Enders for the beginning of their first Northern League season of 1889-90 from Newton Heath where he was largely a reserve player, Kirkham took part in the opening fixtures before switching to Wearside by November. As noted by the Sunderland Echo, when Fred signed up with West End, "it was on the understanding that if he had an opportunity of joining a better club he should be released". Albion were in the Football Alliance at the time, a step up from playing football for West End. Commonly referred to as 'Freddy' and described as a player being "both tricky and judicious in placing the ball", he had been a pioneer footballer in Preston as the game began there, then in North End's second-string when they developed a star-studded line-up. At the Blue House Field on Wearside with Albion, Kirkham took part in 12 games of the Alliance programme. During the early 1890s he began to officiate matches, first as a linesman, then as referee. Kirkham started off in the Lancashire League and eventually developed into a first-class official – in charge of nine international fixtures as well as the 1906 FA Cup final between Everton and Newcastle United.

Fred held a reputation as a "fearless official" and unusually jumped into club management when he took charge of Tottenham for 1907-08. That was not a success, one Spurs history noting he was "unpopular with players and fans alike having an autocratic style, as he did as a referee". Away from the football field, Kirkham was employed as a commercial traveller residing in Preston. He settled near Lytham St Annes, active in the sport of golf being a well-known personality as chairman of the Northern Section of the Professional Golfers' Association, a post he occupied for 23 years.
App & Goals: 8 app 0 gls.

KIRKPATRICK J

1891 Centre-forward
Career: Trafalgar by 1890/**WEST END** 1891/Trafalgar 1891-92/Rendel 1891-92/Wallsend North East Rangers 1892-93.
Also appeared for Rendel Wed.
Striker Kirkpatrick appears to have been a Trafalgar footballer and perhaps had a trial or filled-in for West End for a single fixture against Rendel during April 1891.
App & Goals: 1 app 0 gls.

KNIGHT W

1887-1888 Full-back, Half-back
Career: White Rose Jnrs 1886/Elswick Leather Works 1886-87/**WEST END** 1887/Gateshead NER by Dec 1888/Elswick Rangers cs 1890/Newcastle Albion cs 1891.

Skipper of the West End Swifts team, Knight was promoted to the senior line-up for a handful of games during 1887-88 and 1888-89. When the player joined Newcastle Albion, he had moved full circle, then recently renamed from White Rose.
App & Goals: 4 app 0 gls.

KNOX William

1890, 1891-1892 Full-back, Half-back
b. [Glasgow, c1864]
Career: Partick Thistle/Elswick Rangers Aug 1888 (**WEST END** guest May 1890) to cDec 1890/Partick Thistle briefly by Jan 1891/**WEST END** Feb 1891 to cs 1892. Also appeared for Victoria Wed.
Most likely born and raised in Govan, working in the shipyards like several footballers to move from the area to Tyneside, he was a riveter and one of Partick Thistle's young reserve players who crossed the border. Knox landed at the Mill Lane ground, home of Elswick Rangers where many Scots found a home, including a few who had played for Thistle. At Graingerville, Knox became a sterling footballer, appointed captain of Rangers and in their defeated line-up when they reached the 1889 Northumberland Senior Cup final. Knox played for Northumberland County before he moved to St James' Park with the West Enders where William registered a couple of appearances in the Northern League. He remained at Barrack Road until the club folded in the summer of 1892. It is likely he had a spell back home in Glasgow after leaving Rangers when he possibly appeared once for Thistle at their Inchview ground before joining up with Newcastle West End, maybe as a result of the anti-professionalism regime in Scotland.
App & Goals: 3 app 0 gls.
(Note: Another Tyneside footballer with the same surname appeared for Birtley and Rendel during the era; T Knox. Additionally, there was also a W Knox at Linthouse in Glasgow, but not the same player.)

L

LAING W

1886-1888 Half-back
Career: Marlborough (Newcastle) 1883-84/**WEST END** 1886 (Rendel guest Jan 1887) to 1888.
A West End reserve player who received four call-ups to the first-eleven as winter took hold during season 1886-87, the club's first with a base at St James' Park. Laing also assisted Benwell outfit Rendel against Scottish visitors Linthouse, along with a namesake or possibly a relation from West End, B Laing. The following day he was in action against another touring side, Albion Rovers from Coatbridge.
App & Goals: 4 app 1 gl.

LAMBERT George

1884-1888 Full-back, Committee
b. Chollerton, Northumberland, 1862/d. Newcastle upon Tyne, February 1931

Career: Tyne Ass/Elswick Ordnance Works 1884/**WEST END** 1884 & committee 1886-87 to c1888.

George Lambert was a steadfast defender who started playing the game for the region's pathfinder club, Tyne. With Newcastle West End, he was selected on five occasions during 1884-85 including twice facing rivals East End in the semi-final of the Northumberland Senior Cup during March. On West End's management team, he was born in Chollerton near Hexham and when a teenager Lambert worked as an apprentice blacksmith, settling in the Elswick district of Newcastle. Also a well-known cricketer on Tyneside, playing for the West End club during the summer, skipper and a committee member, George also appeared in whites for Elswick Works CC through the 1880s and 1890s. He was an effective fast bowler, becoming captain of the Elswick side too. When he died at his home in Pendower, Benwell, the Newcastle Evening Chronicle's tribute noted that as a West End footballer he was a "powerfully built man and was a sturdy defender at full-back".

App & Goals: 5 app 0 gls.

(Note: At the same time as George Lambert played cricket, a namesake, Tom Lambert also appeared for the same Elswick Works CC – a prominent professional cricketer in the region who appeared for the Durham County XI. As far as can be traced the two Lamberts were unrelated.)

LAWS H

1882-1884 Goalkeeper, Half-back

Career: **WEST END** 1882-83/Brunswick (Newcastle) 1883-84/**WEST END** 1884-85.

H Laws seemingly had two spells with West End, during 1882-83, the club's first in football, then during 1884-85. Initially, he appeared in the half-back line then as a goalkeeper as the new season commenced in September 1884. Laws also turned out between the sticks for the Brunswick club that played on the Town Moor then at a pitch on Bath Lane.

App & Goals: 3 app 0 gls.

LAWTHER C

1883-1885 Goalkeeper, Forward

With the West Enders during the mid-1880s, Lawther was often selected for the club's reserve sides during 1883-84 and 1884-85 when he played with J Lawther, perhaps his brother. He made outings in both campaigns, once as a 'keeper, a stand-in for regular custodian Tom Minnikin.

App & Goals: 3 app 0 gls.

LIGHTFOOT Robert

1882-1883 Full-back, Forward

b. Newcastle upon Tyne, 2 April 1867/d. Newcastle upon Tyne, 17 February 1932

Career: Rosewood (Newcastle)/Stanley-Newcastle East End by Feb 1882/**WEST END** Aug 1882/Newcastle East End 1883 to c1889/[North Eastern].

A member of Rosewood junior club of Byker, Robert Lightfoot joined neighbouring outfit, the recently formed Stanley FC and remained with the new footballing set-up through their development as Newcastle East End,

eventually becoming a force in Tyneside football. He had a short period across the city with West End during the side's first year of action but only recorded two appearances. As a teenager, Lightfoot lived in Byker, at The Cumberland Arms, the son of the publican. He was a versatile player with East End, appearing in defence, midfield, and attack for the early Newcastle United, totalling 62 games in those pioneer seasons. Lightfoot was captain of the reserve team for much of his period there, but found a regular place during seasons 1885-86 and 1886-87. By 1891 Lightfoot was employed as an iron-moulder on Tyneside.

App & Goals: 2 app 0 gls.

LINDSAY Archibald

1890 Forward

b. Scotland

Career: Carrington (Glasgow) 1887/**WEST END** Jan to cs 1890/Carrington (Glasgow) 1891-92.

Archie Lindsay was retrospectively suspended for 12 months by the Scottish FA during September 1890 after crossing the border to play for Newcastle West End. He teamed up in a red-and-black shirt half-way through the 1889-90 season and had a winning start at St James' Park in a 4-2 victory over Gainsborough Trinity. The Scot was a regular choice across the forward line before leaving Tyneside, in due course turning up once more at Carrington in the Dennistoun district of Glasgow, no doubt after his football ban had been lifted.

App & Goals: 11 app 1 gl.

LONGBOTTOM H

1883-1884 Half-back, Forward

A reserve player with West End during season 1883-84, he was picked in the starting eleven on two occasions, initially for an early game with East End in November 1883, then again at the end of the season for a low-key fixture against Lemington Rangers. Longbottom also played cricket for West End from 1885, a period when he was captain, to around 1887. He was also a regular with the Elswick Works CC for several years.

App & Goals: 2 app 0 gls.

LOWE J D

1883-1884 Full-back, Half-back, Forward

Registering six outings for West End during 1883-84 and 1884-85, Lowe filled various roles and his debut in December 1883 resulted in a 5-1 victory over Rendel. Then on New Year's Day 1884, he enjoyed a 10-0 whitewash of Brunswick. In fact, Howe's time playing for the club's first-eleven was eventful, soon also taking part in the first competitive action for the West Enders, a Northumberland Senior Cup fixture with Tyne later in January – that ended in a 7-0 defeat.

App & Goals: 6 app 0 gls.

M

MACKIE Robert Wood

1890 Outside-right
b. Montrose, 3 January 1869/d. Montrose, 5 May 1957
Career: Crown (Montrose)/Montrose 1886/**WEST END**
Nov to cDec 1890/Doncaster Rovers c1893/Aberdeen
c1893/Sheffield Wed Nov 1894/Montrose Nov 1894
briefly/Sheffield Wed Nov to Dec 1894.
*Known as 'Bob' and a well-known player in Angus, after
several years with the Montrose club, he was tempted to
move to Tyneside and his wage at St James' Park was
recorded, the player receiving: "25 shillings (£1 25p) for
a win, 22s 6d (£1 13p) for a draw and 20 shillings (£1) for
a loss, to be paid only when playing." That was good
money for professional footballers then, but West End's
management didn't spend much on the 5'6" tall Mackie,
as he only took part in a single fixture, a 5-0 Northern
League defeat at Stockton during November 1890
although reports noted he looked "very smart at outside
right". After his short period with West End, a later
Montrose biography confirmed he left football for two
years due to a knee injury which affected him during his
later career. It appears Bob attempted a comeback with
Sheffield Wednesday at the top flight of the Football
League without making an impact. Mackie was
described as a "great character" and "great citizen" of
the coastal town of Montrose, during his playing career
he worked diversely as a joiner and trainee dentist, then
joined a local newspaper, eventually becoming a
respected correspondent after his football days, notably
for the Dundee Courier and Glasgow Herald. On his
death, Bob was described as "Scotland's leading sporting
journalist of his day". Mackie also served in the Royal
Navy, immediately after he left the game, joining up in
1896 and was on board ships in the Mediterranean and
Far East, part of the British force to quell the Boxer rising
in China. When he was discharged, Mackie had another
stint in Newcastle where it was noted "he painted the
hulls of ships in Tyneside yards" at the same time
keeping his pen working by compiling reports for the
press on local rugby matches.*
App & Goals: 1 app 0 gls.
*(Note: Royal Navy documents show his birth year as
1872.)*

MARSHALL J [T]

1889-1890 Forward
b. Nottinghamshire
Career: [Notts Co 1887]/[Notts Mellors by April
1888]/Nottingham Forest/**WEST END** Sept 1889 to cs
1890.
*Described as a former Nottingham Forest footballer
when he settled at St James' Park at the beginning of the
1889-90 season, Marshall joined West End with two
other Nottingham-based players, Frank Carnelley and
Richard Danks. Marshall perhaps was the pick of the trio
and was good enough to be selected in attack for the
Northumberland line-up that season. At the end of the
programme during May when Everton arrived on
Tyneside to play a high-profile exhibition game, Marshall
was badly hurt in that clash, reported as being kicked in
the side of his body. He afterwards took ill at home and
began to vomit blood. The player didn't appear again for
West End and it appears he returned to the Trent area.
By April 1892, local newspapers stated he was lying
seriously unwell in Nottingham, due to the same injury
when appearing for the West Enders two years earlier.
Football records do not reveal a Marshall appearing with
Forest, but a JT Marshall did play for Notts County and
Notts Mellors between 1887 and 1889 and this is likely
to be the footballer who joined West End shortly after he
left the County Ground.*
App & Goals: 22 app 8 gls.

MARTIN

1891 Full-back
*Turning out on the football field for West End towards
the latter stages of the 1890-91 season, Martin featured
at full-back in the Tyne Charity Shield meeting against
Willington Athletic during May. He played a handful of
games for the reserve side at that time and seemingly
left St James' Park by the summer.*
App & Goals: 1 app 0 gls.

MASON W

1884-1886 Goalkeeper
Career: Newcastle Rangers 1883/**WEST END** by April
1884 to 1886.
*A second-string goalkeeper who took part in the
occasional match for trailblazers Newcastle Rangers,
then for West End too. He appeared in a single game at
the end of the 1883-84 programme, maybe as a guest,
then a season later during 1885-86, very much as a
stand-in custodian during the New Year holiday fixtures.
He could well be W Mason to appear during 1887
between the posts for Coundon Grays in Durham. Mason
also played cricket for West End, noted as being
appointed as treasurer during November 1885.*
App & Goals: 2 app 0 gls.

MATHER John Armstrong

1882-1890 Half-back, Forward, Committee
b. Newcastle upon Tyne, 5 September 1860/d.
Newcastle upon Tyne, 19 May 1940
Career: Elswick Ordnance Works/**WEST END** Aug 1882
to c1890 & committee 1886 to 1889/Also occasionally
with Elswick Ordnance Works 1884-85.
*A real pioneer of football and rugby in Newcastle as
those sports developed during the 1870s and 1880s.
John Mather was the son of a local glass-maker and a
prominent character of both codes, also playing cricket
during the summer. He was involved in the very first
organised game of football in Newcastle on 3rd March
1877 at the Elswick Rugby Club when a match was
arranged between two scratch teams; Mather being in
Team A which faced Team B. Firstly a rugby player, an
early captain and treasurer of the Elswick club (soon to
be renamed Northern) an organisation which included
several ex-public-school lads who brought the
association code to the region. Born and raised in
Westgate, Mather then played for the Ordnance Works*

side, employed at the vast Armstrong factory alongside the River Tyne as a machinist. He became involved in the formation of the West Enders during August 1882 and with his younger brother Walter Mather (qv), was a most enthusiastic member of the new club. Captain of the side for a period and noted as being tall at 6'0", Mather played at half-back and up front over four seasons, taking part in the 1886 Northumberland Senior Cup final.

After he stopped playing around 1886, Mather was a regular committee man with West End. And in those later years, he acted as a referee and continued to play cricket, for periods with the Albion, Ordnance Works and Benwell Hill clubs. In addition, John was involved in the region's popular rowing sport on the Tyne, secretary of the Tyne Amateur Rowing Club by March 1882. For many years he resided at Colston Street near the West Road in Newcastle.

App & Goals: 50 app 3 gls.

MATHER Walter

1882-1887 Full-back, Forward, Committee
b. Newcastle upon Tyne, December 1862/d. Newcastle upon Tyne, 1935 (Q2)
Career: Elswick Ordnance Works/**WEST END** Aug 1882 & committee 1882-3, 1886-87/Newcastle Albion/Gallowgate Leather Works 1887.
Younger brother of John Mather (qv), Walter was also a sporting ground breaker on Tyneside and one of the founders of Newcastle West End. An original committee member when the club was formed, he was on the field with his elder sibling for the side's earliest fixtures during 1882. Walter was also the club's captain and took part in the 1886 Northumberland Senior Cup final as well as being selected for the County eleven. Totalling over 60 games for the West Enders, he can be recognised as one of the mainstays of the side along with his brother, Billy Tiffin and the four Waggott footballers. Mather was one of the original Crown cricketers before deciding to form a football offshoot, playing also for the Ordnance Works and Albion sides during the summer. By trade, Walter was originally a glass-blower, like his father, while records also indicate he turned his hand to being a brass finisher in one of the shell-shops of the Armstrong Works. Just before his death and when suffering from ill-

heath, he attempted suicide in January 1934 by cutting his own throat with a bread knife.

App & Goals: 64 app 8 gls.

MATHIESON [Alexander]

1891 Outside-right
b. Scotland
Career: [Northern (Glasgow) 1888]/[Cowlairs 1890-91]/[Thistle (Glasgow) 1890-91/**WEST END** March 1891/[Leith Ath cs 1891]/[Northern (Glasgow) cs 1892 to 1895].
A Scottish forward who crossed the border for Tyneside as the end of the 1890-91 season approached. Reported to be from the "Glasgow district", he is likely to be Alexander Mathieson of the Northern outfit based in Springburn, one of several players from that club to arrive at St James' Park. Mathieson only remained in Newcastle for a few weeks and had departed when the season concluded, registering a single outing against Rendel. When playing with Leith Athletic, he was described as a footballer who "played many brilliant games" in Scotland.

App & Goals: 1 app 0 gls.

MATTHEWS William

1887 Centre-forward
b. Buckland, near Tavistock, October 1865/d. Hartford, Northumberland, 23 December 1895
Career: Shankhouse Black Watch 1884 & committee (**WEST END** guest April 1887)/Bedlington Turks cs 1894.

Billy Matthews was the younger of three brothers to prominently appear for the Shankhouse club since their formation in 1884. With George and John, the trio were top footballers for one of the principal sides in the region during the 1880s. Billy lifted the Northumberland Senior Cup on four occasions, in 1886, 1887, 1891 and 1893 – twice facing West End – and was runner-up for 1888. He also played in the famous FA Cup-tie at St James' Park against the mighty Aston Villa in December 1887, while he took part in another big FA Cup meeting, this time with Notts County at Trent Bridge during 1893. Capped by Northumberland and a danger at centre-forward, he appeared for other local representative elevens and helped out West End by taking the leader's role when the club faced Darlington at Feethams during April 1887. Born over 400 miles from the North East in Devon, his family moved to the Shankhouse area to work in the coal mines by the start of the 1870s. Matthews was a miner at the Amelia Colliery, Shankhouse and died of pneumonia when living at Hartford village nearby. That was a little over a year after the demise of his brother

George following an accident at the same pit. Both footballers were only in their early thirties.
App & Goals: 1 app 0 gls.

MERRILEES Henry Fletcher

1890-1892 Forward
b. Stirling, 19 December 1866/d. Tynemouth, 1936 (Q2)
Career: King's Park Nov 1885/Vale of Forth by Jan 1886/King's Park Oct 1887 (Alloa Ath guest March 1890)(Vale of Bannock guest Jan 1889)/**WEST END** July 1890 to c1892.
Also appeared for Newcastle Wed.
An experienced forward who played his football in and around Stirling during the mid-1880s, notably for the King's Park club at their Laurelhill ground. Born in the historic castle city, during his teens Henry worked as an apprentice plumber. Merrilees was reported as an "old chum" of Robert Johnstone who also arrived in Newcastle for the start of the 1890-91 season and the pair appeared together on the left flank. Johnstone though departed quickly, Merrilees stayed a good bit longer, noted as a lodger in Arthur's Hill. He was usually to be found in the reserve side, yet still appeared for Northumberland. Sometimes criticised during his career for "piano playing" as it was described, he started in West End's attack for the first game of 1891-92, but then vanished from all football reports only noted as being reinstated as an amateur player during September 1892. He married a Wallsend girl and after his stint with West End possibly played on in Yorkshire, by 1901 working as a plumber in Doncaster. Merrilees returned to the North East to reside in Wallsend, then Tynemouth.
App & Goals: 4 app 0 gls.

MILLAR George

1889 Full-back
b. South Shields, c1867
Career: Grove Hill Jnrs (Middlesbrough)/Middlesbrough 1885 (Darlington guest March & April 1887)/Birtley Jan 1888 (Middlesbrough guest March 1889)(**WEST END** guest May 1889)(Sunderland guest Jan to March 1890)/Ironopolis Aug 1890 (Sunderland Albion guest Oct 1890)(South Bank guest Sept 1891)(Middlesbrough guest occasionally 1891-92)/Retired c1894.
Also appeared for Bede College/Corinthians.
George Millar was one of the most celebrated footballers in the region during the later 1880s and early 1890s. The defender was prominently with Middlesbrough and Ironopolis on Teesside and with the Birtley club near Gateshead. During both January of 1888 and January 1889, he was good enough to appear in full international North v South trial matches, just failing to win a coveted England cap. Admired as skipper of Birtley, he joined the Tyne minnows as 1888 opened when he had concluded his teacher-training at Bede College in Durham, being appointed as a master at Bewick Main School nearby. Once described by the North Star newspaper of Darlington as "a veritable Eiffel Tower of strength", George was a dependable and solid full-back and carried the status of an amateur footballer, although it appears he often was a semi-professional as well – taking money for playing. He assisted several

clubs at varying times during his career in the North East, many one-off games. Included was a single appearance for West End against Elswick Rangers at the end of the 1888-89 season.

Millar lifted the Cleveland Cup twice when with Boro in 1885 and 1886, then again with Darlington during 1887. He appeared for the Durham County team as skipper, as well as for Cleveland, Yorkshire and the Newcastle & District elevens. The Tynesider also pulled on the famous Corinthians shirt during 1889. Once George had finished playing the game, he officiated at matches in the region, including at Northern League level.
App & Goals: 1 app 0 gls.

MILLER C

1882-1886 Goalkeeper
With Newcastle United's founders in South Byker, joining Stanley FC during 1881, Miller registered one game at full-back in the club's significant opening season of 1881-82, then soon joined a new club which had been formed on the opposite side of the community for the 1882-83 season, Newcastle West End. He remained with West End, a reserve fixture but did appear on senior duty in three outings as a 'keeper during 1885-86 as the season began.
App & Goals: 3 app 0 gls.
(Note: During the 1880s, a C Miller was a regular rugby player for Benwell.)

MILLER Peter

1888 Full-back, Forward
b. Scotland
Football correspondents with the local press noted that Peter Miller landed at St James' Park to join the West Enders having being with a "Midlothian club" near Edinburgh. He took part in two games during November 1888 but wasn't seen in any West End line-up, first-team or reserves after that.
App & Goals: 2 app 0 gls.

MINNIKIN Thomas

1882-1890 Goalkeeper, Full-back, Half-back, Forward, Secretary (reserve team), Committee
b. Chester-le-Street, c1866/d. Newcastle upon Tyne, November 1927
Career: **WEST END** 1882 to 1890, also asst-secretary & committee 1883-84.

Residing in Newcastle's All Saints district at an early age, Tommy Minnikin appeared in all roles for West End over eight seasons of the club's ten-year existence. A West Ender through and through from the very start, Minnikin was especially prominent during seasons 1883-84 and 1884-85 when he claimed 32 appearances while he was the second-string captain and secretary for period as well. Tommy kept goal in the side's first competitive match against Tyne during January 1884, although he conceded seven goals in the process. By the 1920s, Minnikin was still living in Newcastle, at Wesley Street in Ouseburn. He was also recorded as being a keen local swimmer with the Elswick Swimming Club.

App & Goals: 48 app 1 gls.

(Note: During the 1900s to 1920s there was a prominent athlete running for Heaton Harriers and Wallsend Harriers by the same name, Tom Minnikin, but it appears there is no relationship to the West End footballer.)

MOAT W

1883-1886 Full-back, Half-back, Forward, Committee

Initially with the West End Juniors side, Moat was connected to the club through the mid-1880s, a committee member for at least one season, during 1884-85. As a player, he was selected on a handful of occasions over four seasons before West End moved to St James' Park, his first outing being in the Temperance Festival on the Town Moor in June 1883.

App & Goals: 12 app 0 gls.

MOORE Isaac

1890 Forward

b. Dundee, 8 April 1867/d. Burton upon Trent, 10 December 1954

Career: Our Boys (Dundee) c1884/Aston Villa Oct 1899 to Jan 1890/**WEST END** Feb 1890 (Newcastle East End guest April 1890)/Lincoln City Sept 1890/Burton Wand cs 1893/Swindon Town Dec 1893 to cs 1896/The Engineers, Bass & Co (Burton).

Newcastle West End player Isaac Moore was a noted Dundee forward who after a good spell with the Our Boys club on Tayside moved south to Aston Villa before heading north to join West End in February 1890. And he proved to be a decent centre-forward for the rest of the season. Only 5'6" tall, Moore was something of a prize signing at St James' Park and despite only scoring one goal, at times impressed wearing West End's colours. The Scot also appeared once for Newcastle East End

against Sheffield United during April 1890. Moore then joined Lincoln City, nicknamed 'Ikey' he later settled in Burton, employed at the Bass & Co brewery as an engine-fitter for 30 years. Athletic News described Moore during his playing days as having "great command over the ball, a perfect knowledge of short crossing, and shoots brilliantly". When on Tyneside, Isaac represented the Northumberland XI, then later during the Great War he served in the army and played and refereed services matches on the Western Front.

App & Goals: 12 app 1 gl.

MORRIS A

1886 Half-back, Inside-forward

In West End's ranks during 1885-86 and 1886-87, Morris took part in a single fixture of each campaign, first against Morpeth Harriers during April, a Charity Shield semi-final, then against Newcastle FA the following September.

App & Goals: 2 app 0 gls.

Mc

McCANN Edward

1890-1891 Forward

b. Uphall, near Broxburn, 18 April 1870/d. Broxburn, 13 July 1929

Career: Broxburn Emmet by Feb 1888/Broxburn 1889/Hibernian April 1890/Broxburn Aug 1890/**WEST END** Dec 1890/Broxburn Shamrock Aug 1891/Celtic March 1893/Broxburn Shamrock June 1893 to 1898.

One of two McCann brothers to land at St James' Park who both performed with much credit during season 1890-91; the pair being prominent footballers in their native Linlithgowshire. Edward McCann was the younger of the brothers, known as 'Ned' and he followed his elder sibling John (qv) to Tyneside. He was a regular forward in West End's largely Scottish attack during a campaign when the red-and-blacks hit plenty of goals. Ned and John appeared in the same line-up in Broxburn and Newcastle, while the duo also appeared for Celtic, playing a small part as the Glasgow club lifted the Scottish League title. At St James' Park, unusually both recorded their first and last games together for West End. The McCanns returned to Broxburn and Ned was recorded as employed at the paraffin works for the Broxburn Oil company then became a shale miner.

App & Goals: 27 app 9 gls.

Honours: SL champs 1893 (1 app).

McCANN John

1890-1891 Half-back

b. Uphall, near Broxburn, 6 September 1867/d. Broxburn, 10 July 1944

Career: Broxburn 1889, also secretary/Bathgate Rovers Sept 1890/**WEST END** Nov 1890/Broxburn Shamrock Aug 1891 (Celtic loan Jan 1892)/Hibernian March 1893/Celtic June 1893/Preston North End Oct 1893/Broxburn Shamrock Dec 1893.

John McCann was the senior of two brothers from Uphall and together with Ned McCann (qv) was influential for West End during season 1890-91. When the Scot moved to Tyneside his wage structure was recorded in the newspaper columns, noted as: "£10 down, and is paid £1 per match, with an extra 5 shillings (25p) should the match end in a win."

Within a couple of weeks of settling at St James' Park, McCann headed back to Broxburn to poach his brother, as well as another player from the town, Fergus Byrne – and received a "finder's fee" noted as having a deal of £7 for every approved recruit. When lodging in Newcastle, the trio stayed with the family of West End's Harry Hardman in Westgate. McCann was occasionally captain of West End that season and at the end of the programme departed back to Broxburn. Like Ned, he played with Celtic for a short period, in their title winning side during 1892-93. As a youngster, John worked alongside his brother at Broxburn Oil as well as down his local pit. He was a well-known personality of the town after his footballing days, becoming a respected public servant, a councillor and heavily involved in education for the community. McCann was described as, "a justiceman" ie a magistrate, and a founder of the St Andrew's Catholic Total Abstinence Society as well as an enthusiastic Rechabite, being much involved in the Catholic Friendly Society. When McCann died in 1944 it was estimated that several thousand lined the route to his burial. A cousin, Dan Gordon, was briefly with Everton and Southampton and later notably at Bradford Park Avenue before World War One.
App & Goals: 30 app 1 gl.
Honours: SL champs 1893 (3 app).

McCOLL Donald

1887-1890 Forward
b. [Lismore, Argyll, 18 February 1866]/d. Cramlington, 27 December 1949
Career: Renton/Sunderland 1884-85/**WEST END** cs 1887/Newcastle East End Sept 1890/Rendel April 1895.
Donald McColl's three-year period with Newcastle West End can be assessed as one of the best by any of the many Scots to stay on Tyneside at that time. An automatic choice up front, mainly at inside-forward, he was a frequent goalscorer, grabbing 32 in 98 appearances. He was selected for the County side as well as the Newcastle & District XI while Don's form was eye-catching as the Northumberland Senior Cup was secured during 1888. He then played in the club's first Northern

League match during September 1889. A former Renton player before moving to Wearside, McColl has the distinction of scoring Sunderland's first goal in either the FA Cup or Football League – a strike against Redcar during 1884. He appeared in several matches for the Wearsiders – mainly friendlies – once even as a goalkeeper when he conceded all of 11 goals against Port Glasgow. McColl featured in the Newcastle East End reserve set-up during season 1890-91 season and when at Rendel, ill-health restricted Donald's football around 1895 when severe rheumatism affected his play, being handed a benefit match at St James' Park during February 1896. McColl worked as a machine-man on Tyneside and by 1911, the Scot was still living in Newcastle, lodging with the family of ex-teammate William Swinburne at Westgate. He then settled in Cramlington and was employed as a council workman, during World War One being part of the army labour force which constructed Cramlington airfield.
App & Goals: 98 app 32 gls.

McCOMBIE William

1889 Forward
b. Glasgow, 26 September 1868
Career: Shettleston [Star] (Glasgow) 1888-89/Elswick Rangers Nov 1888/**WEST END** March to cs 1889/Carlton (Greenock) 1889-90/Glasgow Wand 1890-91/Partick Thistle Aug 1891/Glasgow Wand Oct 1891/Northwich Victoria cs 1892/Stockport Co by March 1893 to cs 1895.
The news-packed Scottish Referee weekly of the era reported during November 1888 that "McCombie of the Star, has gone to Newcastle". Frustratingly, no further details revealed which Scottish club he was with, but one further line much later confirmed he had been with Shettleston in Glasgow, moving south to Tyneside with team-mate John McCrimmon. The pair didn't join West End then, but rivals Elswick Rangers, a club that brought in many players from Scotland. They both did well with Rangers and moved to St James' Park within a year. Brought up in the Anderston district of Glasgow, William's career path was a bit of a challenge as he jumped around from club to club, but the jigsaw fell into place after his short stay during March and April 1889 with West End. He appeared in Greenock, traced in the same line-up with ex-colleague at St James' Park, Alf Porterfield – likely the duo moving to the Renfrewshire coast together. Following a brief period with Partick Thistle, McCombie was lured back to English football turning out for Northwich Victoria in the newly formed Football League Division 2, then had two seasons with Stockport in the Combination League and Lancashire League. By the start of the 1900s, William was back in Glasgow employed as an iron plater.
App & Goals: 2 app 1 gl.

McCRIMMON John

1889 Centre-forward
b. Glasgow, 8 November 1866/d. Glasgow, 10 February 1915
Career: Shettleston [Star] (Glasgow)/Newcastle East End Nov 1888 briefly/Elswick Rangers Nov 1888/**WEST END**

March to cs 1889/Darlington by Sept 1889/Nelson cs 1893/Cowlairs Feb 1894/Distillery 1894-95.

Born in the Hutchesontown area of Glasgow, John McCrimmon spent some time residing in Edinburgh with his family before returning to Clydeside to begin his career as a footballer. Moving to West End from Elswick Rangers with fellow Scot William McCombie during March 1889, McCrimmon became noted as a decent forward appearing with several clubs, always grabbing goals, notably with the early Quakers at Darlington.

The Scot initially arrived on Tyneside to join Newcastle East End, breaking amateur rules in his home country to receive payment as a professional. He made a single outing at centre-forward for East End, scoring once against Bishop Auckland but then switched to team up with Elswick Rangers. And McCrimmon proceeded to look good up front at their Mill Lane ground, talented enough to be selected for the Northumberland side during 1889 before heading to sign for the West Enders. Described as a forward "smart at dribbling and shooting", after his good spell with Darlington over three seasons he went onto turn out with Nelson, Cowlairs and Distillery where he played in the 1895 Irish Cup final. When with Darlington, census documents record John as a lodger with another Quakers footballer, Dave Campbell, and note his trade as a "printer-compositor". By the time of his death, he was employed as an "engineer's timekeeper" in Glasgow.

App & Goals: 4 app 2 gls.

Honours: Ire cup final 1895.

(Note: Newspaper reports and official registers variously state his name as McCrimmond and McCrimmon, his birth and death certificates state the latter.)

McCRORY Michael

1891-1892 Half-back, Forward

b. Belfast, c1868/d. [Newcastle upon Tyne, April 1929]

Career: Trafalgar 1888/Worswick Rovers (Newcastle) by April 1890/**WEST END** March 1891/Blyth cs 1892/Trafalgar cs 1893/Blyth Oct 1893/Trafalgar Nov 1893/occasionally for Blyth and Morpeth afterwards. Also appeared for Heaton Wed/Newcastle Wed.

Known as 'Micky' McCrory, an Irishman who was brought up in Newcastle from an early age when his family relocated to Tyneside as the 1870s began, initially in Gateshead then in the very heart of the city on The Side.

McCrory began his football with the Trafalgar set-up, playing alongside several players to graduate to both West End and East End. He was added to the St James' Park ranks with colleague Rodger Patten towards the end of the 1890-91 season and was described in West End colours as "blossoming into a smart player". Micky continued to impress during the club's final campaign and when West End became defunct, joined Blyth with team-mate James Gilmour. He was talented enough to earn a move south to play for Walsall Town Swifts, but decided to remain in the North East finding work at Blyth Dry Dock. McCrory played alongside his brother Patrick for Newcastle minor side Worswick Rovers before his spell with West End. During his second stint with Trafalgar, Micky became club skipper and was described as "a grand tackler and runner", being noted for his "big throws".

App & Goals: 42 app 9 gls.

McCURDIE Alexander H

1892 Half-back

b. Gartmore, Perthshire, c1865

Career: Clydebank c1888/Newcastle East End Jan 1889/**WEST END** Jan to cs 1892.

Although born in Gartmore near Aberfoyle, Alex McCurdie's family moved to Govan then Hutchesontown in Glasgow when he was a youngster. McCurdie was one of three Newcastle East End players who moved from Heaton to help the West Enders at the start of 1892 as they struggled badly. His one and only match in a red-and-black jersey was back at the Chillingham Road ground and he suffered a 7-1 defeat by his previous employers. Before West End's collapse, McCurdie had been a big favourite in Heaton, joining East End from Clydebank with Joe McKane as 1889 opened. Operating in midfield with distinction, he was recorded as a boiler-maker, living at lodgings in the suburb with Scottish colleagues Collins, Creilly and Miller. Alex appeared for the Northumberland County team and at one point the Newcastle Daily Chronicle of the day made the compliment towards McCurdie, that in the region, "few finer lads have graced the football field". He totalled almost 100 games for East End in all matches and was

awarded a benefit match during April 1893. During his period on Tyneside, Alex married a Byker girl and returned to Clydeside. By 1901 he was working as a marine boiler-maker living in Old Kilpatrick.
App & Goals: 1 app 0 gls.

McDERMID Robert

1887-1890 Full-back, Half-back, Forward
b. Bonhill near Alexandria, 15 August 1866/d. Southampton, 14 May 1941
Career: Renton Thistle/Renton 1886/**WEST END** Nov 1887/Sunderland Aug 1888 (**WEST END** guest May 1889)/Sunderland Albion cs 1890 (**WEST END** guest May 1890)/Accrington Aug 1890/Burton Swifts cs 1891/Stockton May 1892/Lincoln City April 1893/Renton July 1893/Dundee Wand July 1894/Newcastle Utd Nov 1894 £15/Hebburn Argyle Feb 1897/Warmley (Bristol) Jan 1898/South Shields Sept 1899 to c1902/[Hebburn Argyle by Dec 1902].

Bob McDermid was a popular and early disciple of the game, especially in the North East where he served Newcastle West End, both Sunderland and Sunderland Albion, then at Newcastle United. Usually operating at full-back or half-back, the Scot appeared for the County sides of Northumberland and Durham, as well as when learning the game with Renton, for Dunbartonshire. On his day, McDermid was a reliable and occasionally brilliant defender, at 5'7" tall, he was comfortable on the right or left side of the field. Appearing at St James' Park for the West Enders when they lifted the Northumberland Senior Cup during 1888, Bob was a formidable competitor during that successful campaign. He then moved on, stepping up a level to play for both Sunderland clubs – apparently signing for each team and receiving a fine for his troubles. Bob took part in Albion's season in the Football Alliance during 1889-90, the breakaway Wear club finishing in third spot. McDermid became a regular for two seasons with Newcastle United as they became established as a Football League side during 1894-95 and 1895-96, registering 64 senior appearances for the Magpies. He was described as a "player devoid of all bravado", and that he preferred "to show his worth by deeds". Bob later became a publican in South Shields and at the Oddfellows Arms on Wearside, also working as a boiler-maker and plater in a steel works. During May 1905, it was reported that McDermid appeared in court accused by his ex-United

captain Jimmy Stott of theft by way of issuing worthless cheques in Newcastle.
App & Goals: 30 app 0 gls.

McDONALD A

1886-1887 Inside-forward
b. Scotland
Selected to appear in West End's side alongside namesake Jock McDonald during 1886-87, he was notated as A McDonald and arrived at St James' Park during December 1886. The Newcastle Daily Chronicle reported he was a Dunbartonshire footballer, as was team-mate Jock, and likely he played for one of the half-dozen or so clubs in that district of Scotland. McDonald was favoured in attack over three months, an ever-present as West End reached the Senior Cup final during March 1887.
App & Goals: 10 app 4 gls.
(Note: There were several footballers called McDonald appearing for North East sides at the time; three for West End, two for Elswick Rangers and two more with Sunderland.)

McDONALD John

1887-1891 Forward
b. [Clydebank], Scotland
Career: Clydebank/**WEST END** Feb 1887 (Newcastle East End guest Dec 1887)/Doncaster Rovers Nov 1891 to c1893.
Alongside Donald McColl, who also began his football in Dunbartonshire, 'Jock' McDonald can claim to be recognised as a top West End signing from Scotland. Over his three-and-a-half seasons at St James' Park, he displayed a good level, scoring plenty goals; 43 in 94 outings. McDonald was a key figure as the West Enders lifted the Northumberland Senior Cup during March 1888, hitting two goals in the semi-final then another in the final – this after claiming a runners-up medal during the previous year. The Scot holds the honour of netting West End's first goal on their debut league fixture, a Northern League derby with Newcastle East End during September 1889 while he hit four in a 9-1 rout of Port Clarence during the same season. McDonald represented Northumberland when in West End colours and during April 1890 it was reported that he returned home to Clydebank, due to "domestic afflictions" and such was his popularity team-mates presented him with a purse of gold. It is likely he returned to the West End club after being suspended by Scotland's authorities during September of that year and remained at St James' Park as a reserve player. By 1891-92, Jock had joined up with Doncaster Rovers in the Midland League for a couple of seasons.
App & Goals: 94 app 43 gls.
(Note: A different Jock McDonald appeared for Sunderland, 1881-85, and Elswick Rangers, 1886-88.)

McDONALD W

1888-1889 Half-back
b. Scotland
Career: Glasgow University/**WEST END** Dec 1888 to cs 1889.

One of three Scots by the name of McDonald with West End during the late 1880s, he arrived on Tyneside at the very end of December 1888 from Glasgow University FC, then a noted club on the football scene in Glasgow. It was reported that McDonald "came through from Glasgow specially to play" in the headlining clash with West Bromwich Albion during February – so it appears he must have been a talented footballer. The Newcastle Journal stated that his profession saw him on Tyneside for a few weeks and he had linked up with the West Enders for the rest of the season.
App & Goals: 6 app 0 gls.

McDOUGALL R

1885-1887 Full-back, Half-back
Career: Jesmond 1884/**WEST END** 1885/Elswick Rangers by Jan 1887/North Eastern.
During the annual summer Temperance Festival of 1885, McDougall first appeared for West End in the holiday football tournament. The following season he became a fixed asset in the side at half-back reaching the final of the Northumberland Senior Cup during April 1886. He was capped by the County, alongside the unrelated Newcastle East End player of the same surname, goalkeeper Alex McDougall. The West Ender was also selected for the Newcastle & District XI side during the same year of 1886.
App & Goals: 22 app 0 gls.

McFARLANE J

1888-1889 Outside-left
With the Newcastle Press FC in the mid-Eighties on Tyneside, a side made up of employees of the Tyneside newspaper companies, McFarlane teamed up with West End for season 1888-89 and was called up as a reserve to the first-eleven during November. He then made his debut, and sole outing, against Middlesbrough as December opened. It was reported that he was due to face Rendel the following week but was "replaced" at the last moment.
App & Goals: 1 app 0 gls.

McFARLANE W

1891-1892 Forward
b. Scotland

Career: Glasgow Rangers 1888-89/**WEST END** Sept 1891/Darlington Sept 1892/Willington Ath 1893-94 to c1897.

Tyneside's football correspondents of the day wrote that McFarlane was a Rangers player when he was recruited for West End during September 1891. A reserve in the main at Ibrox, he made a handful of first-eleven appearances in friendly matches, just as Scottish League football had started. McFarlane then proved to be a good player at St James' Park, selected in attack for the majority of the season as an inside-forward. On West End's closure, he moved the 35 miles to Darlington then returned to Tyneside to appear for Willington Athletic. Alongside another ex-West Ender, Robert McLucas, he enjoyed three seasons in their colours and won a Northumberland cap. During 1893 it was stated that McFarlane had met with a nasty accident when employed at a Tyneside works, losing fingers of his right hand. Despite that mishap, he continued to play football to around 1897.
App & Goals: 34 app 5 gls.

McGIRL Edward (McGill)

1886 Centre-forward
b. Scotland
Career: Dundee Harp 1883/**WEST END** Nov 1886/Elswick Rangers Dec 1886 (Rosehill guest May 1887) to cs 1887/Dundee Harp by Jan 1888 to c1891.
One of several one-off outings for Newcastle West End, on this occasion in an important Tyne versus Wear clash with Sunderland during November 1886. Newspaper accounts, likely syndicated to several titles, including the respected Athletic News, published that West End "tried a new centre-forward J McGill". However, that was a naming error, the player wasn't "McGill" but Edward McGirl from Dundee. It had been noted in the Scottish press the week before the game with Sunderland that McGirl was presented with a gold watch "on his departure to Newcastle" where he was to work for five months. The Newcastle Daily Chronicle confirmed that West End's new man was "from Dundee". Known as 'Ned', he was described at one point as being "a famous Harp player", and had been "for a number of years one of the most active and enthusiastic players of the Harp club". For whatever reason, McGirl didn't stay with West End, transferring quickly to Elswick Rangers, perhaps for better wages or because he knew some of the other Scots at Mill Lane. During his period wearing Rangers' colours, Ned appeared for the Newcastle & District XI. Earlier in his career on Tayside with the Dundee club, he took part in the headlining 35-0 Scottish Cup victory over Aberdeen Rovers during September 1885, scoring six goals. Remarkably, that was on the very same day as Arbroath's record 36-0 thrashing of Bon Accord.
App & Goals: 1 app 0 gls.

McINNES Thomas Fair Macauley

1891 Outside-left
b. Bowling, Dunbartonshire, 8 July 1873/d. Dalmuir, Dunbartonshire, 1 December 1937
Career: Dalmuir Thistle/Newcastle East End Dec 1889 (**WEST END** guest April 1891)/**WEST END** Aug 1891/Clyde Sept 1891/Nottingham Forest June 1892/Bristol Rovers Oct 1899/Lincoln City Sept 1900/Port Glasgow Ath May 1904 to May 1905.

A potent outside-left during the Victorian era of football, Tommy McInnes served both sides of the Newcastle football community when working as a riveter in the Tyne shipyards and became a distinguished player elsewhere. He was quickly an automatic choice for Newcastle East End and always a danger in attack. During his two seasons in East End colours, for all games, he bagged over 40 goals in a little over 50 outings. The Scot became the first player to register what could be called a 'league' hat-trick for the club when he grabbed three goals against West End in a Northern League derby during September 1890, a 7-1 victory. Still a teenager, Tom then went on to score the first ever FA Cup hat-trick for the East Enders, against Shankhouse during November 1890.

McInnes was poached (with team-mate James Collins) by West End the following January, although a dispute between the clubs saw the player remain in Heaton until the close-season. His stay at St James' Park was short though, only appearing in practice matches during August. Whitewashed by the Scottish FA in the same month, so able to appear back in Scotland, he returned north with Clyde as the 1891-92 season began having recorded just a single outing for West End as a guest during the previous April, in Jack Barker's benefit match against Sunderland. McInnes moved south again when he joined Nottingham Forest during June 1892 and proceeded to perform with much credit over seven seasons, totalling 195 senior games (57 goals), regarded as one of the best wingers at the top level. Tom played in the Reds' inaugural Football League fixture and reached the 1898 FA Cup final with Forest, gaining a winners' medal before being transferred to Lincoln City during 1900. McInnes, who appeared for the Scottish League XI, was also included in international trial matches during 1897-98. He was described as a Scottish "Little'un" at 5'6" tall, being "tricky" and having a "fine shot" who "plays the combination game to a nicety". Tommy eventually settled back in his native Clydeside, working for a period at the Singer sewing-machine factory.

App & Goals: 1 app 0 gls.

Honours: FA Cup winner 1898.

(Note: There has been much confusion over McInnes, as another player of the same name appeared for Notts County, Everton, and Luton Town during the same era. And he was born in Glasgow in the same year. However contemporary records and extensive family history research show that the Newcastle player is linked to Nottingham Forest and that he did not play for Scotland, instead the Notts County forward being capped.)

McINTYRE John James

1888 Half-back
b. Hexham, 25 January 1867/d. Newcastle upon Tyne, 17 February 1950

Appearing for Newcastle West End only once against Bishop Auckland Town during November 1888, reports noted that John McIntyre was one of "two new players" given an opportunity by the club. It was also stated that he was a Tynedale rugby player and on that day his club did not have a game, so perhaps he was handed a trial outing. From Hexham, the home of the Tynedale club, he doesn't turn out again for the West Enders so must have reverted to the oval game in which he was a prominent player. With his local club during the mid-Eighties onwards, McIntyre first played for their 15 at the start of the 1885-86 season and was in the line-up which lifted the Northumberland Rugby Challenge Cup during April 1887, Tynedale's first victory in the prestigious competition. Referred to as JJ McIntyre, he was selected for the Northumberland side and became club captain at the Hexham ground for 1890-91. By 1897, McIntyre joined the management committee and was revered as being an ex-skipper and famed trophy winner. John was born and raised in Hexham, later residing in Lemington along the Tyne, working at the nearby steel smelter works.

App & Goals: 1 app 0 gls.

McINTYRE Robert

1891 Half-back
b. Kilmaronock, Dunbartonshire, 1866/d. Dunblane, 21 November 1935
Career: Dunblane/Gateshead NER Sept 1889/Elswick Rangers by Dec 1889 (**WEST END** guest April 1891)/[Sunderland Albion]/Dunblane cs 1891.

West End played a testimonial fixture against Rendel for the benefit of the Benwell club's groundsman during April 1891 and fielded Elswick Rangers half-back Robert McIntyre. A Scot, born in a hamlet near Drymen, McIntyre settled in Dunblane and when working as a joiner became one of the best players in the Dunblane club's ranks. Robert helped the side lift the Perthshire Cup during 1888 and also played for the Perthshire XI before having a go at professional football when he moved to Tyneside. Initially, he was all set to join Elswick Rangers, home to many a fellow countryman, but as was described, "was seduced across the river" to join Gateshead NER.

But he did soon link up with the Rangers at Mill Lane and went onto appear in the FA Cup with the Elswick side. Moving back to Dunblane, when he died in 1935, a short obituary in the Strathearn Herald noted he also had a period with Sunderland Albion but no appearance can be traced, possibly only on trial.

App & Goals: 1 app 0 gls.

McKAY (McKIE) George

1889-1890 Half-back, Forward
b. Glasgow, 18 December 1860/d. Stockton, 1909 (Q2)
Career: Partick Thistle cs 1884/Burnley Oct 1885 briefly/Woolston Works (Southampton) cs 1886/Elswick Rangers cs 1887/**WEST END** Sept 1889/Elswick Rangers cs 1890 to c1891/Ironopolis Sept 1893 to 1894.

An unnamed Woolston Works group which lifted the Hampshire Cup. McKay was captain and perhaps the player with the ball.

One of three Scottish footballers named McKay with the West End club during season 1889-90, unravelling the trio has at times been a challenge. During his early days as a player in Glasgow, McKay turned out for Partick Thistle over a couple of seasons before joining the exodus of Scots to England to become a professional. George tried his luck at Burnley, perhaps brought to Lancashire by ex-Thistle colleague Jack Beattie who had joined Burnley. However, it appears he departed quickly and found himself outlawed by the Scottish FA for breaking the amateur rule-book, suspended from playing in Scotland. McKay joined Woolston Works, a football

club from a large shipyard in Southampton who were rated one of the best sides in the area at the time. They attracted several footballers from the North of England and Scotland then, also being employed at the Oswald & Mordaunt yard. McKay became skipper of the team and lifted the Hampshire & Dorset Cup in February 1887. He was rated highly, noted as a "diminutive captain" and although left-footed could play on either flank at full-back. With a down-turn of shipbuilding work by the end of 1887, most of the imports to Woolston left, and McKay landed on Tyneside with Elswick Rangers and met other ex-Thistle players there from Glasgow. He likely was found work at the club-associated Armstrong factory nearby. George became a key figure for Rangers at half-back, captain at the Mill Lane ground as they challenged Newcastle's West End and East End. He reached the final of the Northumberland Senior Cup with Rangers and was selected for the Northumberland County side as well as for the Newcastle & District XI. McKay was poached by the West Enders during the close-season of 1889 as they made their debut in the new Northern League competition. Playing in a half-back role too and sometimes described as having a rough edge to his game, he enjoyed a good season, registering 10 of the 18 games as they finished as runners-up to Darlington St Augustine's. George totalled 30 outings all told during that campaign and scored a hat-trick for West End in the Senior Cup final too. At the end of his career, George joined Ironopolis for their debut in the Football League during 1893-94 and played on five occasions. Census information reveals McKay had moved from Tyneside where he worked as a ship riveter's labourer, to Teesside, residing in Stockton where he died.

App & Goals: 30 app 4 gls.

(Note: His surname, like the other McKays, is variously stated as McKay, MacKay, McKie or McKee. George's official death register in Stockton notes "McKie" while the birth of his daughter Cecilia in Southampton when at Woolston proved invaluable in tracking his movements from Partick to Southampton, then Newcastle and Stockton.)

McKAY John

1889-1890 Half-back, Forward
b. Scotland
Career: Dumbarton Ath 1888/**WEST END** July 1889 to cs 1890.

John McKay played alongside his namesakes George and T McKay for West End on several occasions, and remained at St James' Park for only a season. A reserve with the Dumbarton club and usually a forward, he was versatile to all attacking roles. Like most of the footballers who ventured to England from Scottish football, he was suspended by the Scottish FA for professionalism and reinstated in September 1891. He likely returned to play around the Dumbarton and Glasgow area.

App & Goals: 16 app 6 gls.

McKAY (McKIE) T

1889 Half-back, Forward
b. Scotland

Career: Cambuslang by Jan 1886/Sunderland c1887/Sunderland Albion Sept 1888/Gainsborough Trinity Oct 1888/Burnley Dec 1888/Sunderland May 1889/**WEST END** July 1889/Stockton Dec 1889 to cs 1890/[Heywood Central (Manchester) Sept 1890 to c1891].

Shining on the football pitch for Cambuslang when they toured the North East over the festive holiday period of 1887-88, McKay was described as "a very tricky player". His side hammered Sunderland 11-0 when it was noted that nothing gave him "more pleasure than amusing the spectators at the cost of an opponent". McKay soon joined up with the Wearsiders, indeed he turned out for both Sunderland clubs before moving to St James' Park as one of the trio of McKays to join West End at the same time. The Scot scored in the club's opening Northern League fixture against East End and grabbed a hat-trick when Port Clarence were demolished 9-1 in the FA Cup. But McKay didn't stay long, true to the comment of the Glasgow Evening Post when he joined West End…"a typical rolling stone which gathers little moss"! The Scot travelled the short distance to sign for Stockton during December 1889 and when playing there represented the Cleveland XI. It is likely he is the same T McKay who appeared for Heywood Central during 1890-91, alongside fellow Caledonian and West End forward Tom Nicholson. The player is also referred to as T McKie.
App & Goals: 14 app 9 gls.

THE McKAY PUZZLE
Several players named McKay or McKie were on the football circuit during the era and a few were also linked to West End, Sunderland, Sunderland Albion and Burnley. As a result, it has been testing to piece together the puzzle and unravel the careers of these footballers. There were three at West End (if not four), three on Wearside and several other McKays who crossed the border to England. It appears the press of the day also found it hard to sort them out while news columns gave a variety of initials for each. Additionally, the McKays are also linked closely to the Scottish Bradys of West End, Sunderland and Burnley, seemingly moving around together. A quandary also exists with William/RW McKay who, as it was reported during September 1891, was granted permission by the Scottish FA to play for the Aberdeen Orion side, noting he was a past Newcastle West End player. No trace of a McKay with these initials can be traced. It appears he was certainly from Edinburgh, appearing for Hearts, Burnley and St Bernard's.

McKECHNIE Donald

1888, 1890 Half-back
b. Renton, c1863
Career: Renton 1883-84 (Third Lanark guest May 1888)/**WEST END** Sept 1888/Sunderland Nov 1888/Port Glasgow Ath Nov to Dec 1890 (**WEST END** guest May 1890)/Sunderland Albion Jan 1890/Renton 1892-93/Dundee Wand coach Aug 1895 for a period.
During season 1888-89 West End's line-up was packed with Scottish imports, Donald McKechnie was one who pulled on the club's shirt, albeit for only a brief period.

McKechnie was a top footballer in Dunbartonshire, having twice won the Scottish Cup with Renton. He was a past colleague of Bob McDermid who previously had settled on Tyneside and Donald followed him to the North East. Described as a tough customer on the field and a team-mate of Bob Kelso, the pair were instrumental when the Scottish club were labelled as "Champions of the UK and the World" after defeating West Bromwich Albion in 1888.

McKechnie pictured at Renton, together with his Scottish Cup medal from 1887-88.

Donald arrived at St James' Park with his famous international team-mate after reaching a third cup final with his Scottish club. During the early weeks of that season, it was reported West End fielded "six Rentonians", McKechnie being part of a celebrated half-back trio with Kelso and James Kelly for that side. When he arrived in Newcastle though, the press gave an opinion as to his condition, noting "he will be seen to better advantage when he has reduced the rotundity of his corporation" while Athletic News made the comment that he "would be a real good man if he would train"! While it is not known if it was his attitude to fitness that saw his departure to Wearside, Donald became a regular with Sunderland for a period during their pre-league days, but jumped to rivals Sunderland Albion who had joined the Football Alliance league. He made a comeback with the West Enders for a glamour match with Everton at the end of the 1889-90 season. During the mid-1890s McKechnie was employed in Dundee for a period working as a painter on the Tay Bridge.
App & Goals: 10 app 0 gls.
Honours: SC winner 1885, 1888/SC final 1886.

McKELLAR Dugald

1890-1892 Forward
b. Rothesay, Bute, 1 January 1869/d. Greenock, 14 September 1921
Career: Dumbarton/**WEST END** Aug 1890/Trafalgar cs 1892/Dundee Wand Aug 1894.
Another footballer from the district north of the River Clyde in Scotland, Dugald McKellar showed his worth to West End over a short two-to-three-month spell in the first-eleven at St James' Park. A forward with an eye for goal, he scored in the opening three Northern League fixtures of the 1890-91 schedule but had lost his place as winter approached and was more often a reserve selection. When the club folded, McKellar was traced turning out for the Trafalgar club on Tyneside before returning north of the border to team up with Dundee

Wanderers. When living in Newcastle, census documents record Dugald as a boarder at Hamilton Street in Westgate and noted his trade as an upholsterer – information which links back to his days on the Isle of Bute, his family moving to Helensburgh where he started to play for one of the nearby Dumbarton sides. As the 1900s began, McKellar was residing in the Partick area of Glasgow, later moving to Greenock and employed as an upholsterer once more.

App & Goals: 12 app 4 gls.

(Note: Both McKellor and McKellar are used in newspaper reports, as is Mc or Mac, and Dugald or Dougald. Birth and death records show Dugald McKellar)

McKENZIE T

1890-1891 Forward
b. Scotland
Career: Renton/[Burton Wand Aug 1890]/**WEST END** Sept 1890 to 1891.

McKenzie reached Newcastle with Alexander Graham from Dunbartonshire, seemingly on a mini-tour of English football clubs in a bid to secure a professional deal. Both were described by reports as "capable players" and the switch to Tyneside was characteristic of the influx of Scots at the time. The Newcastle Daily Chronicle noted that the "new men were from Renton, having just arrived in the town on spec the previous evening". It is likely that McKenzie first landed with Burton Wanderers in the Midlands when he was described in their local newspaper as a "clever and cool player" but only appeared in a couple of matches at centre-forward. On teaming up with Graham on Tyneside, the pair showed up well, the Chronicle's reporter writing, "both are really good men". The Scot made his debut for West End in FA Cup action, at the Mill Lane ground against Elswick Rangers, a 5-2 victory, and went onto record a decent return at St James' Park.

App & Goals: 18 app 7 gls.

(Note: There was another McKenzie with Newcastle West End in season 1891-92, a full-back normally who arrived from Northern in Glasgow and remained only a short time with the reserve eleven.)

McLEOD David

1887 Inside-forward
b. Scotland
Career: Dumbarton Ath 1887 (**WEST END** guest Jan 1887)/Dumbarton Aug 1889 to c1894.

Having been capped by the Dunbartonshire XI, David McLeod played most of his football with his native clubs, Dumbarton Athletic, then the stronger Dumbarton side when they were amalgamated in 1889. When his team took part in popular tour matches in the North East, David was one of a few Dumbarton men to assist West End in a contest against Albion Rovers during January 1887.

App & Goals: 1 app 0 gls.

McLEOD R

1891 Half-back
b. Scotland

Career: Northern (Glasgow) by 1889/**WEST END** Aug to Oct 1891.

McLeod was one of Newcastle West End's new imports for the start of the 1891-92 season, joining the St James' Park set-up during August. He was picked in the half-back line for the opening fixtures of the Northern League programme as the management tried to forge a successful line-up. But when the side only won one contest and conceded 12 goals, McLeod lost his place and wasn't seen again. By October he had returned to Scotland.

App & Goals: 4 app 0 gls.

McLUCAS Robert Robertson

1891 Centre-forward
b. Glasgow, 5 November 1867/d. Newcastle upon Tyne, 12 May 1901
Career: Partick Thistle 1886/Elswick Rangers cs 1889/**WEST END** Feb 1891/Willington Ath Sept 1891 to 1897.

Robert McLucas was one of several ship workers from the Glasgow area to settle on Tyneside during the mid-to-late 1880s and ply their trade in the Tyne yards, as well as on the football field. One of Partick Thistle's reserve forwards, he became a regular with Elswick Rangers for two campaigns after joining the club during the close-season of 1889 – and having faced both West End and rivals Newcastle East End when a Thistle eleven toured the North East. At the time of his stay with Rangers, McLucas lived in Elswick, working as a ship-plater in the neighbouring dockyards. McLucas switched to St James' Park during February 1891 and made his debut for West End against Wishaw when certain reports in the local press noted him with an alias as, "A Mann". The Scot didn't do badly in West End colours, performing well during a run of games through the spring. Robert then moved to the other side of the city for the start of the 1891-92 season and joined Willington Athletic. Having relocated to Byker, closer to new employers at one of the many shipbuilding companies around Willington Quay, he continued his football for six seasons with the strong Athletic club and the Glaswegian was selected for the Northumberland XI, becoming skipper of the Tyne club. He was described as a "capital general" during his period there. McLucas also lifted the Northumberland Senior Cup after defeating Shankhouse in the 1896 final, while he also appeared in the FA Amateur Cup for the club. He died at a young age when in his early thirties.

App & Goals: 7 app 3 gls.

McNICHOL T/J

1891 Outside-right
b. Scotland
Career: Northern (Glasgow) 1888-89/Sunderland Albion Sept 1889/Stockton June 1890/Darlington Nov 1890/**WEST END** Aug to Oct 1891.

Inconsistently reported as T or J McNichol, it is probable this footballer hailed from the Northern club in Glasgow like several North East recruits, including West End's John Downes. He went on to appear with Sunderland Albion and Stockton before moving to Feethams with

Darlington for a season. The forward played with John McCrimmon there, also to join the St James' Park ranks – indicating the close-knit band of Scots in the North East. McNichol relocated to Tyneside after "having been offered more renumeration" and was described as a forward of "small stature" while he was also "heavily built". McNichol only remained at St James' Park for two months, before returning to Scotland and likely continued his career with one of the dozens of clubs in and around Glasgow. It is possible McNichol was with Vale of Leven Wanderers prior to joining Northern, appearing alongside Dan Kennedy, another player to be with West End.

App & Goals: 4 app 0 gls.

McQUILLAN P

1888 Full-back, Forward

With such an unusual surname, it has been a frustration that this player's identity remains vague. Joining West End during September 1888 for the start of the 1888-89 season, McQuillan turned out at full-back for West End, then on the forward line, for the opening four matches. Following his opening burst with the West Enders, McQuillan does not appear for the club again, even at reserve level. The Tyneside-based Northern Magpie weekly paper gave a hint of where McQuillan came from in their football column, noting by October 1888 that he had "gone home disconsolate...to the Land O'Cakes", otherwise Scotland, and likely the Tayside area. That points to a Patrick McQuillan who appeared with the Dundee Harp and Lochee Shamrock clubs during 1886 and 1887 while the same name crops up registered for season 1889-90 with Duntocher Hibs. This may be the same footballer who arrived at St James' Park. Resident in Newcastle then was George B McQuillan who appeared for Tyne and later was captain of Gateshead during the same era, but no family linkage can be ascertained, but as a Scot, maybe he was associated to the West End player.

App & Goals: 4 app 0 gls.

N

NEWBERY Henry Christian

1890-1891 Inside-forward
b. Broxbourne, Hertfordshire, 25 February 1867/d. Cambridge, 25 August 1955
Career: Cambridge University 'blue' 1887 to 1888/St Oswald's College (Tynemouth) 1889/**WEST END** Dec 1890 & Feb 1891/Sunderland Albion Jan 1891.
Also appeared for Corinthians/Old Foresters/Newcastle Wed/Tynemouth.
From a distinguished family in Hertfordshire, both Henry Newbery and his brother Francis, headed for a university education then joined the clergy and played football to a high level. He first attended Forest School in Walthamstow – an early public-school which pioneered football – and gained entry to Cambridge during 1885. Newbery gained a BA and MA at St John's College while during his stay at the renowned university he earned a

Cambridge 'blue' at football. Henry then ventured north, married a girl from Cullercoats and settled in Tynemouth at the end of the 1880s. A master at St Oswald's College there, he became curate of the Holy Saviour's Church during 1891. At that time Henry was a keen sportsman, well-known in the region.

Newbery pictured on a marvellous university team group from St John's College, back left. (Courtesy of St John's College, Cambridge.)

Only briefly with West End, yet his two appearances, in December 1890 and then during February 1891, were both impressive – Henry scoring five goals against Stockton on his debut. Newbery stepped up a grade in football when he was quickly offered a position with Sunderland Albion during January, a side then in the Football Alliance. As an amateur, he often made occasional appearances for clubs – including that brief return with West End, as well as for the celebrated Corinthians and Old Foresters. He was described as a forward with "a deadly shot at goal". Newbery also played cricket extensively wherever he stayed including in the North East for St Oswald's, Tynemouth and South Northumberland. It was no surprise either that he played rugby too, for Percy Park where he also sat on the club's committee for a period. In addition, Henry was Vice-President of Tynemouth's Priory Bowling Club. As the 1900s began, Newbery was appointed vicar at Beltingham, near Bardon Mill in the Tyne valley then moved south during 1911 to become reverend at Haverhill in Suffolk. He took another position in Halesworth and then as Rural Dean of North Dulwich from 1923 to 1937. Newbery retired back to Cambridge by 1939.

App & Goals: 2 app 5 gls.

NICHOLSON Thomas

1887-1890, 1892 Forward
b. Renton, 1867 (Q4)/d. Newcastle upon Tyne, November 1934
Career: Renton 1886-87/**WEST END** Oct 1887/Heywood Central (Manchester) cs 1890/West Manchester 1891-92/**WEST END** March 1892/Blyth cs 1892/Shankhouse Dec 1892/Blyth Oct 1893 (Newcastle Utd guest Sept 1896)/South Shields Aug 1897/Blyth (Blyth Albion) Feb 1898.

Tom Nicholson was a first-class forward for Newcastle West End at St James' Park, no other forward has scored more times for the club than his 54 goals. He was especially prominent during seasons 1887-88 (24 app 18 goals) when the West Enders became the district's top side for a short period, then in 1888-89 (12 app 15 goals) and 1889-90 (31 app 19 goals). The Scot hit three in the FA Cup against Bishop Auckland, then another treble also in the FA Cup, this time facing South Bank. And once Tom struck four goals as West End recorded a 15-0 victory over North Eastern during 1888.

He also netted two as Shankhouse were defeated in the final of the Northumberland Senior Cup, going on to figure in the Northumberland & Durham Inter County final against Sunderland. Nicholson operated at inside-forward as well as in the centre-forward role, at 5'8" tall, he was in many ways the archetypal tricky Scot. He represented Northumberland and the Newcastle & District combination while later, during September 1896, Nicholson took part in a single fixture for Newcastle United, as a guest during a benefit match for Johnny Campbell. He was by then a veteran, but still well respected on Tyneside as one of the city's early footballers. Tom was linked to Blyth football for a good period, described as a "real wizard" and "famous Spartan". He had spells with Blyth's pioneer clubs and was later skipper and during the summer of 1894, it was reported he was one of five players swimming at the local beach at Blyth when a team-mate was drowned. Nicholson resided in that area for some time and was on occasion up to mischief, being charged with the theft of an overcoat in the town during the same year, while during 1898 Tommy was back in court for stealing joints of beef, sentenced to 14 days at Blyth prison.
App & Goals: 77 app 54 gls.

NUGENT James

1887, 1889, 1890 Forward
b. Gateshead, 1867 (Q1)/d. Newcastle upon Tyne, 29 March 1958

Career: St Mary & St James 1886/Newcastle Harp/Elswick Rangers cs 1887 (**WEST END** guest Dec 1887)(Sunderland Albion guest May 1888)(**WEST END** guest April 1889)(Newcastle East End guest Nov 1888 & Nov 1889)(**WEST END** guest Jan 1890)(Sunderland Albion guest May 1890)/Newcastle East End-Newcastle Utd 1892-93 briefly.

Also appeared for Newcastle Wed/Elswick Shipyard/Trafalgar between 1887-1893, acting as Junior XI secretary and later committee member. (Note: Appearances with Trafalgar may be his brother John, or both.)

With an Irish family background, James Nugent was regarded as a top-notch striker during the early years of football's development on Tyneside, notably with Elswick Rangers where he was a big favourite at their Mill Lane ground. Nugent appeared for Northumberland and for the Newcastle & District XI, top honours in the region at that time. With Rangers, he starred in the Northumberland Senior Cup final of 1889, runner-up after a controversial three-match contest with Newcastle East End. A potent forward for the Elswick club, James played alongside his younger brother John Nugent, another decent footballer on Tyneside then. James guested for West End on four occasions over three spells, while he also assisted East End in Heaton and Sunderland Albion – for their very first match during May 1888. He resided at Byker Bank, then later in Jesmond into his nineties having worked as a shipyard labourer and lamplighter for a Tyneside gas company.
App & Goals: 4 app 0 gls.
(Note: Although census data reveals he was born in Newcastle, birth registration records confirm he was a Gateshead man.)

O

OLDHAM Robert Alexander

1885-1887 Goalkeeper
b. Newcastle upon Tyne, 1866 (Q1)/d. Durham, 28 December 1917
Career: Grove Jnrs (Newcastle) 1882/Hawthorn Rovers (Newcastle), Elswick Leather Works, Brunswick (Newcastle), all 1884/**WEST END** cMarch 1885, still assisting Elswick Leather Works & Brunswick/Gateshead 1887/North Elswick Nov 1888.

Also appeared for Park Rangers/Drysdale/Greenmarket Wed.

Robert Oldham was the son of an established milliner on Grey Street in Newcastle and later during 1893 he also opened a hat and gentleman's accessories shop for a period in Sunderland. On the football pitch as a teenager, Oldham built up a good reputation as a reliable 'keeper with the Elswick Leather Works side during the mid-1880s. Robert became attached to West End at that time, but still appeared in the Elswick Works line-up. During 1886-87 at St James' Park, he was recognised as a "valuable acquisition" by the press and totalled 24 games for the West Enders but, as it was reported, left due to work commitments. Once in West End colours as a goalkeeper against Tyne, he exchanged places with Jimmy Duns and scored in a 6-0 victory. During his football years, Oldham lived in Elswick and represented Northumberland County as well as the Newcastle & District side. By 1901 he was running a public-house in the Westgate district, later moving to Waldridge Fell near Chester-le-Street. Robert appears by 1915 as landlord of the Neville Hotel in Durham just before he died a couple of years later. On his passing, the Newcastle Evening Chronicle wrote that Oldham was "a well-known figure in golf, football, rowing and billiards" as well as being a "very successful ped-runner". Robert was also a decent cricketer with Hawthorn CC and a cyclist for the Kensington club.
App & Goals: 24 app 1 gl.

ORMOND Charles

1883-1885 Goalkeeper, Full-back, Half-back, Committee
b. Newcastle upon Tyne, c1864
Connected to the West End set-up as a player and committee member during 1883-84 and 1884-85, Charles Ormond was a regular at full-back during the club's second season of football and during the early part of the following campaign. Census documents reveal one resident who likely fits as the West End footballer. In 1881 a Charles Ormond was raised at Westgate and when he appeared for the early West Enders would have been around 19 years of age. A moulder by trade, he resided during the later 1880s and 1890s at Meldon Street near Elswick Road. During the club's second annual meeting in the summer of 1883, Ormond was elected to the West End committee. He was also a cricketer for the Gloucester CC in Elswick.
App & Goals: 28 app 0 gls.

P

PAPE R

1885-1887 Forward
Career: St Andrew's (Newcastle)/**WEST END** 1885 to 1887.
Playing most of his football for the West End second-eleven, Pape was handed four opportunities in the senior line-up during the opening three months of 1886, including early Tyne versus Wear clashes with Sunderland.
App & Goals: 4 app 0 gls.

PATTEN Rodger

1890-1891 Forward
b. Newcastle upon Tyne, 2 January 1872/d. Blyth, 22 January 1941
Career: Trafalgar by 1887 (**WEST END** guest Jan 1890)/**WEST END** cs 1890/Trafalgar cs 1891/Blyth March 1893/Trafalgar Oct 1893 briefly/Blyth Oct 1893/Newcastle Utd Aug 1896/Hebburn Argyle July 1897/New Delaval Villa Aug 1897/Blyth Spartans cs 1901 to cs 1902.
Also appeared for Victoria Wed.

Brought up in the centre of Newcastle during the 1880s, his family resided at Shipley's Court in the city's Bigg Market. Rodger Patten made a name for himself with the Trafalgar club and assisted West End Reserves during January 1890 for a holiday fixture against Dumbarton Rangers. He scored three goals in that outing and West End's management made sure they acquired his undoubted talent up front for the start of the following 1890-91 season. Patten scored on his full debut against another Scottish visitor to Tyneside, Albion Rovers, and he became the pick of the club's forwards for that programme striking 18 goals alongside international player Bob Calderwood. Patten though headed back to join up once more with Trafalgar then served Blyth and later had a spell with Newcastle United as well. He was described during March 1893 when impressing with Blyth as being "a sterling little player" and "one of the trickiest forwards in the Northern Counties". Rodger was included in the County team on several occasions during his career, while he also played cricket for Trafalgar. His elder brother Jack Patten was also a noted footballer, with East End and Newcastle United, later becoming Northumberland FA secretary for many years. The two brothers appeared together for Trafalgar and for the early Magpies 'A' side during season 1896-97. Rodger lived in Blyth, working at Crofton pit and was injured following a mine accident during 1924.
App & Goals: 36 app 18 gls.

PENNY Alexander

1890 Half-back
b. Kemback, Fife, 7 June 1866/d. Arbroath, 4 March 1939

Career: Perseverance Jnrs (Arbroath)/Strathmore (Arbroath)/Gateshead NER/**WEST END** July 1890/Newcastle East End-Newcastle Utd Oct 1890/Gateshead NER by April 1891/Arbroath Wand June 1893/Dundonians Jan 1894/Arbroath c1895 to 1897. Also appeared for Newcastle Wed.

From a Fife village near Cupar, Alex Penny left his job as a flax mill worker to settle on Tyneside during the 1880s. He appeared for railway works side Gateshead NER then Penny moved across the River Tyne to join Newcastle West End during the summer of 1890. Remaining with the St James' Park side for only a few months, he soon was on his travels again, but not far, barely the two miles or so across the city to sign for Newcastle East End.

Appearing for both rivals during the 1890-91 season, Penny never settled at Chillingham Road either. He went on to turn out in midweek football for Newcastle Wednesday and again at Gateshead NER then returned to Scotland. He made home in Forfarshire and was for a long period associated with Arbroath, a player and later supporter. He ran a tailoring business in the coastal town, nicknamed both 'Alick' and 'Sy' Penny, during the Great War he joined the Royal Highlanders while in 1924 it was reported he saved a boy from drowning at Arbroath Harbour. Penny died watching a Scottish First Division match at Gayfield Park during 1939.

App & Goals: 1 app 0 gls.

PORTERFIELD Alfred

1889 Goalkeeper, Half-back
b. Londonderry, 8 June 1866/d. Glasgow, 4 May 1922
Career: Craigbank (Glasgow) & secretary 1888-89/**WEST END** March 1889/Carlton (Greenock) Sept 1889/Greenock Morton April 1890/Blackburn Rovers Sept 1890/Bootle Oct 1890/Thistle (Glasgow) by Sept 1891/Clyde by Dec 1891/King's Park by Oct 1892/Burnley April 1895/Cartvale Aug 1896.

A well-travelled football enthusiast who was born in Ireland, the Porterfield family moved to Glasgow and by the time of the 1881 census Alf was living in the Camlachie district as a 15-year-old, his parents both being school-teachers in the city. Working as a "spirit salesman" then, he started playing football with the Craigbank side, turning out both as a 'keeper and outfield, as well as being the team's secretary. He was at that time also in charge of administration for the Glasgow 2nd XI Junior Association. Porterfield headed to Tyneside towards the latter weeks of the 1888-89 season and was handed a trio of outings, again between the posts and as a half-back. But Alf remained at St James' Park only a short period before moving on, back to

Clydeside then to Lancashire where he joined FA Cup winners Blackburn. But Porterfield made no senior appearances for Rovers before taking part in six games of Bootle's Football Alliance programme. He appeared for the representative teams of both Glasgow and Stirlingshire, as well as when on Merseyside, for the Liverpool & District XI. At one point the Edinburgh Evening News described Alf as "on the small side, but is very active and cute"! When he died in 1922, Porterfield was employed as an "electrician's storeman".

App & Goals: 3 app 0 gls.

(Note: Although press reports show initials of ASG Porterfield, birth and death records only state Alfred as a Christian name.)

PROCTOR David

1883-1885 Full-back
b. Newcastle upon Tyne, 1865 (Q2)/d. Newcastle upon Tyne, 1924 (Q2)

David Proctor was a Newcastle West End cricketer and the club's secretary during the mid-1880s, residing near Westgate cemetery. He appeared once for the football eleven, a match during December 1884 against Tyne at their Warwick Place ground in Jesmond. That was West End's seventh victory in a row at the time. Proctor grew up in Newcastle during the 1880s and 1890s, at the family home in John Street and during his teens worked as a clerk at a supplier of weighing machines. During the 1900s, he became a commercial traveller in the same line of business, recorded as living in Benwell.

App & Goals: 1 app 0 gls.

Q

QUEEN Thomas Bernard

1890-1892 Full-back
b. Newcastle upon Tyne, 29 March 1868/d. Newcastle upon Tyne, October 1951
Career: Newcastle Harp c1888/**WEST END** 1890/Newcastle East End-Newcastle Utd cs 1892 to cs 1893.
Also app for Newcastle Wed.

A full-back who never reached West End's senior eleven, but who took part in the side's reserve team which lifted the Northumberland Senior Cup during March 1892. That was the West Enders last trophy success just prior

to their demise in the summer. Queen afterwards was part of the reserve squad which migrated to the East End club when they set up home at St James' Park and he turned out for Newcastle United's 'A' side during 1892-93. It was noted that Tommy "displayed good tackling powers and judgement". Queen was for several seasons from the late-1880s into the 1890s also attached to the St James' Park-based Newcastle Wednesday, being captain of the side in popular Wednesday games on Tyneside. Queen was born and raised in Westgate and at the time he played football worked as a tailor.

App & Goals: 0 app 0 gls (Reserve app in Senior Cup final 1892).

R

RAYLSTONE (RALSTON) James Buchanan

1886-1888, 1889-1891 Full-back, Half-back, Forward
b. Cardross, Dunbartonshire, 12 October 1863/d. Glasgow, 31 December 1940
Career: Renton 1885-86/[Kilmarnock]/Clydebank 1886/**WEST END** Dec 1886 (Newcastle East End guest Dec 1887, March & April 1888)/Newcastle East End cs 1888/Kidderminster Nov 1888 (Sunderland Albion guest Dec 1888)/Sunderland Jan 1889/**WEST END** Feb 1889/Rotherham Town cs 1890/**WEST END** Feb 1891/Clydebank Aug 1891.

Born and raised around the Dumbarton football hotbed of football, Raylstone soon began playing the sport and joined the Renton club. Noted in the local press as a "tough, uncompromising player", James was an imposing character who served both Newcastle West End and East End after moving from Scotland with his younger brother. He appeared at St James' Park from late in 1886 to 1888 and was capped for Northumberland during that period, lifting the Senior Cup with West End just before moving on. At half-back, he was also selected for the local county when in East End colours, signing for the Chillingham Road outfit during the close season of 1888. Also operating at full-back, and occasionally in attack, the Scot once scored a hat-trick for the club in West End's biggest victory, 15-0 over North Eastern. Raylstone amassed over 100 games for the two Newcastle teams in a belligerent style and was always able to notch a goal. Described as "a very clever half-back" by Athletic News during 1889, James was suspended by the Scottish FA when he joined West End. A controversial character at times, often rough on the field, the Newcastle Chronicle reported that he had "a reputation few would care to possess" and that Raylstone "should not be allowed to play football"! Later moving to Wearside, but the Scot didn't see senior action for Sunderland, at the time a club rapidly developing into a top outfit. Then James rejoined West End, being especially prominent during 1889-90 when he appeared in the West Enders first Northern League season. During April 1889 it was reported that Raylstone had "narrowly escaped drowning" after falling into the water at South Dock in Sunderland; unable to swim, a dock gateman and two river constables arrived to rescue him from his peril in the Wear. By 1891 when residing in Dumbarton,

he made headlines when charged with manslaughter following a fight in the town; the trial in December ending with a 'not proven' verdict. When James died in Glasgow during 1940, he had worked as a plater's helper in the Clyde shipyards.

App & Goals: 95 app 25 gls.

(Note: His surname is spelt various ways, often Raylstone, but confirmed by court papers, Scottish FA registers and birth and death certificates as Ralston. Previous birth information at Kirkintilloch (1866) is a different James Ralston.)

REDPATH John George

1891 Inside-forward
b. Newcastle upon Tyne, 11 March 1872/d. Newcastle upon Tyne, 7 June 1952
Career: **WEST END** 1890-91/Trafalgar cs 1891/Rendel Feb 1892 to 1897.
Also appeared for Science & Art.

Johnny Redpath was a well-known local footballer during the late-Victorian era who had a short period with West End when a teenager during the latter part of the 1890-91 season, likely when studying at the Science & Art College. He appeared once, in the local Charity Shield competition against Willington Athletic during May then joined up with Trafalgar before becoming a stout-hearted and reliable competitor for Rendel. He was a loyal servant in Benwell during the 1890s, as the club reached the Northumberland Senior Cup final in 1892, 1893 and 1895 – all as runners-up. Captain of the side for much of his time there, he was selected for the County eleven. Redpath was also a fine cricketer, associated with Benwell Hill CC for many years as a reserve player then as treasurer as the Twenties began, becoming assistant-treasurer for over 25 years thereafter. The Benwell Hill history records that his "services to the club were immeasurable". He also played cricket for St Phillip's and Elswick Works. John lived in that district and was employed as a turner-engineer's lathe-hand at the Armstrong factory.

App & Goals: 1 app 0 gls.

(Note: Gateshead NER fielded R Redpath at the same time, no family linkage has been traced.)

ROBERTSON William W

1889-1890 Half-back, Forward, Secretary (reserve team)
b. Scotland

Career: Whitefield (Glasgow)/**WEST END** Sept 1889 becoming asst-secretary (Sheffield Utd guest April 1890) to cs 1890.

From Scotland, William Robertson arrived on Tyneside from the Whitefield club of Govan (although the Newcastle press noted the side as "Whitelaw" in error). He had captained the representative eleven of the Govan district and was a decent footballer in Glasgow. That experience saw him appointed as skipper – and noted as secretary of West End's reserve side. The Scot was elevated to senior action during December, at one point displaying top form, notably in an important FA Cup tie against Grimsby Town when it was stated "he played a splendid game". Robertson was selected for Northumberland during February 1890 while he was captain of a local Scotland XI which faced an England XI for an end of season finale match during May. He once stepped in to assist Sheffield United against Newcastle East End during April 1890, probably due to a mishap to one of the visiting players – by co-incidence, another W Robertson was also in the Tykes line-up, he was a Scot as well. During William's stay on Tyneside, he lodged on Westmorland Road in Elswick.

App & Goals: 9 app 1 gl.

(Note: Official Scottish FA Minutes refer to the player as WW Robertson when he was suspended for playing in England, while contemporary Tyneside reports note him as AW Robertson, W Robertson or even T Robertson.)

ROBSON E

1883-1884 Half-back, Forward
Career: Rendel 1882/**WEST END** Dec 1883 to cs 1884. Also appeared for Newcastle Wed.

A Rendel player before joining the early West End set-up at the end of 1883, Robson appeared alongside a namesake, W Robson, in the Benwell line-up, possibly related. With the West Enders' reserve squad for season 1883-84, he made two senior appearances; firstly, against Drysdale as a forward in a 7-0 victory, then at Rosehill as a half-back.

App & Goals: 2 app 0 gls.

ROSS Joseph

1890 Half-back
b. Scotland
Career: Heart of Midlothian 1889/**WEST END** July 1890 to cDec 1890.

When Joseph Ross turned up at St James' Park from Edinburgh with another Scottish player, Dave Walker, the Newcastle Daily Chronicle reported they were "a couple of splendidly built youths". Although registered for Hearts for season 1890-91, he broke amateur rules and had already moved to England, Ross making his debut in West End's red-and-black shirt for what was an eagerly awaited visit of Preston North End to Barrack Road to open the new season. Joseph was selected frequently as the programme got under way, however by the end of 1890, Ross appears to have departed back to Scotland. Another player called Ross progressed to appear for Hearts and Leith Ath, but he is unlikely to be the same footballer, however a J Ross was a regular with

Portobello Thistle, near Edinburgh, during 1891-92 and 1892-93 and could be the player.

App & Goals: 13 app 1 gl.

RULE William Youngson

1887 Half-back
b. Tynemouth, 5 June 1863/d. Gateshead, 7 February 1950
Career: Newcastle Rangers 1880/Gateshead Ass Dec 1884, becoming treasurer by Sept 1886 & committee Aug 1888 (**WEST END** guest May 1887) to c1890. Also appeared for Villa Association (Newcastle)/1st Northumberland Volunteers XI.

A past captain of one of Tyneside's oldest clubs, Newcastle Rangers, William Rule operated as a goalkeeper and defender. When Rangers folded, along with several team-mates, Rule was one of their players to regroup and form the Gateshead Association club. William was also captain of the new side and he guested for West End in one fixture, against Darlington St Augustine's during May 1887. An electrical draughtsman, born in Tynemouth and moving to Westgate in Newcastle then to Gateshead, he became a well-liked figure who remained on Tyneside to his death in 1950. He was a past Battery Quarter Master Sergeant with the Northumberland Volunteer Artillery as well as a keen member of the Lodge of Oddfellows and the Sir Allan Painter Lodge in Gateshead.

App & Goals: 1 app 0 gls.

RYDER Isaac James

1891-1892 Half-back
b. Newcastle upon Tyne, 23 December 1871/d. Newcastle upon Tyne, 26 May 1960
Career: Villa Association Jnrs (Newcastle), becoming secretary by 1887/**WEST END** by April 1891/Newcastle East End-Newcastle Utd cs 1892/Newcastle Albion cs 1894/Willington Ath Jan 1895 to c1896.

From a popular and well-known Newcastle footballing family, Isaac Ryder was one of four brothers to feature in the early Tyneside game. Brought up on Spring Garden Lane near St James' Park, he grew up with Joseph (qv) and William (qv), all three brothers appearing for West End, and for East End as well. The elder brother, Harry, also served Newcastle's early football clubs too, while a younger sibling, George, later appeared for Bolton Wanderers during the 1900s. Isaac played alongside Joe and William for West End during season 1891-92, filling in on two occasions during the early part of the programme. With West End becoming defunct, Isaac

joined up with the Newcastle East End club and was captain of their 'A' side, going onto play for the senior eleven on one occasion, that a historic fixture – in what was Newcastle United's first Football League win, a 6-0 victory over Arsenal at Gallowgate during 1893. Ryder picked up a dodgy knee playing football and was once described as having "suffered a martyrdom from injuries received in the arena". As a youngster, Isaac began work as an iron moulder's apprentice and later was employed at the Vickers engineering complex alongside the Tyne. Ryder kept his association with St James' Park, the family noting that he was United's kit-man for a period after the turn of the century.

App & Goals: 2 app 0 gls.

RYDER Joseph

1890-1892 Half-back, Forward
b. Newcastle upon Tyne, 15 August 1873/d. Newcastle upon Tyne, 19 November 1945
Career: Villa Association Jnrs (Newcastle) 1887/Elswick Rangers 1889/Newcastle Albion 1890/**WEST END** cs 1890/Newcastle East End-Newcastle Utd cs 1892/Willington Ath by Sept 1894/Hebburn Argyle cs 1895/Newcastle Utd Sept 1896/South Shields July 1897.

One of 14 children including eight brothers, with Isaac (qv) and William Ryder (qv) being also at West End, Joe worked as a "plater's helper" on Tyneside. At 5'10" tall, Ryder turned out as a goalkeeper and in outfield positions during his career – as a half-back and forward for West End, but between the posts for East End and Newcastle United. He was elevated from West End's reserve side towards the very end of season 1890-91, making his debut against Darlington St Augustine's alongside sibling William. He figured in 10 games the following campaign, including the West Enders' last ever fixture at Stockton during April. Joe was a respected local character, good enough to appear for Northumberland County. Joining Newcastle United's founder club, Newcastle East End, Ryder had to compete with several players for the goalkeeper's position during those early days at St James' Park. Newcastle tried four other custodians, Whitton, Lowery, Ramsay and Ward, and Ryder only managed two first-eleven matches for the Magpies. He reached the Northumberland Senior Cup final with the United 'A' combination.

App & Goals: 16 app 0 gls.

(Note: Family history information, as well as birth-death records, only show the Christian name of Joseph, however official FA and Football League registration data notes JJ Ryder. This is likely a type-setting error and should be IJ Ryder, his brother Isaac James Ryder.)

RYDER William

1890-1892 Goalkeeper
b. Newcastle upon Tyne, 31 July 1870/d. Newcastle upon Tyne, 28 May 1945
Career: Newcastle Albion/**WEST END** by Nov 1890 (Trafalgar guest March 1891)/Newcastle East End-Newcastle Utd cs 1892 to cs 1893/Newcastle Albion 1894-95.
Also appeared for Elswick Shipyard.
Of the three Ryder brothers to appear with Newcastle West End, William appeared on most occasions; 26 times over the team's last two campaigns of 1890-91 and 1891-92. Given the opportunity between the posts when regular goalkeeper Dave Whitton was out with a long-term injury, Ryder did well and was an able deputy until the Scot returned during November 1891. Afterwards on Newcastle United's staff, he never received a first-team call up, but like all the Ryder lads, remained an enthusiastic supporter of the Black-and-Whites all his life. His family was described as "famed in football" during those years, William resided at Dilston Road in Arthur's Hill at the time of his passing during 1945.

App & Goals: 26 app 0 gls.

S

SADLER Thomas

1888-1889 Full-back, Half-back, Forward
b. Nottingham, 14 March 1862/d. Barrow, December 1934
Career: [St Mary's (Nottingham) by 1882]/Nottingham Rangers by Nov 1883/Jardines (Nottingham) Sept 1886/**WEST END** Oct 1888/Stockton Jan 1889.
Also appeared for Newcastle Wand.
A regular in defence for the Nottingham Rangers club playing in the Midland League, Tom Sadler then joined up with the strong Jardines Works outfit where several employees were also footballers. Skipper at the Nottingham factory team, he moved to the North East two years later during 1888 and settled at St James' Park during the autumn with West End. Athletic News reported that he was a "a good half-back" and added that with West End had "turned out a distinct success". Taking part in seven fixtures, Sadler though moved on as the year turned, down the North East coast to join up with Stockton. From 1891 and 1901 census information, it is likely he returned to Newcastle, living in the Arthur's Hill neighbourhood and employed as an ordnance fitter at Elswick. A decade later he was now a resident of Barrow, noted as a "fitter, gun machinery" where similar factories were based.

App & Goals: 7 app 0 gls.

SAWERS Alexander

1889 Full-back
b. Kilmarnock, 13 November 1865/d. Burnley, 2 March 1925
Career: Kilmarnock Nov 1885/Clyde by Aug 1887/**WEST END** March 1889/Newcastle East End April 1889/Clyde

Dec 1889/Third Lanark 1890/Clyde by Dec 1890/Burnley Sept 1892 to Aug 1893/Abercorn c1893/Clyde Oct 1897. *Alex Sawers was a member of a good Kilmarnock team which lifted the Ayrshire Cup in 1886 and noted as a "Scottish Corinthian". Although a touch insulting perhaps, he was also described in the Northern Echo during 1889 as possessing "carthorse proportions", yet Sawers was a skilled and practised defender. Initially landing with West End, he played once against Sunderland Albion in March 1889, but quickly traded camps to rivals East End where he found colleagues from north of the border. At Heaton Junction with East End, Sawers assisted in the Northern League and while the club needed his experience, Alex did not remain long in Heaton leaving after only nine outings. It was reported that when playing for the Northumberland County eleven on a trip to Lanarkshire, he remained in his native Scotland and did not return. Alex later had a spell back south with Burnley, part of their line-up for a handful of FA Cup and Football League matches. He was the elder brother of Bill Sawers (qv), to briefly appear for West End as well and who was capped by Scotland. The siblings played alongside each other for Clyde, while as a teenager Alex worked as a tailor, a trade he returned to when he settled in Burnley.*

App & Goals: 1 app 0 gls.

(Note: Newspaper reports have his name spelt both as Sawers and Sawyers, family history data also noting both.)

SAWERS William

1890 Centre-forward

b. Kilmarnock, 4 January 1868/d. Glasgow, 24 October 1927

Career: Kilmarnock South-Western/Clyde 1888/Sunderland Albion Dec 1889 (**WEST END** guest May 1890)/Clyde Aug 1891/Preston North End Sept 1891/Clyde Sept 1891/Blackburn Rovers Sept 1892/Stoke Aug 1893/Dundee June 1894/Stoke Aug 1895/Dundee Sept 1895/Kilmarnock Feb 1896/Clyde cs 1896 to c1897.

Like his elder brother Alex (qv), Billy Sawers was a well-travelled Scot. He was a noted forward at the Barrowfield Ground with Clyde, recognised by the Glasgow XI before sampling professional football in England when he joined Sunderland Albion at the end of 1889. Sawers could be a touch feisty on the pitch, while he quickly became embroiled in controversy on Wearside when he played in the FA Cup against Bootle – the

Wearsiders being kicked out of the competition as the Scot had not been registered in time. Playing in their Football Alliance side during 1889-90, he did well, scoring nine goals in 12 outings. Sawers guested for West End before he returned to Clydeside, on a single occasion, when Everton visited St James' Park at the end of the 1889-90 season, one of no fewer than six Sunderland Albion players to wear West End colours. Back with Clyde, he netted 15 goals in 22 appearances during the Scottish League's second campaign of 1891-92 and Billy became a player in demand. He crossed the border once more, a success with Blackburn Rovers during 1892-93, claiming 14 goals in 28 matches. When appearing for Dundee at the end of his career, Sawers enjoyed another good period, reaching the Scottish Cup semi-final, but Bill missed a crucial late penalty against Renton when the match was all level at 1-1. At that time, Sawers was selected for his country, gaining a single cap against Wales during March 1895. He possessed powerful shooting, while the Scottish International Who's Who notes he was "praised as a clever dribbler" yet was "criticised for hanging onto the ball too long". The forward caused a bit of a rumpus when he signed for Preston North End during September 1891, but almost immediately quit the Deepdale club and returned to Clyde. Sawers later settled in Glasgow and ran a well-known sports-outfitters shop in Bridgeton, then afterwards worked as a cabinet-maker.

App & Goals: 1 app 0 gls.

Honours: 1 Scot cap 1895.

(Note: When with Sunderland Albion, press reports referred to him as J, W, or R Sawers, but he is identified as William. Several web and football books note William being born in Bridgeton, Glasgow, but he hailed from Kilmarnock.)

SCHUBERT A

1883 Half-back

Career: WEST END 1883/Elswick Ordnance Works cs 1884, becoming secretary.

In West End's ranks during season 1883-84, Schubert appeared once for the club during October against Rendel. The Newcastle-based sports periodical, Northern Athlete, listed him as being the Ordnance Works secretary for season 1884-85 residing at Stowell Street near to Gallowgate in Newcastle. He played alongside John Mather for the Works outfit. Schubert was also a top runner at athletic meetings on Tyneside during the 1880s, as well as a cricketer for West End CC and later doubling as secretary for the Ordnance cricket and football sides. Frequently taking part in sports events, he once raced in a 110-yard handicap against the celebrated Arthur Wharton, the Darlington footballer and first-class sprinter; a large crowd watched the West End man win a "magnificent race". Frustratingly, having an unusual surname, Schubert does not appear in any local official records between 1870 and 1890 and by the end of the 1880s it seems he left the area, possibly to Kent where an Albert Schubert settled (b. Liskeard, Cornwall 1864, d. Gillingham 1909); this could be the same individual.

App & Goals: 1 app 0 gls.

SCOTT David

1887-1888 Forward
b. Newcastle upon Tyne, c1866
Career: Newcastle East End Oct 1883/**WEST END** Nov 1887/Rendel 1888-89/Newcastle East End 1888-89.
As a teenager David Scott joined the Newcastle East End set-up during season 1883-84 and made his debut in the first-eleven against Prudhoe Rovers. With West End's rivals across the city, he became more a regular fixture in 1885-86 as the Heaton side took part in a programme of numerous friendlies before a league format arrived. Scott totalled almost 80 games (21 goals) in addition to a single first-class outing in the FA Cup. He was good enough to appear for both the City of Newcastle and Northumberland representative sides. Dropping out of senior recognition shortly after his FA Cup outing, David appeared for West End during season 1887-88 then for Rendel, as well as continuing to turn out for the East Enders' reserve combination. Scott lived in Byker during those years before the turn of the century.
App & Goals: 5 app 0 gls.

SCOTT James

1887 Half-back
b. Newcastle upon Tyne, c1869
Career: Elswick Leather Works 1883/**WEST END** cs 1887/Elswick Rangers Dec 1887 to c1889.
A regular selection in the Elswick Leather Works side during the mid-1880s since a teenager, James Scott then joined St James' Park's roster for a couple of seasons. He was a reserve line-up player, but managed a first-team call-up during November 1887 against Morpeth Harriers. Scott switched to Elswick Rangers in Graingerville at the end of 1887, although still appeared for West End Reserves during early 1888. He found himself one of three players at Mill Lane by the name of Scott. Rangers often fielded the trio; James along with goalkeeper Matt and William (junior) (qv) – at West End too – while William Scott (senior) was on the side-lines. The 1881 and 1891 census registers show William Scott aged 46 with sons William (junior) and James, residing at Shumac Street in Elswick, adjacent to Richardson's Leather Works complex where all three worked. James was the younger brother and employed as a leather-finisher.
App & Goals: 1 app 0 gls.

SCOTT William

1887 Forward
b. Newcastle upon Tyne, c1867/d. [Newcastle upon Tyne, September 1898]
Career: Elswick Leather Works 1881/Newcastle FA by Dec 1884/Elswick Leather Works 1885/**WEST END** Sept 1887/Elswick Rangers Dec 1887 (Sunderland Albion guest May 1888) to c1889.
William Scott and James Scott (qv) were brothers from Elswick and appeared for Elswick Leather Works, West End and Elswick Rangers during the 1880s. Both also represented Northumberland. William was a tanner at the nearby Leather Works and sported West End's colours only once, against Redcar at the start of the 1887-88 programme, scoring in a 4-1 victory. Scott assisted Sunderland Albion during May 1888, the

Wearsiders' very first game against Shankhouse at the Blue House Field. A cricket enthusiast as well, William played for West End during the summer months. He was noted occasionally as W Scott (junior), and there was a William Scott (senior), his father, also linked to the West End, Elswick Leather Works and Elswick Rangers clubs in the decade, all residing at Shumac Street, the family home. It is probable that William Scott (junior) is the man who died in Newcastle at the young age of 31 during 1898.
App & Goals: 1 app 1 gl.
(Note: William Scott (senior) hailed from Scotland originally and became the Works XI football secretary, often an umpire or referee at Rangers and West End fixtures, having been the West Enders' first captain without an appearance being traced. Scott (senior) was also part of the Newcastle Temperance Festival organisation management for the Town Moor football tournament and a dedicated member of the Northumberland FA, becoming President before the turn of the century. He also sat on the Northumberland & Durham Referees' Association committee and was one the group to form the organisation in 1896.)

SHAW George [Wardhaugh]

1887-1889 Half-back
b. [Newcastle upon Tyne, 1867 (Q3)]/d. [Southend-on-Sea, 9 January 1925]
George Shaw was attached to West End for season 1886-87 and 1887-88. For the visit of the Glasgow University eleven to Tyneside during September 1888, the St James' Park club were without star Scottish international Bob Kelso and reserve Shaw filled in at half-back, his single appearance for the side. Census documents for the period show three potential lads named George Shaw who could be the footballer. Two lived south of the River Tyne, in Gateshead and Jarrow, but the probable individual was George Wardaugh Shaw who resided at Monday Street in Elswick near to where several West End players were based. A fitter and turner, when he appeared for the club, he would have been around 20 years of age. Shaw later relocated to Southend-on-Sea where he died.
App & Goals: 1 app 0 gls.

SHAW T

1891-1892 Forward
b. Scotland

Career: Glasgow Wand/Third Lanark 1890-91/**WEST END** Nov 1891 to cs 1892.
Described as a "new man from Glasgow" when he arrived at St James' Park to join West End, Shaw was

further noted as an ex-Third Lanark player. He appeared with Glasgow Wanderers then for the Cathkin Park outfit on three senior occasions during 1890-91 before moving to Tyneside – and was given the mandatory suspension by the Scottish FA. He came into West End's line-up for the Northern League fixture at Bramall Lane with Sheffield United during December, a 5-1 defeat, but the Scot remained in the forward line for the club's final few months into 1892. As West End folded, Shaw departed and has not been tracked, although a Scottish player named Shaw appeared with Blyth before moving to Doncaster in February 1893 and could be the same footballer.

App & Goals: 14 app 4 gls.

SIMM John Thomas

1882-1883 Forward
b. Seaham Harbour, 10 October 1863/d. Newcastle upon Tyne, 1946 (Q2)
Career: Stanley-Newcastle East End 1881/**WEST END** Aug 1882/Heaton Ass 1883 to c1885/Later becoming St James' FC (Newcastle) reserve-team secretary by 1889.
Briefly with Newcastle United's founder club, Stanley FC of South Byker, as they kicked off the association game late in 1881, John Simm played once for the new side as a teenager against Newcastle FA during that opening campaign. At that time, he was living at Clifford Street in Byker, working as a "Pattern Maker". Being a reserve with Stanley, he soon joined Newcastle West End for the 1882-83 season and again only appeared in senior action briefly, in the club's first traced line-up against Heaton Association. Simm though can claim to have played in each club's very first season of action. He did not stay long with the West Enders either, as he switched to Heaton Association during 1883. Ten years on from the 1881 census, Simm is recorded as still residing in Byker, and when the 1939 National Register was compiled, Simm remained in that district at Bothal Street, a retired pattern-maker.
App & Goals: 1 app 0 gls.
(Note: Reports have his surname as Simms and Simm, family history information confirms the latter.)

SIMM William

1892 Forward
b. Newcastle upon Tyne, 22 March 1872/d. Newcastle upon Tyne, 27 January 1950
Career: Portland (Newcastle)/Greenmarket (Newcastle) by 1890/**WEST END** Jan 1892/Newcastle East End-Newcastle Utd cs 1892/Newcastle Albion Jan 1893/Christchurch FC (Newcastle) player-secretary June 1893/Newcastle Utd Sept 1893/Trafalgar by Jan 1894/Rendel cs 1897.
Also appeared for Newcastle Wed.
William Simm was a prominent Geordie player during the early years of the 1890s on Tyneside. Capped by Northumberland County, as a youngster Simm was described by one journalist as having "the appearance of one who will develop into a good player" while a couple of years later the Newcastle Daily Journal noted he was, "one of the best local forwards". When barely 20 years of age, William came into the West End line-up for a

Northern League derby with East End at the start of February 1892 and suffered a dreadful debut when the red-and-blacks lost 7-1.

Simm played a handful of games for the club and lifted the Northumberland Senior Cup appearing for West End's reserve side just prior to their demise during 1892. On Newcastle United's books over two short periods, he managed to reach the senior eleven on one occasion before returning to local competition, a Football League fixture against Small Heath during October 1893. Working as a commercial clerk on Tyneside, his elder brother, Richard 'Dickie' Simm was also a competent Tyneside footballer during the same era, playing in the same team at Trafalgar and Rendel. The pair were also together with Newcastle United, Dickie failing to break into the senior eleven. The brothers were brought up residing in the All Saints locality at Russell Terrace in Shieldfield. When the 1939 National Register was published William was living at Thropton Terrace, Heaton and registered as a "Potato Merchant's Manager".
App & Goals: 7 app 2 gls.
(Note: Like his namesake JT Simm, football reports state William's surname as Simm or Simms.)

SMART (SMIRK) Joseph

1887-1888 Half-back
b. Sunderland, 30 March 1864/d. Sunderland, 11 August 1930
Career: Sunderland St Bede's/Sunderland 1885/**WEST END** Sept 1887/Sunderland May 1888 to c1889, becoming asst-trainer.

Registered as Joseph Smirk in official documents, but he was known as Joe Smart through his life. As a teenager

the Wearsider was employed as a blacksmith and joined the early ranks of Sunderland becoming a regular over two seasons in the years before they joined the Football League. Smart appeared in the FA Cup for his club – against West End during November 1886. At the start of the following programme of 1887-88, Joe moved from Wear to Tyne and signed up with the West Enders. He appeared at half-back for most of that season, taking part in the successful run to secure the Northumberland Senior Cup, although he missed the final against Shankhouse. Joe returned to Sunderland during the summer, however he was found more than often in the reserve side at the Newcastle Road ground. By then, Smart was working as a machinist at a local engine works. Remaining on Wearside all his life, he later was a steward at Sunderland Conservative Club, then a publican between 1914 and 1930 at a well-known watering hole, the Aquatic Arms, near Monkwearmouth Station.
App & Goals: 22 app 0 gls.

SMITH
1884 Half-back
With Newcastle West End during 1884-85, little is known about this footballer other than he played once for the club against Newcastle Rangers during October 1884. There is no trace of him appearing in reserve football either.
App & Goals: 1 app 0 gls.

SMITH J
1890 Inside-forward
b. Scotland
Career: Renton/Elswick Rangers 1888/Sunderland Nov 1888/Sunderland Albion Sept 1889 (**WEST END** guest May 1890) to Feb 1891.
One of five Sunderland Albion players to assist West End when they faced Everton during May 1890, the Scot was nicknamed through his career as 'Cutty' Smith – Scottish dialect for short or small. He was often referred to with his nickname to be differentiated from numerous Smiths playing the game then. Indeed, he appeared in Sunderland's forward line alongside another J Smith as well as a Jack Smith, who later played for Newcastle East End. Initially landing on Tyneside with the Elswick Rangers club, Cutty made a quick impact and was snatched by Sunderland and while on Wearside, he was good enough to represent the Durham FA side.
Banned by the Scottish FA when he ventured to England, he was reinstated as a player in Scotland during May 1891 and is likely to have returned to appear again north of the border.
App & Goals: 1 app 1 gl.
(Note: His nickname is not uncommon in Scotland, another 'Cutty' Smith played with Clyde during the 1890s, but he is a different footballer.)

STANGER Thomas William
1886-1889 Outside-left
b. Gateshead, 12 December 1869/d. Newcastle upon Tyne, 20 August 1949

Tom Stanger appeared for Newcastle West End's junior, reserve and senior elevens between 1886-87 and 1888-89. Having skippered the reserve side, he stepped up from being one of the St James' Park understudies for an important clash with Sunderland Albion in the FA Cup during the autumn of 1888 and appeared in what were two controversial matches which West End eventually lost after a protest and replay. Census and family history information somewhat remarkably show two sets of father and sons of the same name, Tom senior and Tom junior, living on Tyneside which posed difficulties in identifying the footballer. It appears the West Enders were served by a younger Thomas Stanger as a player, as well as by an elder Thomas Stanger (qv) as a club official in various capacities, likely a father and son pair. The Stanger duo of Elswick, then Gateshead, with Tom senior from Wetheral originally and working as a cartman, is highly unlikely to have become West End's Vice-President alongside well-known citizens such as Dr I'Anson and Councillor Weidner. Consequently, the Stanger pair who resided firstly, also in Gateshead, then in Heaton, are probably the family associated with West End. Tom Stanger's father was born in Newburn and by the start of the 1870s the family were based in Lamesley just outside Gateshead where Stanger junior was raised before settling in Heaton at the opening of the 1880s. His father worked as a joiner while son, Tom, an apprentice engineer. The Tyneside newspaper columns during 1886 also referred to a referee officiating local games as "JW Stanger", In addition noted as Cheviot FC secretary at the family address in Heaton. This is likely a press type-setting error, and is the same TW Stanger. Tom junior remained in the Heaton district, at Mundella Terrace, to his demise in 1949.
App & Goals: 3 app 0 gls.

STEWART E
1884-1885 Goalkeeper, Full-back, Half-back, Forward
An early footballer to turn out as a 'keeper, in defence, midfield and attack for West End during his eight appearances for the club during season 1884-85. Stewart registered his debut against Lemington Rangers in November between the posts, and was part of the attack for his last outing during April.
App & Goals: 8 app 0 gls.

STEWART Samuel
1889 Forward
b. Renfrew, 2 May 1866/d. Sunderland, 8 November 1950
Career: Renfrew/Sunderland Aug 1887/Sunderland Albion May 1888 (**WEST END** guest May 1889)/Sunderland Olympic cs 1891.
Sammy Stewart arrived in the North East as a 19-year-old from the Renfrew club near Glasgow. Having appeared for the local county eleven, Renfrewshire, at only 5'5" tall, he originally operated as a goalkeeper, but in England was seen more often in the forward line. He did though play the odd game between the sticks on Wearside. In an era before Sunderland played on the Football League stage, Stewart was often seen wearing

their colours in friendlies as well as local cup games, and in the FA Cup too.

The Scot moved to breakaway outfit Sunderland Albion during the close-season of 1888 and was a regular in the forward line for their Football Alliance campaign of 1889-90. He also played for the Durham County XI, while along with three other non-West Enders, Stewart assisted the St James' Park club when they faced Elswick Rangers at the end of the 1888-89 campaign, a late replacement for Don McColl. Sammy's brother, Jake Stewart, also turned out for Sunderland Albion and played in the same line-up together. He settled on Wearside and was employed as a boilersmith.
App & Goals: 1 app 0 gls.

STOKOE W
1887-1888 Forward
Career: Boundary (Newcastle) 1886/**WEST END** 1887/Elswick Rangers cs 1888/Rendel by Nov 1888/Elswick Rangers 1889.
Also appeared for Rendel Wed.
A player who was labelled as a "substitute" for West End when the side were missing senior names. He recorded his debut versus Morpeth Harriers during November 1887 when Stokoe filled in as a forward, something he repeated at the end of the season, once more against Morpeth. Also with Elswick Rangers and Rendel, he was capped by Northumberland when with the Rendelites. Stokoe was a cricketer for West End during the summer months. There are other players with the same surname reported in the local sporting press at the time; T and G Stokoe, both playing alongside W Stokoe for Boundary and West End. Census records show several men in the age group by that name, but possibly a family residing in Elswick during the 1870s to 1880s could be the source of the footballers; William Stokoe (b. Newcastle upon Tyne, 14 January 1870) and brothers Thomas, John and Joseph.
App & Goals: 2 app 1 gl.

STOREY E
1882-1885 Half-back, Forward
Two footballers took part in Newcastle West End's first season of 1882-83, possibly brothers, E Storey and T

Storey (qv). The pair were selected for the same eleven during February 1883 against Rendel, then faced Newcastle FA, both in the half-back line. E Storey played on two occasions during 1884-85 as well, and is also recorded as appearing on the cricket field for the West End club.
App & Goals: 4 app 0 gls.

STOREY T
1882-1884 Half-back, Forward
Perhaps related to E Storey (qv), a half-back who was picked for first-team duty in February 1883. Local newspaper reports show a T Storey also performing for Sleekburn Wanderers two season later during 1884-85.
App & Goals: 3 app 0 gls.

SULLIVAN M
1891-92 Half-back
Career: Newcastle East End 1891/**WEST END** Oct 1891 to 1892.
Joining the St James' Park set up from West End's Heaton rivals where he appeared for the East End Amateurs, Sullivan was described as a "new recruit" and he stepped into a half-back role against Darlington for the injured Mick McCrory soon after changing camps. The player was immediately embroiled in a bit of controversy as his "eligibility for Northern League matches" was questioned in the Northern Echo, Sullivan allegedly not being registered in time to play. Yet he appeared nevertheless and it was noted he caught the eye and "showed fairly good form".
App & Goals: 2 app 0 gls.

SURTEES Edward
1882-1888 Full-back, Half-back, Forward, Committee
b. [Newcastle upon Tyne]
Career: **WEST END** August 1882 to 1888, becoming a committee member 1883-84.
Edward Surtees took part in West End's venture into the football world during the first two seasons of 1882-83 and 1883-84, a regular and on the pitch for the side's earliest fixtures. He soon also became a member of the management committee of the new club. Surtees remained with West End for most of its lifespan through the 1880s, with the club for six seasons. He was captain for a period during 1887-88 when he made his last first-team appearance against Morpeth Harriers. During the early years, Edward was also a cricketer for West End. Records for the 1880s show only two or three possible men to be the West End footballer; two would have been too old to play the game and the most likely individual is Edward (or Edmund) Surtees, born in Newcastle who resided at Stanhope Street near St James' Park. A factory clerk, at the time of first playing for West End he was only around 15 or 16 years of age. He may have been Edmund Cockburn Surtees (b. Newcastle upon Tyne, 12 March 1867) who later became a marine engineer and died in 1938.
App & Goals: 48 app 2 gls.

SUTHERLAND Donald James

1887 Half-back
b. Lerwick, Shetland, 1 July 1866
Career: Edinburgh St Bernard's 1885 (**WEST END** guest April 1887)/Grimsby Town May 1888/Burton Swifts Aug 1891 to c1894/Hull Albany Feb 1896.
The son of a Shetland-based sailor, Donald Sutherland was a good footballer with Edinburgh St Bernard's when the Stockbridge side was recognised as one of Scotland's finest. When his club was on a tour of the North East, Donald assisted the West Enders against Redcar over the Easter holiday of 1887.

Having appeared for the Edinburgh FA XI, Sutherland was rated highly as a versatile forward and he moved to Grimsby Town for the 1888-89 season, totalling 47 league and cup matches for the Mariners including in the Combination League and Football Alliance – two rival competitions to the recently created Football League. With Burton Swifts, the Shetlander turned out on 30 occasions, including through the club's first Football League campaign of 1892-93. At that time, Donald was described by the Grimsby press as the "Indian Rubberman" because of his twists and turns beating opponents with tricky play. He later resided in Cleethorpes working as a joiner.
App & Goals: 1 app 0 gls.
(Note: Two other footballers named Sutherland played in the same era; Daniel Sutherland (Darwen, Liverpool, Dundee) and Malcolm Sutherland (Burnley as well as St Bernard's like Donald).

SWINBURNE William

1886-1892 Full-back, Half-back, Forward
b. Hexham, c1867
Career: Hawthorn Rovers (Newcastle)/South Elswick/**WEST END** Dec 1886 (Newcastle East End guest Dec 1887) to cs 1892.
Also appeared for Newcastle Pelicans.
Billy Swinburne was born in the Tyne valley at Hexham, by the time of the 1891 census his family had moved to Newcastle, living on Stanhope Street next to St James' Park. One of their lodgers was fellow West End and East End player, Donald McColl, who appears to have been a long-term friend of Swinburne. Employed as a machine-man, Billy was skipper of the St James' Park club during 1887-88 after Jack Wardale departed, and through 1888-89 and 1889-90. He took part in West End's first Northern League fixture during 1889, against great rivals Newcastle East End. Swinburne did appear for East End

as a guest during December 1887 against Darlington, but was a far more prominent West Ender, a dominant force for three seasons, usually at full-back or half-back. Swinburne was honoured with County caps and as a member of the Newcastle & District line-up. A proficient rugby and cricket sportsman, he appeared for West End over the summer months, at rugby for Benwell during 1886 before joining a newly formed rugby club, Newcastle Rangers and was prominent during the 1886-87 season.

The Newcastle Daily Chronicle at that time debated players who appeared in both the rugby and association codes and noted: "We need not go far to find one who is adept at each game, for in Swinburne, the West End captain, we have a player is a first-class man in both the dribbling and handling games." Billy turned out for both West End and Rangers as skipper in the football and rugby Northumberland Cup tournaments; beaten by holders Percy Park for Rangers in 1887, then winning the Senior Cup trophy with the West Enders a year later. He was a more than decent rugby exponent, described as "one of the best drop kickers in the county" and good enough to be "a candidate for county honours".
App & Goals: 131 app 5 gls.
(Note: Other individuals with the surname of Swinburne were involved in rugby on Tyneside to a high level during the 1880s. West End's William Swinburne should not be confused with Northern and Northumberland player W Swinburne, or other players in Gateshead of the same name to appear for the North Durham club.)

T

TAYLOR John

1884-1892 Full-back, Half-back, Forward
b. South Shields, 1863 (Q4)/d. Newcastle upon Tyne, 28 October 1928
Career: Drysdale (Newcastle) c1884/**WEST END** Dec 1884 (Newcastle East End guest Dec 1887)(Sunderland Albion guest Aug 1888) to cs 1892/Rendel.
'Jock' Taylor as he was known, was a prominent player on Tyneside, appearing for Newcastle West End in over a century of games. A dependable full-back and half-back, he became a regular in their red-and-black colours for season 1885-86 and remained with the club until their demise during the summer of 1892, especially

conspicuous from 1886-87 to 1888-89 when he was at the very heart of the side. At his peak, Taylor was capped by the County while he also represented the Newcastle & District XI. Jock lifted the Northumberland Senior Cup during 1888 with the West Enders, playing in two finals as runners-up as well. Along with some of his colleagues from the St James' Park base, Taylor guested for Newcastle East End against Darlington for a Christmas fixture during December 1887, while he also assisted Sunderland Albion the following year when he stepped into a role vacated by the celebrated Dan Doyle for a practice game on Wearside. Described as a "cheery and jovial" character, Taylor was awarded a benefit match during 1892 when an England XI faced a Scotland XI at St James' Park. He was also a regular cricketer in the area, playing for the West End, Bath Lane and Newcastle Working Men's Club teams. Taylor was employed as a clerk and resided in Elswick.

App & Goals: 122 app 2 gls.

TELFORD William

1885-1887 Goalkeeper, Committee
b. Newcastle upon Tyne, 1860
Career: Newcastle FA 1882/Jesmond 1883/**WEST END** 1885 & committee 1886-87 to c1887.

An early football and rugby enthusiast in Newcastle, William Telford played both codes during the early 1880s, a goalkeeper for West End in season 1885-86. Reported as being the captain of the Jesmond club for 1883-84 and 1884-85, he was a reserve for the Northumberland County side and represented a Newcastle upon Tyne XI. Telford was also a keen cyclist, a sport hugely popular on Victorian Tyneside, riding with the Newcastle Cycling Club. Often described as "W Telford junior", which points to a family residing initially in the St Andrew's district then in Byker; father William (senior) and son, William (junior). The younger Telford became a print engraver.

App & Goals: 8 app 0 gls.

THOMPSON H

1887 Goalkeeper
Career: Gateshead Ass 1886 (**WEST END** guest April & July 1887)/Gateshead NER 1888-89 to c1890.
A top-rated goalkeeper with both Gateshead clubs in the mid-to-late 1880s, Thompson assisted West End against Redcar during April 1887 when the red-and-blacks also fielded his Gateshead namesake Jack Thompson as well

as a couple more guests from St Bernard's. He then played two more fixtures for the side before the end of the season when regular custodian Robert Oldham wasn't available. All three outings ended in victories. Noted as vice-captain of Gateshead Association, and to also play in an outfield role, Thompson had earned a good reputation in football at the time, the Morpeth Herald once describing him as a "first-class goalkeeper". He also played cricket with the top-ranked North Durham club and reports indicate that he was the brother of Jack Thompson (qv), both playing the winter and summer games together.

App & Goals: 3 app 0 gls.

THOMPSON John

1887 Forward
Career: Gateshead Ass 1886 (**WEST END** guest April 1887)/Gateshead NER 1889 to c1890.
Referred to usually as 'Jack' Thompson, he was an effective and at times dangerous forward in the Gateshead attack during the latter seasons of the 1880s. It was noted that Thompson was "one of the fastest on the wing in the district", had "performed brilliantly if somewhat selfishly" while his "dribbling is a marvel of speed and grace". At the time he guested for West End, there appeared to be a close relationship with the Gateshead side, several players turning out on occasion for both clubs. He was twice in West End's ranks during April 1887, against Derby St Luke's and Redcar, once alongside his goalkeeper brother H Thompson (qv). Jack played cricket to a high standard with North Durham and represented his county, making nine appearances as a stylish batsman for Durham between 1887 and 1891. In addition, he played rugby for North Durham.

App & Goals: 2 app 0 gls.

THOMPSON J/D

1888-1892 Half-back
One of potentially three players named "J Thompson" to appear for West End, it is probable the footballer to turn out briefly for the club during seasons 1888-89, 1890-91 and 1891-92 was a reserve half-back to fill in on three occasions. It was also reported that another squad player in season 1888-89, "D Thompson", played against Birtley during November 1888. This could be a newspaper mis-print being the same J Thompson or a different individual altogether.

App & Goals: 3 app 0 gls.

THOMPSON William Pringle

1887 Centre-forward
b. North Seaton, Northumberland, October 1867/d. Bedlington, 10 September 1928
Career: Bedlington Burdon 1882/Ashington Rising Star c1886/Shankhouse Black Watch Aug 1886 (**WEST END** guest July 1887)/Morpeth Harriers 1888 briefly/Newcastle East End-Newcastle Utd Dec 1889/Jarrow July 1897/Ashington Aug 1898/[Wallsend Park Villa May 1900]/[Bedlington Town Nov 1900].
When the West Enders travelled to Ashington to face the town's Rising Star outfit in July 1887, they found themselves two players short, "Chalmers and Angus not

arriving in time". The club's management located substitutes in Tom Minnikin – likely a travelling reserve – and a "W Thompson". The latter is almost certainly Willie Thompson who at the time was living and playing in the area for Shankhouse. He became a celebrated local centre-forward. Working as a blacksmith, Thompson was a dashing goal-getter during the early years of Tyneside football. Popular with all his clubs, he was an especially renowned striker with a powerful Shankhouse line-up before he joined Newcastle East End's set-up. Willie won Northumberland Senior Cup medals with the noted Black Watch combination and took part in one of the biggest games staged in the north

during those pioneering years, when his side faced Aston Villa in the FA Cup at St James' Park during 1886-87. Thompson wasn't too big at 5'7" tall, but was swift and possessed a sure shot in either foot, as well as a magnificent moustache in the style of the day. Willie became a Northumberland County player and took part in Newcastle United's debut St James' Park fixture when they moved there, as well as the club's initial Football League match against Arsenal during September 1893. He is also registered as scoring the club's first senior hat-trick, also against the Londoners later in the same month. A formidable player, firstly as East End developed, then during United's first three years of Football League action, Thompson grabbed 65 goals in 135 games, a goal every second match for the Tynesiders. In addition, Willie played in the many friendly and miscellaneous fixtures programmed during the era, passing 230 games and registering almost 125 goals for the club overall, an admirable record. He later suffered from injury, being described as having, "a dodgy knee" by the local press. The Northumbrian is also recorded as scoring the very first penalty for East End during January 1892 in a friendly against Middlesbrough. Thompson played on well into his thirties as a veteran in the East Northumberland League. On retiring from the full professional game, Willie returned to his trade as a blacksmith, by 1911 working at one of Northumberland's pits.

App & Goals: 1 app 1 gl.

(Note: Family research has established his middle name being Pringle, his initials being WP rather than WK or WR as in the press. He was baptised at Woodhorn during 1867.)

TIFFIN William Wilson Tatham

1882-1890 Half-back, Forward, Secretary
b. Newcastle upon Tyne, 16 March 1866/d. Whitley Bay, 7 November 1925
Career: WEST END Aug 1882, retiring as a player 1889, also secretary & treasurer Aug 1882, having various

roles as financial secretary and match secretary 1882 to Aug 1890/Northumberland FA secretary Aug 1890 to May 1911 & FA Council member 1896.

Player, captain, secretary and treasurer of Newcastle West End, Billy Tiffin could be recognised as the club's driving force during those early to middle years of the 1880s. He was an influential and key figure when West End were founded in August 1882, described in one profile much later during 1933 as the man "who started the Newcastle West End club". As a player, Billy was usually a left-sided forward, but played across the attack and featured in the side over seven seasons, prominent on the field from 1883 to 1887. Tiffin represented Northumberland and the Newcastle & District XI while he was a cricketer for the club during those early days, likely also for the original Crown CC in Elswick. The son of a Newcastle-based tailor, he was raised in the Westgate area of the city, and became a clerk and book-keeper living on Northcote Street then Wingrove Avenue until retirement when he moved to the coast at Whitley Bay. After playing the game, Billy officiated at local matches for several years helping to create the Northumberland & Durham Referees' Association in 1896. Before that, during August 1890, Tiffin was offered the high-profile position of Secretary at the Northumberland FA and for the next 21 years became hugely admired in football, not only in the North East but also nationally. The early seminal text, Association Football & The Men Who Made It, published during 1905, described Tiffin as giving "ardent, energetic and tireless work" to the area's football development and noted that "his services to football have been conspicuously valuable". With a "cheerful and optimistic disposition", he was awarded the FA's Long Service Medal and on his death the family received numerous letters of condolence including from Frederick Wall, Secretary to the FA, as well as Frank Watt at Newcastle United who wrote that Tiffin was "highly respected by everyone, with his genial manner, his excellent abilities as a legislator on football and his gentlemanly behaviour at all times".

App & Goals: 83 app 13 gls.

TINDLE

1884-1885 Half-back
Representing West End once during October 1884, Tindle played for the club against Newcastle Rangers. In the reserve ranks during season 1884-85, it is possible he

was the same lad who appeared with the Science & Art College side during 1888, reported as "F Tindle".
App & Goals: 1 app 0 gls.

TINN William

1888-1889 Forward
Career: White Rose/**WEST END** 1888/Newcastle East End cs 1889 to cDec 1889.
Appeared also for Victoria Wed.
A local player who stepped up from the reserve team to appear in the forward line for West End against Bishop Auckland Church Institute during April 1889. He moved on during the summer to be part of Newcastle East End's Swifts line-up, that club's second-string. With the Heaton side, Tinn was called up for two Northern League fixtures during season 1889-90, at Darlington, then against Elswick Rangers. He also appeared for White Rose cricket club during the mid-1880s. Census data for 1891 shows only two possible men of that name in the age group; William John Tinn (b. c1867 Newcastle) living in Elswick, and another William Tinn from Heaton (b. 1869, Dublin) who was from a noted family of dentists in the city and a keen cycling enthusiast.
App & Goals: 1 app 0 gls.

W

WAGGOTT Edward MBE

1882-1890 Goalkeeper, Half-back, Forward, Committee
b. Newcastle upon Tyne, 8 April 1867/d. Newcastle upon Tyne, 8 June 1945
Career: **WEST END** Aug 1882 to 1890, becoming a committee member 1883-84.

One of four early West End servants named Waggott to be influential as the club developed. Of the two sets of brothers, 'Ned' Waggott appeared for the West Enders the longest, from 1882 to 1890, almost the side's complete life-span. Usually playing as a half-back, but also in the forward line and as a goalkeeper on occasion, he stood out during 1884-85 and 1885-86. The younger brother of Thomas Waggott (qv) and thought to be related to both John (qv) and Henry Waggott (qv), a different pair of brothers. Ned was brought up on Scotswood Road and spent his entire life residing in that Elswick district. As a teenager he started working as an apprentice fitter at engineering company Donkin & Nicholson near Gallowgate then joined the giant

Armstrong Works during 1888. Waggott was employed at the armament factory in Scotswood for over 50 years, and by the time of the 1901 and 1911 census records was noted as a foreman engineer, then assistant-manager of the Shell & Tube Dept. Due to his outstanding effort in shell production during the Great War, Ned was honoured with the MBE during January 1918.
App & Goals: 58 app 0 gls.

WAGGOTT Henry

1882-1887 Goalkeeper, Full-back, Half-back
b. Newcastle upon Tyne, 29 December 1867
Career: **WEST END** Aug 1882/Wellington Rovers (Newcastle) 1887.
Henry Waggott was the younger brother of John (qv), the family living in the Arthur's Hill district. Henry was a regular player for West End during their debut season of 1882-83 and only missed a handful of games. An engine-fitter working in the shipyards, Waggott later resided in Walkerville. Certain family history reports note that Henry later moved to Australia and died in Victoria on 23 March 1946, but this is not confirmed.
App & Goals: 10 app 0 gls.

WAGGOTT John Amory

1882-1888 Full-back, Half-back, Forward, Finance-Secretary
b. Newcastle upon Tyne, c1865/d. Newcastle upon Tyne, 1933 (Q4)
Career: **WEST END** Aug 1882 to 1888, becoming finance-secretary 1886-87/Wellington Rovers (Newcastle) c1888.
A founder member of Newcastle West End during the summer of 1882 when the Crown Cricket Club was renamed as West End Juniors CC, at that time the cricket team's treasurer. Alongside the Mather brothers, he was a significant figure in the rise of the new football club, appearing on the field in six of West End's ten seasons, usually at full-back. John was noted in the press as West End's captain during their first season, continuing as skipper for part of 1885-86 when he appeared in the side's first Northumberland Senior Cup final. Capped by Northumberland, like the other Waggott footballers he enjoyed playing cricket in the summer months, also captain and secretary of West End CC for periods. The 1891 census records John as an engine-fitter, like his brother, both living at Jefferson Street near St James' Park. With his younger sibling Henry (qv), it is likely (although not confirmed) that both Thomas and Ned Waggott are part of the same wider family.
App & Goals: 71 app 0 gls.

WAGGOTT Thomas William

1882-1887 Full-back, Half-back, Forward, Committee
b. Newcastle upon Tyne, 21 October 1864/d. South Shields, September 1941
Career: **WEST END** Aug 1882 to 1887, becoming a committee member 1884-85.
Captain of Crown Cricket Club in Elswick when the side became West End and formed a football outfit, Thomas

Waggott was only in his teens then and an enthusiastic player at both sports.

A family photo of the Waggotts. Ned is pictured at the centre of the back row. His brother John is not identified, but likely to be one of the others.

The elder brother of Ned Waggott (qv), he took part in West End's debut fixtures during 1882-83 and was a regular choice over the following two seasons when he totalled 39 matches. Born and raised in Elswick like so many of West End's players and officials, he is recorded as an iron-moulder in both the 1881 and 1901 census documents. Thomas continued to appear for the cricket eleven – now West End CC – and by 1883 was the team's secretary and treasurer. He also turned out in whites for Drysdale CC and Bath Lane CC at times.
App & Goals: 48 app 0 gls.

WALKER David
1890 Half-back
b. Scotland
Career: Our Boys (Dundee) 1888/**WEST END** July to cDec 1890/Our Boys (Dundee) 1891 to c1893/[Dundee Harp].
David Walker appeared with one of the pioneer teams of the present Dundee club, Our Boys FC. He was selected for the Forfarshire County XI and was described as a versatile player, being well-built and sturdy. David arrived at St James' Park along with fellow Scot, Joseph Ross over the close-season of 1890. Walker was a starter for the West Enders as the season began however by December wasn't selected again, maybe moving on as the year turned. The Scottish FA released a schedule of banned footballers who had been reinstated during May 1891, included was "D Walker, Dundee Harp-Newcastle West End", which contradicts press reports when he moved to Newcastle, being an Our Boys player. Walker may have also turned out for Harp prior to joining their Dundee rivals.
App & Goals: 13 app 1 gl.

WALKER James
1889 Inside-forward
b. Scotland

Career: Dundee football/Elswick Rangers 1889 (**WEST END** guest Nov 1889)/Our Boys (Dundee) Oct 1891.
Another footballer from Tayside named Walker and when West End found themselves short of five of their regular starters due to call ups for the Northumberland County line-up at the end of November 1889, reserves were drafted in, including a "J Walker" at inside forward. No player has been traced with this surname in West End's ranks at the time, and it is probable that James Walker of Elswick Rangers assisted West End for the meeting with the newly formed Dumfries club on a visit to Newcastle. Walker had joined Rangers during the first half of season 1889-90, a half-back who had learnt his trade in Dundee and teamed up with the band of Scots at Mill Lane. He helped West End to a rout over the Dumfries team, winning 11-1. There were several players with the surname of Walker to appear in Dundee football during the period; James later turned out for Our Boys, at the same time as David Walker.
App & Goals: 1 app 0 gls.

WALTON John
1891 Half-back
b. [Newcastle upon Tyne]
Career: Trafalgar 1887 (**WEST END** guest May 1891)/Newcastle Utd July 1895 to 1898.
Also appeared for Newcastle Wed.

A long serving footballer with Trafalgar, one of Newcastle's top sides below the likes of West End, East End, Elswick Rangers and Rendel, Jack Walton became vice-captain and captain during his near-decade with the club. With many player connections in that period between Trafalgar and West End, he guested in a red-and-black jersey at the start of May 1891 against Willington Athletic. Walton was described "as a very cool player", being instrumental in Trafalgar lifting the Tyneside League title for season 1891-92. He was selected for Northumberland, then Jack was one of several Trafalgar players to later be signed by the Newcastle United 'A' team for season 1895-96. Walton's experience saw him made skipper of the side and he spent two-and-a-half campaigns with the Magpies but didn't get near to United's Football League line-up. Jack was badly injured playing in black-and-white stripes during October 1897 and only appeared occasionally afterwards. The Newcastle Evening Chronicle ran a line

just after World War One that he had returned to Tyneside "after some years spent in Canada".
App & Goals: 1 app 0 gls.
(Note: There was also T Walton (qv) and J Walton associated with West End's cricket XI in the mid-to-late 1880s, they may be linked to Jack. The former was also a West End football official.)

WARD Frederick

1891-1892 Goalkeeper
b. Barnard Castle, 1869/d. [Daventry, near Northampton, 1936 (Q2)]
Career: **WEST END** c1891/Newcastle East End-Newcastle Utd cs 1892 to 1893/Barnard Castle by Feb 1896.
Also appeared for Newcastle Wed/Newcastle Garrison.

Fred Ward was a Barnard Castle man and featured between the posts in Newcastle West End's Northumberland Senior Cup victory with the reserve team during March 1892. He never reached the first-eleven for the club before their demise, then became part of Newcastle East End's 'A' side. During the 1880s and 1890s, Ward was a serving army recruit based at the Newcastle upon Tyne garrison like team-mate Charles Cattell. By 1892 he held a sergeant's rank and was described at that time by the Blyth News as "a soldier and a very smart man". He returned to his native Barnard Castle for a period where he played football and cricket for the local club then settled in Burton-on-Trent employed as a driver's fitter. By the time of the 1911 census, he worked as an engineer and boiler mechanic in Northampton.
App & Goals: 0 app 0 gls (Reserve app in Senior Cup final 1892).

WARDALE John Dobson

1887 Half-back, Forward
b. Newcastle upon Tyne, 16 April 1868/d. Hayden Bridge, 7 December 1958
Career: Newcastle Rangers/Gateshead Ass 1884-85 (Tyne Ass guest Oct 1886)(**WEST END** guest April 1887)/**WEST END** cs 1887/Gateshead Ass later in 1887 to c1890/Also Bishop Auckland Church Institute briefly.
Also appeared for Durham University/Newcastle Medicals.
A half-back of repute during the mid-years of the 1880s, notably with the Gateshead Association club, John Wardale began playing football as the Newcastle Rangers club struggled to survive. Wardale was recognised by Northumberland, winning County honours

while he also was selected for the Newcastle & District XI. He guested once for West End at the end of the 1886-87 season then teamed up permanently at St James' Park as captain for the following season. But Wardale didn't remain long with the West Enders heading back to Gateshead and at that time concentrated on his medical studies in Newcastle and Durham. He still appeared with Gateshead when he could though, and for Durham University too. A top all-round sportsman, like many university lads then, he also played rugby and cricket, for the North Durham club and for Bridgewater when in Somerset for a period after his studies. Raised in Gateshead, the son of the chief-draughtsman at the famed Robert Stephenson Company, his great uncle was John Dobson, a celebrated North East architect. And Wardale himself was to become an eminent northerner too, in the field of medicine. Initially educated at Market Rasen Grammar School in Lincolnshire, Wardale qualified as a doctor during 1891 and became House Surgeon at Newcastle Infirmary, later a General Practitioner as well as Registrar at the city hospital. John became a renowned ophthalmic surgeon (eye specialist) and was Professor of Ophthalmology as well as being a founding officer of the region's Northern General Hospital in 1909, afterwards at the unit during the Great War with the rank of major in the RAMC. He retired from full-time medicine during 1928 but then was appointed Director of Surgery at Sunderland Eye Infirmary by the 1930s and served at the RVI Eye Department in Newcastle during World War Two. John lived on Jesmond Road and later at Hayden Bridge. He married into the distinguished Lord Joicey family.
App & Goals: 5 app 0 gls.

WARDROPPER James Robert

1891-1892 Forward
b. Newcastle upon Tyne, 12 May 1871/d. Birmingham, 25 July 1946
Career: Rendel c1888/**WEST END** Dec 1891/Rendel June 1892.
Also appeared for Elswick Works.

The younger of two outstanding footballers with Benwell club, Rendel, James Wardropper joined West End during December 1891 shortly after his elder brother Joe (qv) had signed for the club. Following a trial match against South Bank in which he scored twice – although some reports note he netted a hat-trick – James teamed up with his sibling in an attempt to halt the slide in form at St James' Park during season 1891-92. A regular player with Rendel, James appeared in the 1891

Northumberland Senior Cup final and represented his County as well. Wearing a red-and-black shirt, although he netted five goals in 15 games, his efforts were not enough to stop the club's demise and Wardropper returned to Rendel during the summer where he went on to reach another Senior Cup final, although his team decided not to turn up for the show-piece against Shankhouse in 1893 following a dispute! Raised in the Elswick and Benwell district of Newcastle, Wardropper was employed with Joe at the ordnance factory alongside the Tyne, later following his brother to Barrow then to the Midlands on munition work. He was described during May 1915 as "Chief foreman, submarine engine machines" at the Vickers factory becoming a "commercial traveller" for the engineering company. When residing in Barrow, he continued involvement in the game of football, recorded as being President of the Furness FA for a period and associated with Vickerstown FC. During World War One, James served with the Loyal North Lancashire regiment.

App & Goals: 15 app 5 gls.

WARDROPPER Joseph W

1887, 1891-1892 Full-back, Half-back
b. Newcastle upon Tyne, 16 August 1866/d. Sutton Coldfield, 21 March 1947
Career: Rendel by Dec 1884 (Newcastle FA guest Dec 1886)(**WEST END** guest Jan & May 1887, March & April 1891)/**WEST END** Sept 1891/Rendel June 1892 to April 1894 when he retired.
Also appeared for Elswick Works.
The respected national sports paper Athletic News once described Joe Wardropper as "a very fine half-back" being a well-known footballer in the North East for over a decade. With Rendel for nine seasons, he was their leader on the field as an influential captain. Joe steered the team in two Northumberland Senior Cup finals and remained an amateur footballer with the Benwell club – only turning professional when he joined West End for the 1891-92 season. Following a handful of games for the West Enders as a guest player, Wardropper became skipper at St James' Park from February 1892 onwards, playing alongside his younger brother James (qv), the pair being regulars together for Rendel. He was a

reliable and solid player, capped by Northumberland – indeed, playing more games than anyone else for the county during the era. Joe was very well respected in the game, appointed the first President of the Northern Alliance League when it was formed in 1890, while once he finished playing, the Geordie turned to refereeing in the north, a founding member of the Northumberland

& Durham Referees' Association. With Russian parentage, he resided in Benwell near Elswick Park and by 1901 at Dunston. Joe was employed at the Armstrong Works, an engine-fitter and later foreman for over 20 years before relocating to Barrow where he was employed with another well-known ordnance and engineering company, Vickers. During the Great War, Joe was appointed to a management role in the Midlands, residing at Sutton Coldfield. Apart from his brother James, two other siblings of the Wardropper family, Thomas and William, also assisted Rendel while their father, James (senior), was the club President and secretary for a period. All worked at the huge Armstrong facility too. Joe's son, Fred, played football for Barrow but sadly died from tetanus, following a leg injury when training with the club.

App & Goals: 40 app 2 gls.

WATSON William James

1886 Goalkeeper
b. Willington Quay, 1861 (Q1)/d. [Willington Quay], Tynemouth district, 3 July 1931
Career: Rosehill by 1884/**WEST END** April 1886 briefly/Willington Ath 1886 to c1890.
William Watson began playing football with the Rosehill club near to his home alongside the River Tyne, and during April 1886 was drafted into the West End eleven against Morpeth Harriers but never reached first-team action again. He probably made a one-off appearance as he isn't traced as turning out for the West End club in reserve matches. Watson had played for Rosehill against the West Enders in the Tyne Charity Shield clash during the previous season and was a regular goalkeeper for that club. He later was found between the posts for Willington Athletic and acted as a referee and linesman during the 1890s. Watson was also a cricketer for the Rosehill-Willington side through the 1880s, becoming captain by 1885. Born and raised in Willington Quay, he was employed as a ship-plater and it appears he lived in that working-class community all his life.

App & Goals: 1 app 0 gls.

WATTS J

1888-1889 Half-back
b. Scotland
Career: Renton/**WEST END** Oct 1888 (Elswick Rangers guest April 1889) to 1889.
Described as both Watts and Watt in contemporary newspaper reports, this half-back commenced his football in Dunbartonshire and by the time he joined West End was described in the weekly Northern Magpie football column as "late of the Renton reserves" and noted as one of the best recruits "picked up for a long time". Watts impressed officials enough to justify being elevated to the senior eleven and he played on 11 occasions at varying intervals during the programme.

App & Goals: 11 app 0 gls.

WELFORD Joseph A

1884-1888 Half-back, Forward
b. Newcastle upon Tyne

Career: Elswick Leather Works 1883/Drysdale (Newcastle) 1884/**WEST END** cs 1884/Gateshead NER 1888.

Joining up with Newcastle West End for the annual Town Moor Temperance Festival in the summer of 1884, Welford was a trusty footballer over two seasons for the club, during 1884-85 and 1885-86. He was skipper of the red-and-blacks for a period and led the side to the Northumberland Senior Cup final during 1886, scoring in the meeting with Shankhouse, a 3-2 defeat. Joseph was also a Northumberland County player.

App & Goals: 41 app 5 gls.

WHEELER J
(see FIGURES WH)

WHITE Alexander Henry
1888 Half-back

b. Glamis, Forfarshire, 1860/d. Newcastle upon Tyne, 18 May 1940

Career: Newcastle Rangers cOct 1880/Newcastle East End Dec 1884 (**WEST END** guest April 1888) retired cs 1889, to return as a player occasionally to June 1891, returning again Feb 1892, finally retiring cs 1892, also East End secretary June 1889 to Dec 1889, committee member c1888, director Feb 1890 to cs 1891/Northumberland FA in various capacities, becoming treasurer 1913 to May 1938, and an Honorary Life Member as well as FA Council Member.

Also appeared for Chester College/Corinthians.

One of the most distinguished individuals during the early years of Newcastle East End and Newcastle United, Alexander Henry White also played a single fixture for West End as a guest during April 1888 against one of the country's top sides then, West Bromwich Albion. A school-teacher who hailed from the district around Airlie and the historic village of Glamis near Dundee, White settled in the Heaton area of Tyneside. He started playing the fledgling game of football with Newcastle Rangers as they switched base from Gateshead to Newcastle and soon became the strongest club on Tyneside, twice winning the Northumberland & Durham Challenge Cup during its earliest years of 1881 and 1882. Although the footballers present are not recorded, White was probably on the field when they played the first game of football at St James' Park, a practice match during October 1880. When Rangers folded, Alec joined Newcastle East End and was to become their leading figure. A frequent selection for the County eleven and Newcastle & District side, White operated in various roles, at the back or as a tough and clever midfielder from the old-style centre-half position, once described by one journalist of the day as showing "effective rushes" in attack. White was soon appointed captain and reached national recognition by being selected as reserve for the North versus South match during 1886, an unofficial international trial contest, while the following year he also appeared for the celebrated Corinthians eleven, both tremendous accolades considering that football on Tyneside was still very much in its infancy. At 5'10" tall, the Scot was always able to score goals, once when playing at centre-forward hitting seven in a 19-0 romp

over Point Pleasant during 1888 in East End's highest ever victory. White did much to develop the East Enders into Newcastle's foremost club and by the time they had switched to St James' Park, the Scot had guided the side in two Northumberland Senior Cup victories (1885 and 1889) as well as the prestigious inter-county title against Sunderland Albion during 1889.

White as a footballer with East End (left), and in later years (right).

That highly successful 1888-89 season was to be Alec's last as a regular. By then, aged almost 30, he concentrated more on his profession as a teacher. He retired in that summer, but then returned to the field, to bow out once more during 1892 shortly before East End were to change their name to Newcastle United. White clocked up over 100 appearances for the East Enders in all matches and received a marvellous send-off at the time, portrayed as being "the life and soul of the club". Alec was afterwards often to be seen at St James' Park over the following decades and was associated with the Northumberland FA as an administrator and distinguished local character for over 50 years – awarded the FA's Long Service medal. White was one of the original shareholders in the East End (and Newcastle United) company when equity was launched during 1890, a signatory to the first Articles of Association, and was also elected as one of the club's first directors. Alec also acted for a short time as East End secretary, while additionally he played cricket in his younger days, for White Rose and East End, acting as secretary of both clubs for periods. On retiring from football, the Scot was a referee in North East football during the 1890s, becoming treasurer of the Northumberland & Durham Referees' Association when it was formed in 1896. His teaching career ran parallel to that of football, starting at Newcastle's Royal Jubilee School, then at Chester Training College, returning to schools on Tyneside at Dudley and West Walker, before being appointed Head at Walkergate then Royal Jubilee once more in 1917. He retired during 1924. His son Alex H White (junior) died in a Luftwaffe air-raid on Newcastle a year after his father's death.

App & Goals: 1 app 0 gls.

(Note: Although all documents since he settled on Tyneside as a young man, including death and probate records, note his middle name as Henry, the birth certificate of Alexander H White (b. Airlie, near Glamis, 1 August 1862) states "Hardy", taking the maiden name of his mother. As Airlie and Glamis are very close communities, this is likely to be the celebrated early footballer.)

113

WHITTON David Rutherford

1889-1892 Goalkeeper
b. Blairgowrie, 23 June 1867/d. Blyth, 7 October 1938
Career: Clydesdale (Dundee)/Dundee Wand April 1885/**WEST END** Aug 1889 (Sunderland Albion guest May 1890)/Newcastle East End-Newcastle Utd May 1892 £10/Shankhouse Sept 1893/Blyth Spartans Sept 1894 to c1897/later Blyth Shipyard 1906.

Known as Davie Whitton and once described as "the Little Demon" when he arrived at St James' Park for the start of 1889-90, he was noted as a 'keeper of "medium height and stocky build". Yet despite his lack of inches, when at Dundee Wanderers, Scottish Referee considered

that he was in the reckoning for a Scotland call-up during season 1887-88. Colin Veitch recalled Whitton as "a capital goalkeeper" when he watched football as a youngster on Tyneside during the mid-1890s. A popular character on Tyneside, also labelled by the local press as a "bundle of energy",

Whitton took part in West End's first Northern League contest and their initial FA Cup proper fixture against Grimsby Town during 1890. The Scot was almost an ever-present for West End during his three seasons at St James' Park and only missed a period when he broke his leg in a derby meeting with East End during March 1891. Out for six months, it was reported that in that clash he was hurt "running out among the players", receiving "a serious injury to his leg below the knee which caused him to be carried off the field". Totalling almost 100 games for the club, on one occasion during a meeting with the decidedly inferior Blackpool Olympic team during February 1891, Whitton left his goal area at one stage and joined the forwards in attack. Appearing for Northumberland, when the West Enders folded, he joined Newcastle East End, soon to be Newcastle United, and Whitton appeared during the 1892-93 Northern League programme just prior to the club's entry into the Football League. He also took part in their first home game on the Leazes turf, against Celtic. Whitton later settled in Cowpen and was killed when working as a plater's helper at a local Blyth shipyard following an accident in which he sustained head injuries.
App & Goals: 98 app 0 gls.

WILDE George Martin

1887-1892 Half-back, Secretary (reserve-team)
b. Newcastle upon Tyne, 4 August 1869/d. Newcastle upon Tyne, 1952 (Q3)
Career: White Rose Jnrs 1885/Percy Ironworks (Newcastle) 1887, also secretary/**WEST END** Aug 1887, becoming reserve-team secretary 1888-89/Newcastle East End-Newcastle Utd cs 1892.
Also appeared for Newcastle Wed/Science & Art/Newcastle Rovers, also as secretary.

George Wilde only totalled two games for West End's first-team during 1888-89 and 1891-92, as a deputy to big-name players in Bob Kelso and Joseph Wardropper. A regular junior and reserve half-back, Wilde looked after the admin of the second-string as secretary for a time and was part of the side when the club's reserve line-up lifted the Northumberland Senior Cup in March 1892. Standing out at that level, the Tynesider soon appeared for Northumberland during that period.

Originally skipper of White Rose Juniors, he played cricket for that club and for Bath Lane while he was a keen runner at meetings for Elswick Harriers during the 1890s. George was brought up in the Arthur's Hill quarter and resided near to Gallowgate at Back Lane and was associated with Percy Ironworks at the same address. Wilde was noted as being a "whitesmith" and by the start of World War Two was living in Benwell.
App & Goals: 2 app 0 gls.

WILLIAMS J

1887 Outside-left
Virtually nothing has been traced regarding J Williams. He appeared for West End during April 1887 when the club faced Darlington.
App & Goals: 1 app 0 gls.

WILLIS Robert Holland Blyth

1892 Outside-right
b. Peters Marland, Devon, 1870/d. Shankhouse, 16 May 1935
Career: Shankhouse Jnrs 1886/Shankhouse Black Watch/**WEST END** March 1892/Blyth cs 1892/Newcastle Utd amat Dec 1893/Shankhouse Aug 1895/[Ashington Nov 1899].

The Willis family moved the long distance north from Devon to work in the coalfield when Robert was a youngster, being brought up in the Cramlington area. He was employed as a coal-trimmer and became a hugely popular footballer in South Northumberland, described as a player with "quick, energetic dribbles". In a final bid to halt the slide during the closing stages of 1891-92, West End brought in Willis having been a stalwart player for the Shankhouse club. But Bobby only appeared once for the troubled West Enders, against Sunderland Albion, losing 7-1, one of several heavy defeats in that final season. Afterwards, the Newcastle Daily Chronicle described Bobby Willis as a "well known forward" when he joined Newcastle United's staff for the Christmas programme of 1893. An amateur player, he had already appeared for the Northumberland County side and as the local press recorded, "proved a great acquisition" for the team. Coming into United's forward line during the club's first Football League season, Willis struck a goal on his debut and in a Tyne-Tees encounter with Ironopolis over the New Year celebrations, scored twice as United hammered the Middlesbrough club 7-2. At 5'10" in height, Bobby did well the following season too, hitting 13 goals in only 20 games, then left the club to return to non-league football. His son Bobby (junior) was on Newcastle United's books as well, and later appeared with Dundee and Rochdale during the 1920s.

App & Goals: 1 app 0 gls.

WILSON J

1887-1889 Inside-forward, Secretary (reserve-team)
Career: White Rose Jnrs/**WEST END** Aug 1887, becoming reserve-team secretary cApril 1889/Newcastle Rovers.
Chiefly a reserve footballer at St James' Park, Wilson also took over the second-team's secretarial role towards the end of the 1889-90 season when he was residing at Hedley Street in Gosforth. He appeared on a single occasion in a West End shirt, against Stockton during November 1888.

App & Goals: 1 app 0 gls.

WILSON William A

1889-1890 Full-back, Half-back
b. Dunbartonshire, c1867
Career: [Renton]/Vale of Leven 1885/Jamestown Sept 1887/Greenock Morton Aug 1888/**WEST END** July 1889/Newcastle East End-Newcastle Utd Aug 1890 to cs 1892.

An unyielding 5'8" defender who had played the game to a high standard north of the border with Vale of Leven over two seasons. Capped by Dunbartonshire, Wilson settled on Tyneside for the start of the inaugural Northern League competition during 1889-90, intending to appear in East End's blue shirts. But rivals West End poached his services and he ended up playing in a red-and-black jersey for the 1889-90 season. In a composed and steady manner, he claimed 27 appearances including in the final of the Northumberland Senior Cup when West End lifted the trophy with a 5-0 victory over Rendel. The Scot though moved from St James' Park to join the Heaton outfit the following summer as the East

Enders prevailed in the Tyneside rivalry between the two clubs. Wilson became captain and an ever-present for East End during 1890-91 and was a dependable player for the club. At times the centre of attention, during December 1891 against Sheffield United, colleague Bobby Creilly walked off the field in protest after a row with Wilson, who apparently, was showing no interest and giving little support to his team-mates. Wilson was suspended afterwards and left the club as they relocated across the city during the summer of 1892. When lodging in Newcastle at Argyle Place near Manors Station, he was recorded as an "athlete" in the census, a rarity in those days when usually occupations were a trade of one kind or another.

App & Goals: 27 app 0 gls.

WOOD Samuel Philips

1891 Forward
b. Greencroft, Co Durham, 1869 (Q1)/d. Morpeth, 20 December 1945
Career: Heaton Ass 1882/Elswick Leather Works 1884/Boundary (Newcastle) 1884/Rendel 1887 (Newcastle East End guest April 1887)/**WEST END** March 1891/Middlesbrough Sept 1891/Rendel cs 1892 to 1896/Stanley Utd by Oct 1897 to 1899/Later, Morpeth Working Men's Club 1904-05/Morpeth Harriers Feb 1905.
Also appeared for Elswick Ordnance Works/Dipton occasionally/Newcastle Wed.

Sam Wood was a well-known figure in North East sport during the Victorian era, especially with Newcastle's western football clubs although Wood did cross the city divide when a Rendel player to turn out for Newcastle East End as a guest during April 1887. Living in Elswick, then nearby Benwell, Wood was employed as a milling machinist and was once described in the football news columns as a "dashing forward with good shooting power" while Athletic News termed the 5'10" tall striker as "a speedy forward". Sam was a popular footballer with Benwell outfit Rendel over several seasons, he played for Northumberland at County level and moved to West End's set-up for a short period at the end of the 1890-91 season, showing up well in his six games. He then appeared with Middlesbrough for season 1891-92 and Sam later became a local referee during the 1890s. Wood was also a prominent cricketer in the region for a lengthy period, a wicket-keeper with several clubs, notably Boundary where he was also secretary.

A Middlesbrough group from 1892 featuring Wood, far right, back row.

115

Wood also appeared for local teams during the summer into the 1920s; for East End, Rendel, Elswick Ordnance, Stanley & District as well as prominently with Morpeth, Hartford Hall, Longhirst and even the cricket club at the County Asylum. He represented Northumberland at cricket too, playing seven matches between 1884 and 1887, later coaching the summer game. Sam's brother, Thomas Wood, also played both sports on Tyneside. Later in life Wood became a school-attendance officer living in Morpeth.
App & Goals: 6 app 2 gls.

WYNN E

1884-1885 Full-back
Career: WEST END 1884-85/Worswick Rovers (Newcastle) 1885-86/Elswick Leather Works by March 1886/Elswick Rangers 1886-87.
A stand-in full-back for John Waggott when West End played Rosehill alongside the Tyne as November opened in 1884. Reports also note his surname as Winn, while Darlington also fielded a J Winn, as did Newcastle East End against the Quakers (maybe as a guest), both during 1885. The Darlington player was later with Middlesbrough and could be the same footballer.
App & Goals: 1 app 0 gls.

NEAR MISSES

Notable Newcastle West End 'arrivals' who never appeared for the first-team.

COLEMAN John
A Scottish full-back who joined West End from "Edinburgh Hibernians" during September 1886, noted in the press that he would "partner Taylor at the back". Coleman never registered an appearance on Tyneside and seemingly the deal fell through and he was back at Hibs for season 1887-88. It is likely he is the same player with Celtic between 1888 and 1893.

DANKS Richard
One of three footballers to arrive at St James' Park from Nottingham during August 1889, Danks played reserve football for West End as a forward then teamed up in Benwell with the Rendel club. The brother of Nottingham Forest's England international Tom Danks, he had appeared with Forest too and several teams in the Midlands including Trent Valley, Notts Wanderers, Jardines and Sneiton Rovers. It was reported that Richard was partially deaf and dumb yet did well in the ranks of the Rendelites.

JOHNSTON Thomas
A former St Mirren striker, Johnston held a big reputation in Paisley having appeared with the Saints between 1882 and 1889, with a spell at neighbours Abercorn in between.

His arrival in December 1889 would have been a coup for West End, described in Athletic News as a "really good centre-forward" when due to be at St James' Park. But he never pulled on the West End shirt and was seen playing for Middlesbrough instead over seasons 1889-90 and 1890-91.

McCUDDEN Peter
During October 1892 Scottish Referee's correspondent in the North East, TT Mac – a knowledgeable Tyneside hack – reported that Peter McCudden of Arthurlie had once signed for West End, and had recently left Ironopolis. He had apparently joined the Tees club from Barrhead in Glasgow but left very quickly after receiving a £10 signing-on fee. Mac wrote: "The trick of receiving other people's money under false pretences has not even merit of being original or funny." He may well have duped West End's management in a similar way?

OFFICIALS

West End Management

West End Football Club's management began with a customary 'committee' and 'secretary' in charge of activities. These were the original enthusiasts of the club, mainly cricketers from Crown Cricket Club, including Walter Mather and Billy Tiffin. Over the decade, West End seemingly could not hit upon a satisfactory way of structuring the club's management. There was a lack of stability, which, no doubt, had a major impact on why the West Enders ultimately collapsed.

Once established, they tried several different arrangements; run by a committee, a hybrid council & committee combined, becoming a limited company with a board of directors, then returning to a committee-cum-board, all in less than 10 years.

With several well-known dignitaries supporting the club from the neighbourhood, West End boasted esteemed figureheads as Patron or President. Joseph Cowen and Arthur Henderson were both noted Parliamentarians and William I'Anson, a well-known doctor from Westgate, was the principal for over five seasons. When he stepped down in 1890, it perhaps was no coincidence that the club quickly went downhill.

Many on the club's management over the period were close friends or business colleagues. Other distinguished characters to be prominent who lived in the district were Councillor John Weidner, a leading local politician and future Lord Mayor, John Pease and Matthew Carverhill, both from eminent families, while towards the end of the club, William Nesham arrived, to later serve Newcastle United.

From the mid-decade onwards, all was not well behind the scenes with certain individuals who ran and backed the club refusing to stand for re-election as officials, many came and went. There were long and heated discussions. It looked as if disagreements continued season on season. The departure of Tom Watson as secretary – and manager in all but name – at the end of 1887 was a major loss.

During May 1889 it was decided upon a new method of running the club. The press reported that 30 members agreed to subscribe £5 each and a "syndicate" was created to take over the assets and liabilities. An inventive 'council' was to be set-up from those members to manage affairs. In addition, a 'committee' would be formed. The *Newcastle Journal* reported that at a further meeting held at the Northumberland Restaurant, the committee was elected consisting of "four vice-presidents, three members of the council, and three ordinary members". That appeared a bureaucratic hierarchy. William Nesham was elected Chairman of both the committee and council.

By the late 1880s, a handful of clubs around the country considered switching to company status and running football on business lines. Included were both West End and Newcastle East End. Over in Heaton, during February 1890 the East Enders were the first to take the plunge becoming a Limited Company of 2,000 shares at 10s 0d (50p) each, capital of £1,000. West End soon followed. Discussion took place during the same month at a meeting of members at the Bath Lane Hall to make arrangements to form the "West End Football & Athletic Company Limited". The club's prospectus was released with the objective to raise funds, the sale of 2,000 shares at £1 each being double the capital of East End. The change was all finalised during July at the Clock Restaurant on Clayton Street.

The move resulted in a Board of Directors, 12 in total, and Nesham was elected Chairman again. However, that formation of a company was nothing short of a disaster for West End. There was only a mediocre uptake in purchasing a stake in the club. The *Newcastle Daily Chronicle* wrote that West End had around "700 members" but that "only about 80 have taken shares". Probably, they were overpriced. At the end of season 1890-91 a meeting of shareholders proposed to wind up the new company, but decided to carry on for another season. Yet by June, they had changed their mind and it was reported that the company had been voluntarily wound up. West End, as was stated, would be managed "on old lines" and by September the *Daily Chronicle* reported that West End "is vested in the hands of a quartet of the oldest, most ardent, and enterprising members of the old association". The men were not named, but likely to be led by Nesham.

Another considerable factor to cause the club's decay were outgoings to both players and visiting clubs, a twin policy that was also to be unsuccessful. There were substantial costs as West End tried to elevate the club to be the best on Tyneside. Apart from paying top wages for the constant churn of footballers to arrive at St James' Park, they also had to lay out pledges to visiting clubs when teams from out of the region came to Tyneside. This substantial expenditure had a key effect on the club's downfall.

West End had already received a warning during the 1887-88 season. That year Billy Tiffin recorded they had lost between £25 and £30 on the opening fixture, a substantial sum, and had spent most of the season in financial trouble, around £40 in debt. Salvation came when West Bromwich Albion visited Tyneside during early April. As FA Cup winners, they were a big attraction. Suddenly West End found themselves in profit and, indeed, ended the season with a balance in hand of £21 15s 11d (£21 80p). It had been a close-run thing but they did not heed the warning.

During March 1891 it was stated that the "heavy guarantees" given to clubs to come to Newcastle had taken its toll. Often West End made a loss at the gate, even when they had raised admission prices   not a popular decision. Several visiting teams were hardly so-called top sides, but they still received such guarantees.

As the new decade opened shareholders and supporters were dissatisfied with how the club was being run. Performances on the pitch deteriorated and so did finances. More changes in executives took place, but none made a difference. The club declined and ultimately were forced to close the shutters.

Finances

West End's secretary and treasurer looked after the club's finances and from time to time the Newcastle press reported on annual results which gave an indication of football's economics in those early days of the game. And there were no great profits. Like many clubs then, it was a struggle to balance the books.

For season 1886-87, West End's first at St James' Park, a small profit of £45 16s 4d (£45 82p) was reported. It was stated at the annual meeting in St Andrew's Hall on Percy Street that "the future prospects are bright indeed and the people of Tyneside are rapidly becoming enthusiastic over the game". A schedule of income and expenditure was published:

Income
Subscriptions/Members £21 8s 6d (£21 43p)
Match receipts £175 6s 7d (£175 33p)
Use of ground £13 8s 0d (£13 40p)
Sundries £6 2s 0d (£6 10p)
Expenditure
Entrance fees £4 0s 0d
Match expenses £124 1s 10d (£124 9p)
Rent £33 5s 0d (£33 25p)
Sundries £9 1s 11d (£9 10p)

The following season also resulted in money in the bank, while during May 1889 it was reported the past season of 1888-89 showed Income of £721 2s 1d (£721 10p), and expenditure of £715 14s ½d (£715 70p), another modest profit. A year later, income rose substantially to £1,494 2s 9d (£1,494 14p), yet so did expenditure, to £1,515 0s 8d (£1,515 3p), resulting in a loss. Cash through the gate was increasing but not showing a profit unless the match was important or high-profile. Christmas Day football was invariably well supported and the clash of West End and East End at St James' Park at Christmas 1890 was no exception, producing gate receipts of over £115, stated at the time as the best recorded. Similarly, when Aston Villa arrived for a Good Friday contest, receipts were in excess of £90. Sadly, revenues of that size were the exception rather than the rule.

West End Officials 1882-1892

1882-83
Patron-President: *Not traced*
Vice-President: *Not traced*
Committee: *Blair J, Mather W, Wray CA*
Secretary-Treasurer: *Tiffin WWT, Williams JA*

1883-84
Patron-President: *Not traced*
Vice-President: *Not traced*
Committee: *Fawcett T, Minnikin T, Ormond C, Surtees E, Waggott E*
Secretary-Treasurer: *Best A, Tiffin WWT*

1884-85
Patron-President: *I'Anson WA*
Vice-President: *Fawcett SF, Snell BJ*
Committee: *Fawcett T, Middlemiss T, Moat W, Ormond C, Waggott TW*

Secretary-Treasurer: *Barker J, Best A, Tiffin WWT*

1885-86
Patron-President: *I'Anson WA*
Vice-President: *Not traced*
Committee: *Mather JA*
Secretary-Treasurer: *Barker J, Tiffin WWT*

1886-87
Patron-President: *Cowen J, I'Anson WA, Pease JW*
Vice-President: *Maughan I, Robinson J, Stanger T*
Committee: *Barker J, Best A, Divine M, Johnston H, Lambert G, Mather JA, Mather W, Morpeth T, Robinson J, Stanger T, Telford W, Walton T*
Secretary-Treasurer: *Robinson J, Waggott JA, Watson T*

1887-88
Patron-President: *I'Anson WA*
Vice-President: *Stanger T, Robinson J*
Committee: *Barker J, Best A, Divine M, Haig JS, Johnston H, Lambert G, Mather JA, Woof T, Wotherspoon G*

Secretary-Treasurer: *Haig JS, Robinson J, Tiffin WWT, Watkins TJ, Watson T*

1888-89
Patron-President: *I'Anson WA*
Vice-President: *Carverhill M, Jamieson SB, Robinson J, Stanger T*
Committee: *Barker J, Divine M, Stanger T, Watkins TJ, Woof T*
Secretary-Treasurer: *Haig JS, Phillips G, Stanger T, Tiffin WWT, Wilde GM, Wilson J, Woof T*

1889-90
Patron-President: *I'Anson WA*
Vice-President: *Carverhill M, Johnson WJ, Robinson J, Stanger T*
Council-Committee: *Black J, Gibb, Henderson A, Jamieson SB, McIntosh D, Nesham W (chairman), Scott RA, Spittle R*
Secretary-Treasurer: *Eddy JJ, Graham GT, Robertson WW, Tiffin WWT, Watkins TJ*

1890-91
Patron-President: *Henderson A*

Vice-President: *Not traced*
Director-Committee: *Aynsley M, Black J, Carverhill M, Eddy JJ, Graham GT, Hannah, Hudson H, Johnson WJ, McIntosh D, Nesham W (chairman), Robinson J, Scott RA, Stanger T, Weidner JF*
Secretary-Treasurer: *Aynsley M, Spittle R, Dagg J*

1891-92
Patron-President: *Not traced*
Vice-President: *Not traced*
Director-Committee: *Black J, Jackson, Nesham W (chairman)*
Secretary-Treasurer: *Bennett M, Dagg J, Dixon JW, Graham GT*

Note: *At certain times during Newcastle West End's existence, information on the club's management is sketchy and where officials' time-spans with West End are noted, these are only the dates which have been traced, but may in fact be longer.*

SEE ALSO PLAYERS: *Several players also acted as West End officials, see player biographies; Barker J, Best A, Fawcett T, Lambert G, Mather JA, Mather W, Minnikin T, Moat W, Ormond C, Robertson WW, Surtees E, Telford W, Tiffin WWT, Waggott E, Waggott JA, Waggott TW, Wilde GM.*

AYNSLEY Michael

Director: 1890-91/Treasurer: 1890-91
b. Newcastle upon Tyne, 1845 (Q4)/d. Newcastle upon Tyne, 2 June 1932
Appointed to Newcastle West End's first Board of Directors during July 1890 when the club's management was restructured, Michael Aynsley was a resident of Brighton Grove in the club's heartland and aged in his 40s at the time. He ran a plumbing and heating business on Stowell Street and Bath Lane, then later at Heber Street. Aynsley was also involved with St Paul's Cycling Club as captain while he also played bowls for Nun's Moor in the popular Tyneside league.

BENNETT M

Secretary: 1891-92
Living in the Benwell area at Buddle Road, a change in personnel at the West End club during the summer of

1891 saw Bennett appointed to the important administration role as secretary. He remained with at St James' Park until its liquidation a year later, then during June 1894 Athletic News reported that he had joined Rendel in a similar role.

BLACK John

Committee: c1889/Director: 1890-91, 1891-92
b. Newcastle upon Tyne, c1839/d. Newcastle upon Tyne, 13 June 1909
One of the earliest devotees of football's development on Tyneside, John Black lived at Buckingham Street not far from St James' Park and had interests in the licensing trade. From a Scottish family, he was associated with the running of the Duke of Buckingham and Lord Hill Inn, two of several pubs in proximity of the ground. He was

also a publican at the Bacchus Inn on Newgate Street for a period, described in census records up to his death in 1909 as an "innkeeper". During the sport's early days on Victorian Tyneside, the Lord Hill was a favourite location in football circles, associated with what was even then a fervent supporter base. West End used the Lord Hill as a headquarters for a period when the club was based at St James' Park. They changed in the pub before games, walked across Barrack Road in full kit before taking to the field. They were even nicknamed the 'Lord Hill Men' for a time by certain members of the local press. Black was initially very much a West Ender becoming a committee member and then a director as the club became one of the game's earliest limited companies during July 1890. John was a key figure in West End's cause, and financially more than once helped keep the club afloat over those difficult fledgling years, once in 1890 offering to pay for the erection of a stand at St James' Park.

On the club's demise, Black was joined by William Nesham at the famous meeting to arrange the transfer of West End's assets to Newcastle East End. He also joined up with the East End club, purchasing shares almost immediately and helped forge the single football

identity of Newcastle United, supporting his new organisation with cash when needed. Indeed, during October 1893 it is recorded in the club's official Minutes that he paid debts owing to Derby County, Liverpool and West Bromwich Albion totalling £18 6s 8d (£18 33p) to halt a storm with the Football Association. And a year later it was his gratitude which loaned the club £7 10s (£7 50p) to purchase Bob McDermid. He remained on United's early hierarchy until 1899 and later resided in Forest Hall. Black was also Vice-President of Newcastle Wednesday FC during the 1890s, a club closely linked to West End. His son, noted as "John Black the younger" also managed public-houses around Tyneside.

BLAIR John

Committee: 1882-83

An original member of the West End club, with the management of Crown Cricket Club in 1882 when they decided to form a football side, Blair also sat on the new organisation's committee. He played cricket for the Elswick-based side, captain of their second-eleven during 1883. Census and Electoral Register documents reveal two men named John Blair living in Elswick, likely to be the West End committee man; one living at Sidney Grove, the other at Gloucester Street, both near Crown Street where the club's origins are found.

CARVERHILL Matthew

Vice-President: 1888-89, 1889-90/**Director:** 1890-91

b. Newcastle upon Tyne, 1841 (Q2)/d. Newcastle upon Tyne, 30 March 1920

A popular figure in the Elswick and Westgate districts of Newcastle, residing near Elswick Park during the 1880s and 1890s, then at Crown Street – where West End's founding club took its name. When a teenager, Matthew became interested in most sports, Northern Gossip magazine noting that "football in particular claimed him as an enthusiast". He played a bit of football and cricket, captain and secretary of the SS Mary & James club as well as being later a Vice-President of North Elswick Wanderers. His father was an established businessman in Low Elswick, running the Gloucester Iron Foundry, but Matthew advanced his own career, employed for 53 years at the Armstrong Works, managing foreman of the Projectile Dept by the 1890s. He was still an engineer manager in Elswick at the time of the 1911 census and

worked alongside several West End players, notably Ned Waggott, at the Armstrong ordnance plant. Following West End's demise, it seems Carverhill retained an interest in football, linked to his local club of Rendel in the Benwell neighbourhood. It is likely another and younger member of the family, noted also as "M Carverhill", appeared for Rendel during 1890 and 1891 and as a stand-in guest for Rosehill when they visited Benwell outfit Boundary in 1887. His brother's daughter married John Weidner (qv) also a prominent West End official.

COWEN Joseph

Patron: 1886-87

b. Blaydon-on-Tyne, 9 July 1829/d. Blaydon-on-Tyne, 18 February 1900

One of Newcastle's foremost citizens of the era, Joseph Cowen was born and raised at Stella Hall in Blaydon where his father, Sir Joseph Cowen (senior) ran a major brick manufacturing business. Becoming Liberal MP for Newcastle, elected in 1874 and serving until 1886, Cowen was something of a radical figure described in the Tyneside Celebrities text as "a consistent, unflinching, and devoted political reformer". He supported the working-classes and did much to improve conditions for the under-privileged at the same time encouraging co-operative societies in the region. One profile noted that Joseph possessed "marvellous intellect, keen perception" and was "held in great respect". He could voice Churchillian-style and gave marvellous speeches to the public and to Parliament in what was described in one biography as "a gift of rough but genuine eloquence". Nicknamed the 'Blaydon Brick', Cowen attended Edinburgh University and for a while managed the family business before entering local then national politics where he soon became a dynamic player. Joseph also enjoyed being involved with sport on Tyneside, including both football and cricket. Apart from acting as a Patron of Newcastle West End during 1886-87 (and likely for a longer period), he also held similar positions for the Northumberland FA and Northumberland County CC while he was President of the Newcastle Press CC and of Rendel FC for periods too. Apart from his political life, Cowen was also the proprietor of the Newcastle Chronicle, the leading newspaper in the region.

Purchasing the various titles during 1859, he took a leading role in the paper's editorial while he was one of the prime movers in creating the Tyne Theatre Opera House and Newcastle Public Library. A lasting tribute to a man of Tyneside was erected during 1906, a handsome bronze statue on Westgate Road in the city.

The Cowen statue on Westgate Road in Newcastle.

DAGG Joseph

Secretary (reserve team): 1890-91, 1891-92
b. Newcastle upon Tyne, 1858 (Q4)/d. [Tynemouth, 1935 (Q2)]
A fervent supporter of West End's cause, Joseph Dagg looked after the club's reserve eleven during the latter seasons of their time in Tyneside football, likely building the side which lifted the Northumberland Senior Cup in 1892. He was described as working hard to obtain a line-up "of purely local talent" and that trophy victory was evidence of that, containing young and upcoming players from the city. Recorded as being a joiner and later a general builder, Dagg was the son of a Newcastle policeman. He resided at Elswick and took part in popular pot-share bowling contests in the district, challenges for top money through the 1880s. Following the First World War, Joe relocated to the coast at Monkseaton.

DIVINE M [Michael]

Committee: 1886-87 to 1888-89
b. [Portobello, near Edinburgh, c1855]
A scarce Newcastle West End Rule Book from 1886 shows one of the club's committee men as 'M Divine'. The spelling of the surname with an 'i' rather than an 'e' points to one man residing in the St John's area of city as recorded in census documents. The likely individual is Michael Divine, born near Edinburgh and by the 1870s living in Newcastle as an apprentice engine-fitter and when West End had started to play football was in his thirties residing at Orchard Street near the city's Central Station.

DIXON John William

Secretary (reserve team): 1892
b. Newcastle upon Tyne, 9 November 1867/d. Newcastle upon Tyne, 18 January 1943

John Dixon was the older brother of West End player Harry Dixon (qv), born in Westgate and a commercial clerk for a wholesale grocery business. Better known as 'Johnnie', he was described as "a most energetic and enthusiastic official" and had been linked to the West Enders for several years, occasionally acting as an umpire at matches. Noted as "Honorary Secretary" of the team, he was with the reserve squad when they secured the Northumberland Senior Cup just before the club folded – maybe working alongside Joe Dagg or as a replacement. Dixon played a bit of football himself as a younger man, for White Rose Juniors during the mid-1880s, captain of the side. He also turned out for Science & Art as well as Rendel.

Living on Pitt Street near St James' Park, by the time of the 1911 census Dixon had moved to the Fenham suburbs, now a commercial traveller still in the grocery trade. Along with his younger brother, Johnnie was a keen cricketer with White Rose and later Bath Lane CC where he became secretary. The Tynesider was also elected to the Northumberland County CC committee for a period.

EDDY John James

Director: 1890-91/**Financial Secretary-Treasurer:** 1889-90
b. Newcastle upon Tyne, 1855/d. Newcastle upon Tyne, 3 April 1933

A long-term employee of the Newcastle Chronicle newspaper, for over 60 years Eddy worked for the organisation becoming Chief Dispatch Manager. He played cricket for the well-known Newcastle Press & Athletic club during the late 1870s and early 1880s, being recorded as their secretary and treasurer, while he also sat on the organisation's football committee. A West End official at the turn of the decade, he was involved in various sporting activities, while in addition, Eddy was a Vice-President of Newcastle Wednesday during the 1890s. John resided on Jefferson Street during

the 1880s, later based at Brighton Grove, two locations where several West End personalities lived.

FAWCETT Selby Forster

Vice President: 1884-85
b. Heddon-on-the-Wall, 1828/d. Newcastle upon Tyne, 31 August 1899

One of Newcastle upon Tyne's top policemen, and somewhat celebrated as a detective in the city, Selby Fawcett served the constabulary from the 1850s until he retired from the force during 1878. Fawcett was involved solving many serious crimes in Newcastle and earned a reputation as a distinguished officer. The Newcastle Evening Chronicle wrote on his death just before the turn of the century that he "was held in certain dread" to the "wrong-doers of past generations". Selby lived in the Westgate area and was stationed for several years at the local police station on Westgate Road, no doubt being in contact with many of the West End club's personalities. He supported the side and joined their management during the mid-1880s. His son, Thomas Fawcett (qv) was a player in the red-and-black jersey.

GIBB

Committee & Council: 1889-90
Little is known about Mr Gibb, noted as being on the club's management then part of a newly created council for season 1889-90 as well as a Vice-President of the Newcastle Wednesday club. No definite information on Gibb has been traced and census papers show several options living in Newcastle at the time. The best match is David Gibb from Elswick originally, aged around 24 and a grocer's manager, living at Stanhope Street by 1891.

GRAHAM George Thomas

Director: 1890-91/**Treasurer:** 1889-90/**Match Secretary:** 1891-92
b. Newcastle upon Tyne, 1858 (or 1857, records differ)/d. Cape Town, South Africa, 13 July 1922
A member of West End's initial Board of Directors during July 1890 as management attempted to place the club on a sound footing, George Graham ran a glover and hosier business with a shop on the corner of Clayton Street and Nun Street in the city. He resided near to St James' Park at St Thomas' Street, then moved to Cullercoats by the 1890s. At some point Graham emigrated to South Africa and family history trees note he died there in 1922.

HAIG John Samuel

Committee: 1887-88/**Secretary:** 1887-88
b. Edinburgh, 18 March 1865/d. Leeds, 11 September 1948 (or 7th, records differ)
Having previously played football for Tyne, becoming the team's Pilgrims junior XI secretary during 1881, John Haig was later also associated with Jesmond as a footballer, acting as their secretary when the club was formed during 1883. Haig was appointed to the prominent role of secretary at West End during December 1887. The Scot was employed as a clerk when a young man, later becoming an accountant and was recorded as based at 38 Northumberland Street when in charge of the West Enders. He was deeply involved in football at this time, also sitting on the Temperance Festival organisation committee. But Haig decided to part company with the St James' Park club at the start of the 1888-89 season during August, then around 1890 it was noted that he had moved to Spain. By 1902, John was living in Linares, Andalucía, but returned to Britain and settled in the Headingley district of Leeds. When based at St James' Park, it was reported during April 1888 that Haig was in the West End line-up for the Inter County Championship meeting with Sunderland. However, as secretary his name was used as an alias for a mystery player handed the surname of "Hunter" (qv).

HANNAH

Director: 1890-91
Noted in the news columns of the period as being appointed a director of West End during March 1891, Hannah only remained in post a short time. With West End's rivals and close neighbours Elswick Rangers toiling behind the scenes, he left St James' Park to join up with Rangers as a director in an effort to revitalise the Graingerville club. With little information traced, identifying who Hannah was has been problematic. There are a few possibles in the area during the era and with his link to Elswick Rangers, it is probable he resided in that district. That points to four individuals, including three brothers, residing at two addresses on Dilston Road near the Mill Lane ground, home of Rangers. They were all born in the city and may all be related. The 1891 census records the four as; William Hannah (aged 36, commercial traveller in tobacco), John W Hannah (32, accountant), Richard Hannah (30, piano dealer) and Henry Hannah (28, musician). It is likely the West End official is one of them, probably either of the older pair, William or John Hannah.

HENDERSON Arthur

President: 1890-91/**Committee & Council:** 1889-90
b. Glasgow, 13 September 1863/d. London, 20 October 1935
Born in Anderston, Glasgow, Arthur Henderson's family relocated to Tyneside during the early 1870s when he was around 10 years of age. As a teenager Henderson worked as an apprentice moulder at the famed works of Robert Stephenson & Co on Forth Banks, then had a short period at a Southampton shipyard before heading back to Newcastle and Stephensons once more. He soon became a prominent union man, holding the position of

Delegate and Secretary for the Ironfounder's organisation in the region. Arthur entered local politics during the early 1890s and became a Liberal councillor for the Westgate North ward in Newcastle. Like his fellow West End supporter, Joseph Cowen, he was well-known in the city, and a speaker of distinction. At this time during the late 1880s and early 1890s, he resided at Croydon Road in Arthur's Hill. Henderson became a Methodist preacher and supported various causes in the Elswick and Westgate districts.

He was also an avid supporter of football, notably Newcastle West End. Leading journalist TT Mac recalled that Henderson "did much work in furthering the game in Newcastle" while the great Colin Veitch recalled in his memoirs that Arthur was a guiding figure as football took hold, noting that he "played a prominent part". It is also recorded he refereed occasional matches during the early 1890s. Arthur was appointed as President of the Northumberland FA from 1890 to 1893 and moved to Darlington during that decade where he became a councillor and mayor of the town. His political career rapidly progressed, reaching national level by 1903 when he was elected as Labour MP for Barnard Castle, then later for Widnes – and Newcastle upon Tyne East in 1923 – before representing Burnley and Clay Cross. By then Henderson was a major figure in the Labour Party and during 1915 had been elevated to ministerial level in government; taking roles at the Board of Education, as Paymaster General and Home Secretary in 1924, then Foreign Secretary between 1929 and 1931. The former West End director reached the top of the tree of the Labour Party, holding various posts as Chairman, General Secretary, and Leader. Arthur became known on the world stage during the 1930s, being appointed President of the Geneva Disarmament Conference between 1932 and 1935 and was awarded the Nobel Peace Prize during 1934 for his international efforts in that forum. Once nicknamed 'Uncle Arthur', Henderson was honoured as a Freeman of Newcastle upon Tyne.

HUDSON H [Henry]

Director: 1890-91
b. [Newcastle upon Tyne, c1844]
The Newcastle West End official named as a director for season 1890-91 is probably Harry Hudson, a longstanding licensee of The Lowther Inn at "Nun's Gate" near the junction of Newgate Street and the Bigg Market – the pub remains in that location even now. Hudson's establishment was a popular meeting place and he lived in Elswick during the 1880s and 1890s.

I'ANSON William Andrew

President: 1884-85 to 1889-90
b. Newcastle upon Tyne, 6 June 1848/d. Newcastle upon Tyne, 23 April 1908
Residing in West End's football breeding ground, at Westgate Hill House, William I'Anson was likely the foremost supporter of the club during the mid-to-late 1880s. He became West End's figurehead as President for six seasons as the team developed into a force in the region. The son of a respected surgeon in the city, William also studied medicine, in Edinburgh, and by 1870 had returned to Tyneside and ran a GP's practice on Westgate Hill. He was, like his West End colleagues, Carverhill and Weidner, a prominent citizen in the area. William was also connected to Grove Juniors football and rugby teams in North Elswick. Later in life, I'Anson resided at the historic 17th century Denton Hall on the West Road, still an imposing building on the route to the Tyne valley. He is buried in the grandiose family tomb at Westgate Hill cemetery. The wider I'Anson family included others named William I'Anson; a father and son pair, both celebrated racehorse owners and trainers from near Malton in Yorkshire.

The I'Anson tomb at Westgate cemetery.

JACKSON

Committee: 1891-92
Almost nothing has been discovered of Mr Jackson apart from a brief line during December 1891 when it was noted that as a West End committee member, he "had severed his connection with the club".

JAMIESON Stuart Boyd

Vice-President: 1888-89/**Committee & Council:** 1889-90
b. Belfast, c1858/d. Newcastle upon Tyne, 28 November 1932
Although certain press columns note this official as SM Jamieson or SR Jamieson, West End's Vice-President is Stuart Boyd Jamieson who ran a watch-maker's and jewellery business on Grainger Street West. It was reported that his firm presented players with mementoes from his shop. He also acted as a referee and umpire at various local fixtures at St James' Park. Originally from Ireland, his family crossed the Irish Sea to set up house in Glasgow by the start of the 1880s, then Jamieson moved to Tyneside. He resided at Victoria Street in Westgate and by the 1920s at Elswick Row nearby.

JOHNSON William J [Jacob]

Vice-President: 1889-90/Director: 1890-91
b. Dalton, Northumberland, 1861/d. Dalton,
Northumberland, 4 July 1910
*The son of a Tyne valley farmer, William Johnson
became a keen early fan of West End's fortunes, also
associated with the club's cricket set-up during the mid-
1880s. A clothier and tailor, Johnson ran shops on
Northumberland Street and Clayton Street and his
business during the late 1880s and early 1890s held the
copyright of fixture cards for the West Enders – in the
form of a diary booklet available at his outlets. When
William died at the family home of Broomy Hill Farm in
Dalton near Stamfordham, now a Grade II listed
building, the Newcastle Journal described him as being
"very well-known and highly esteemed in the city". At
that time, he was a resident of Jesmond.*

JOHNSTON H

Committee: 1886-87, 1887-88
*Another Newcastle upon Tyne resident connected to
West End, but who remains unknown and mysterious. He
sat on the club's committee over two seasons.*

MAUGHAN Isaac

Vice-President: 1886-87
b. Kirkhaugh, Northumberland, c1837/d. Cullercoats,
near Whitley Bay, 28 January 1905
*Appointed to the position of West End's Vice-President
at the AGM during May 1886, Isaac Maughan was a live-
stock dealer and farmer. He was based at High
Gowlands, a 50-acre farm on the West Road in
Newcastle, before the area was developed. With his
brother Thomas, he operated T & I Maughan, which was
still trading into the 1950s. From an Alston Moor family,
Isaac was living on Elswick Road by the beginning of the
1880s and became a supporter of West End throughout
the decade and moved in the same business and social
circles as other Westgate and Elswick worthies.
Following the club's demise, Maughan became an early
shareholder in Newcastle United, recorded in the club's
share-ledger as purchasing four 10s 0d (50p) shares
during July 1895. He later resided in the Jesmond and
Gosforth suburbs, then retired to Cullercoats where he
died. His son George Maughan, a solicitor, was a noted
cyclist with the Elswick Bicycle Club.*

MIDDLEMISS T [Thomas]

Committee: 1884-85
*Variously stated in the Tyneside press as Middlemiss or
Middlemas, at the time during the mid-1880s two
Newcastle upon Tyne police officers named Thomas
Middlemiss served the city. Both were aged in their mid-
Twenties when a West End player "T Middlemiss"
appeared for the club at reserve level between 1883-84
and 1885-86. He was elected to the management
committee alongside Vice-President Selby Fawcett, also
a senior policeman. Perhaps the relationship at the
Westgate police station brought Middlemiss to West
End. It is probable he is one of those two officers;
Thomas Middlemiss (b. Elsdon, 3 July 1860/d. Newcastle*

*upon Tyne, 1939 (Q1)) who became an inspector, or
Thomas Middlemiss (b. Newcastle upon Tyne, 1859/d.
Newcastle upon Tyne, 24 February 1916) a constable
and later when he left the force, inspector at the Elswick
Armstrong works.*

MORPETH Thomas

Field Committee: 1886-87
b. Newcastle upon Tyne, 1860 (Q2)/d. [Newcastle upon
Tyne, June 1908]
*A past footballer with Newcastle Rangers and Gateshead
Association during the mid-years of the 1880s, Tommy
Morpeth was also associated with West End during the
same period. In addition, he also played cricket for West
End as well as the Brighton, Gloucester and West Elswick
clubs, all in the city's western districts. For season 1887-
88, Morpeth acted as club auditor with Gavin
Wotherspoon. He also was an umpire at various West
End matches during the late 1880s. Born and raised in
Westgate, at Pitt Street and Swinburne Place, Tommy
was engaged as a clerk and by the 1891 census was
noted as living in Heaton employed at a stockbroker's
office.*

McINTOSH D [David]

Committee & Council: 1889-90/Director: 1890-91
*Chairing West End's annual meeting during May 1889,
McIntosh also presented the celebrated Bob Kelso with a
parting gift when he left Tyneside after a season at St
James' Park. He was another supporter of the club seen
as an umpire during the late 1880s. Census data reveals
two or three individuals living in Newcastle between
1881 and 1891 who could be "D McIntosh". The best
match is David McIntosh residing in the All Saints area
near to West End's ground. He was originally from
Scotland, settling on Tyneside by the 1860s and would
have been around 49 years of age when part of West
End's management. A commercial traveller, he remained
living in Newcastle (b. Edinburgh, 1841/d. Newcastle
upon Tyne, 1899 (Q2)).*

NESHAM William

**Chairman: 1889-90 to 1891-92/Committee & Council:
1889-90/Director: 1890-91, 1891-92**

b. Newcastle upon Tyne, 4 June 1828/d. Newcastle upon
Tyne, 8 January 1902

Appointed Newcastle West End's first Chairman during the summer of 1889, William Nesham has the unique distinction of being Chairman of both West End and Newcastle United, a position he held from August 1895 to January 1901. Nesham owned the lease for 5.25 acres of land on Leazes, known as St James' Park and passed that to the West Enders to fortify the site as a home for football. Residing in the historic Leazes Terrace overlooking the ground since the 1870s, he was an aficionado of the early game in the region. Along with John Black, as a committee member then director, Nesham did much to see that West End survived during their troubled later years before a cash crisis eventually saw their collapse. Nesham was then invited to join the East End directorate and for almost a decade served Newcastle United with esteem. It was noted that he assisted the early Black'n'Whites financially in times of need during the 1890s and was a man "widely known and universally respected". Nesham was a wealthy local dignitary from a prominent Tyneside family, the son of a physician and surgeon, William (senior), and he sported a marvellous set of whiskers in the fashion of the Victorian era. A successful merchant importing various goods with a base near the Quayside, at the time of the 1901 census, it was noted he was dealing in "gunpowder, and other explosives". William was also President of the Northumberland FA to his demise. The Tynesider had been a highly respected cricketer in his youth appearing as a wicket-keeper for the pre-county Northumberland XI and for the Northumberland club, later being for a period President of Northumberland County. He retained a close connection with the summer game in Jesmond, officiating as an umpire on occasion. His younger brother, Thomas Nesham, also a doctor like their father, played cricket on Tyneside to a similar high standard as well. William was linked with running minor local club Newcastle Wednesday as a Vice-President, his brother being President. For 30 years he was Foreman of the Newcastle upon Tyne Grand Jury at the city's quarter-sessions. The prominent Novocastrian died at his Leazes Terrace home and on his death Northern Gossip magazine's tribute was of high praise, noting he was a "thorough English gentleman, a keen lover of sport, and had done much for the good of football in the North of England".
(Note: Several reports spell his surname as Neasham, however family history and Newcastle United documentation confirm it as Nesham.)

PEASE John William

Patron: 1886-87
b. Darlington, 13 August 1836/d. Newcastle upon Tyne, 25 March 1901
From a well-to-do family near Darlington, John Pease was a successful businessman, a merchant-banker and director of the North East Railway Company. He resided at Benwell Towers, a neighbour of fellow West End official John Weidner. Pease also owned a residence at Nethergate in Alnmouth and like his West End colleagues at the time, Weidner, I'Anson and Joseph Cowen, he was an esteemed citizen. Becoming a local

councillor for Benwell, Pease was also a city magistrate as well as a governor of the Royal Grammar School.

For a period, he was also chairman of the Benwell & Fenham local board of Northumberland County Council.

PHILLIPS George

Secretary: 1888-89
b. Glasgow
Moving to Tyneside at the end of 1888 from Glasgow where he acted as secretary to Glasgow University FC, Phillips took over as West End's secretary when Thomas Woof left the position in January 1889. The Scot didn't stay long with West End and handed over the role to Tom Watkins by May.

ROBINSON James

Vice-President: 1886-87 to 1889-90/**Field Committee:** 1886-87/**Treasurer:** 1886-87, 1887-88/**Director:** 1890-91
Although holding important positions with the West Enders over five seasons, little has been traced on James Robinson. Apart from being a football supporter, he turned out on the cricket field for the club in the mid-1880s. There are several options recorded in census documents who were resident in Newcastle during the mid-1880s and early 1890s. To be a Vice-President, it is likely Robinson was a prominent figure. Included was a restauranteur, a pram-dealer, printer's engineer, and a wine-spirit merchant.

SCOTT Robert Anderson

Committee & Council: 1889-90/**Director:** 1890-91
b. Newcastle upon Tyne, 1843 (Q2)/d. Newcastle upon Tyne, 26 August 1917
During the mid-to-late 1880s and opening of the 1890s, West End Football Club could count on several well-respected supporters, all resident in their heartland. Robert Scott was one, and would have been known to his colleagues Carverhill, I'Anson, Henderson, Nesham and Weidner. In his mid-40s then, Scott held an important civic role to the Magistrates Police Court. He became Chief Assistant-Clerk, remaining in that position until his

retirement during 1908 after nearly 40 years. A former solicitor's official, he also worked at the Bankruptcy Court and North of England Trade Protection Society for periods. Living near to St James' Park at Wellington Street in Westgate, then on Leazes Park Road, Scott was honoured as a Freeman of the city.

SNELL Bernard Joseph

Vice-President: 1884-85
b. Earlswood, Surrey, 1856 (Q4)/d. Bowdon, Cheshire, 15 June 1934

Pastor at St Paul's Congregational Church in the Arthur's Hill area of Newcastle, the Reverend Bernard Snell was deeply involved in the local community, one of his roles being as Vice-President of West End. Born and raised in Surrey, Snell was a tall and distinguished looking man and after qualifying with a MA and BSc at the University of London moved into the clergy. Described as a "forceful and independent character", Bernard took a post on Tyneside and was involved in numerous good causes during those pre-Welfare State years. He was often a speaker and lecturer at events in the 1880s and 1890s connected with the temperance movement. Snell left Newcastle to take up a new position at Salford and his farewell gathering was attended by a large number of friends and colleagues, including Joseph Cowen.

Snell became something of a non-conformist preacher and when he moved back to the South East during 1891 was based at Brixton Congregational Church for the next 37 years. He was noted as "a popular and highly-esteemed minister", appointed chairman of the Congregational Union in 1917. The reverend did outstanding work over several years running the Moffat Institute, a mission in North London while he was also a keen cricket devotee, a member of Surrey CCC and a regular at the Oval. Snell retired from the church during 1930 and settled in Cheshire.

SPITTLE Robert

Committee & Council: 1889-90/**Secretary:** 1890-91
b. Newcastle upon Tyne, 1856/d. Newcastle upon Tyne, 2 January 1936

An Elswick man like many of West End's guardians, Robert Spittle was a joiner and builder who became a prominent union man on Tyneside. He was appointed to run the Amalgamated Society of Joiners by 1885, and by

1890, was also leader of the Tyne District United Trade Committee. Spittle did much to support workers in the region and more specifically, in the western suburbs of the city, managing what was known as the "Bath Lane Poor Children's Free Breakfast Fund". Apart from being attached to West End's management, he also became a committee member of the Northern League as the 1890s began. Residing at various times in the years before the turn of the century at Monday Street, Stanhope Street and Dilston Road, he died when living in Fenham during 1936.

STANGER Thomas

Vice-President: 1986-87 to 1889-90/**Field Committee:** 1886-87/**Committee & Director:** 1888-89, 1890-91/**Treasurer:** 1888-89
b. Newburn, near Newcastle upon Tyne, 1841/d. Newcastle upon Tyne, 13 December 1904

Born alongside the River Tyne at Newburn, Thomas Stanger was the father of West End player, TW Stanger (qv), and was associated with the club over a lengthy period in various roles as the management of the side changed. Stanger became a foreman joiner in Lamesley near Gateshead before settling in Heaton and by the time he acted alongside the West Enders' other officials during mid-to-later years of the 1880s, Tom was around 50 years of age. But in the spring of 1891, a year before the club's collapse, Stanger surprisingly departed, joining rivals Elswick Rangers when that club was struggling and in need of new direction.

WALTON T

Committee: 1886-87

During Newcastle West End's decade playing the game there were apparently several individuals named 'Walton' associated with the club, notably Jack Walton (qv) who played during season 1890-91 and was prominent with the Trafalgar side where it was also noted a J Walton (senior) and J Walton (junior) were in line-ups too, likely related. The football columns of the local press also revealed West End's cricket team included I (or IJ) Walton, R Walton as well as J Walton and T Walton – the latter two both being committee members of the cricketers during the mid-1880s.

T Walton was also noted as being on the football club's committee and after chairing a meeting of the West End club during June 1887 to elect officials for the new season, Walton seemingly left the management group. National registers do not identify a family which can readily be linked to the West End Waltons. There was a Thomas Walton associated with the Elswick Ward Constitutional Association during the early 1880s and who is possibly the man living at Gosforth who died in 1893 with a son John Joseph Walton. Alternatively, Isaac Thompson Walton, a clerk from Haltwhistle with brothers Thomas and John, resided in Elswick during 1891 and later in Corbridge.
(Note: The added issue in unravelling the Walton connection is likely type-setting errors in newspapers; I or IT Walton, could be J or JT Walton, or vice-versa.)

WATKINS Thomas John

Committee: 1888-89/Secretary: 1889-90/Secretary (reserve team): 1887-88
b. Derby, 1854 (Q2)/d. Southampton, 1936 (Q1)
For season 1887-88 "TJ Watkins" was reported in the press acting as secretary to the West End junior side, then was elevated to the club's committee taking the key post of secretary during May 1889 to oversee the whole club. Recorded as residing at Langhorn Street, Heaton when occupying that role, there is only one individual of that name in either the 1881 or 1891 census documents. He hailed from Derbyshire and was a fruiterer's clerk initially. Having family links in County Durham, Watkins trained to be an accountant and moved to Teesside setting up a business in Stockton. Thomas was appointed a public auditor in the town as well as auditor to the Hartlepool Gas & Water Company. By the latter years of the 1920s, Watkins had moved his business to the south coast in Southampton.

WATSON Thomas

Secretary: 1986-87, 1887-88
b. Newcastle upon Tyne, 8 April 1859/d. Liverpool, 6 May 1915
While Tom Watson never kicked a ball in anger for Newcastle West End or Newcastle East End, he gave the city's rival clubs first-rate service as secretary and in all but name, manager, before making a huge reputation for himself in charge of Sunderland and Liverpool. Born and raised in the Byker and Heaton districts, he appeared as a footballer and as secretary for Rosehill alongside the Tyne, while he was also an enthusiastic cricketer for Rosehill Star CC. During those days as a younger man and when just becoming involved in football during the early 1880s, Tom was a moulder living on Tyneside.

Having watched a St Bernard's versus Rangers match in Scotland, Watson was so impressed with the sport that he formed the Rosehill club back home, once playing against West End in 1884. Tom joined West End as secretary during the summer of 1886, then after a period establishing the St James' Park club, moved across the city in December 1887 to team up with East End at Chillingham Road. A cheery character with a Geordie twang, Watson was described as silver-tongued and sported a large well-trimmed moustache in the fashion

of the day. As a shrewd administrator, the Tynesider helped form the Northern League during 1889 which was a major catalyst to the development of football in the region, then additionally was the Northern Alliance league's first secretary when it was established the following year. The Newcastle Daily Chronicle noted that Watson had "proved himself a true judge of style" and he did such a good job turning a struggling East End club around, that Tom was lured to join Sunderland in the close-season of 1889 for what was described as a healthy salary of £150 per annum, at the time the Wearsiders being far more advanced than either Newcastle outfit. He was a forward-thinking individual and did much to build the celebrated 'Team of all the Talents' on Wearside. Sunderland went on to lift the Football League title in 1892, 1893 and 1895, as well as being runner-up during 1894, all under Watson's guidance. Sunderland's John Grayston noted that he "could rule his team with kindness and firmness, and always made himself the chum of the rank and file". At one point in 1895, and before Newcastle United appointed Frank Watt, Watson applied for the vacant United secretary's post, but lost out to the Scot. A year later, during July 1896 he moved to Liverpool for twice his salary and again weaved his magic, developing a top-class set-up in a spell of 19 years with the Reds, the Anfield club winning title honours in 1901 and 1906, twice being league runners-up and reaching the FA Cup final as well. It is recorded that he even encouraged players to drink beer and red wine as part of his master plan! At that time Athletic News noted Watson as a secretary-manager who had "few equals, and no superior". Tom was elected to the League Management Committee during September 1891 and to the FA Council in October of that year. He was an outstanding personality of the Edwardian game, being awarded the Football League's Long Service medal during 1910 while he latterly has been included in the League Managers Association Hall of Fame. Watson died on Merseyside during May 1915 and is buried at Anfield cemetery. He married into the Oliver family of Newcastle United directors.

WEIDNER John Frederick

Director: 1890-91
Also appeared for Newcastle Wed/Victoria Wed.

b. Newcastle upon Tyne, 3 October 1853/d. Newcastle upon Tyne, 4 May 1934
Born and raised in Newcastle's Westgate district at Elswick Lodge, then later a resident at Condercum House in Benwell, John Weidner was another of West End's

well-known public figures. He was described at one point in the Newcastle Daily Chronicle as having a love of football, being "an ardent supporter of the game". He also enjoyed cricket and was President of the SS Mary & James club. John had established a business as a steam-ship owner and export merchant, transporting Geordie coal to the world. His business was prominent on Newcastle's Quayside while he also owned a popular tobacconist chain, Finlay & Co Ltd and was associated with Sowerby's Glassworks in Gateshead as well as the Hodgson's Hardware company. His success saw Weidner purchase the West Heddon Estate in the Tyne valley, while he is related by marriage to the Carverhill family, also West End supporters. John entered local politics and governance, he was a magistrate, and a member of the important city Board of Guardians. He was elected councillor of the Elswick East ward from 1887, became Sheriff of Newcastle in 1897, an Alderman during 1906, then Lord Mayor for 1912-13. When Weidner died in 1934, he was remembered in glowing terms, described as the "father of Newcastle council".

WILLIAMS Joseph A
Secretary: 1882-83
When the club was formed as West End Juniors FC during August 1882, Joseph Williams was noted as the first secretary of the new outfit. He was based in the city at Marlborough Crescent near the Central Station. The one man logged in 1881 documents is a Joseph Alfred Williams (b. c1867), from Hebburn originally and living in Byker. He was then only around 16 years of age, which would seem too young to be the club secretary, however the teenager did work at the time in an accountant's office. Interestingly, later records show him scheduled in the ledgers of the Grand Lodge Himalayan Brotherhood, based in Shimla, Punjab where he died during August 1893.

WOOF Thomas
Committee: 1887-88, 1888-89/**Secretary:** 1888-89
b. Washington, October 1858 [5 November 1858]/d. Sutton, near Epsom, 25 April 1924
Raised in Dawdon near Seaham, Thomas Woof later resided in Heaton at Denmark Street, then Headlam Street when connected to West End, recorded being employed as an engine-fitter. On the club's committee, Woof took on the role of club secretary from August 1888 to January 1889 after Tom Watson controversially quit to join rivals East End. But he left the post as 1889 opened, soon relocating to London, and settling in Lewisham, south of the Thames, described as a "traveller, machine-tools". He later was based near Epsom to his death.

WOTHERSPOON Gavin
Committee: 1887-88
b. Airdrie, 15 March 1857/d. Sunderland, 5 July 1908
The only individual in census documents for 1881 and 1891 which fits the West End profile is Scot, Gavin Wotherspoon who originally hailed from Airdrie but who put down roots in Arthur's Hill, Newcastle during the mid-1880s. A clerk with a printing firm at the time, he

was appointed to the West End committee during June 1887 and acted as club auditor for the coming season. Wotherspoon had moved to Wearside by 1901, running a "beer shop" in Pallion and on several occasions unsuccessfully attempted to gain a licence to convert the outlet to a public-house.

WRAY Charles Albert
Committee: 1882-83
b. Newcastle upon Tyne, 13 September 1862/d. Newcastle upon Tyne, 3 November 1946
When the Crown Cricket Club in Elswick decided to form a football club during the summer of 1882, Charles Wray was a resident in the vicinity at Hartington Street. A neighbour there, and probably a friend too during the decade, was James Carverhill, the brother of West End's prominent supporter and official Matthew Carverhill. Likely part of the cricket set-up, he was one of the young men to be active as a committee member and develop football for 1882-83 in that first season. Wray was employed as an ordnance fitter at the Elswick Armstrong factory, later becoming a "telegraph instrument mechanic", spending a period in Bristol during 1911 on what was termed "Government work". At the time of his passing just after World War Two, Charles was still living in Elswick, at Belgrave Terrace and had spent much of his life in West End's heartland.

TRAINERS

SEE ALSO PLAYERS: *Certain players also acted as West End trainers, see player biographies; Kennedy DC.*

LINDSAY James
Trainer: 1890-91
Joining up with the West End set-up during September 1890 after H Nelson defected to rivals East End, James Lindsay was "the right man, in the right place" as described in the Newcastle Daily Chronicle. He was a former trainer to Clyde FC in Scotland as well as other "well-known clubs" frustratingly unnamed. Lindsay had recently arrived on Tyneside "with some of the players from Glasgow" in the hope of finding a post.

NELSON H
Trainer: 1889-90
A former trainer with Aston Villa, Nelson moved to Tyneside and took on a role at St James' Park for season 1889-90, and perhaps before. But prior to the end of that campaign, in April 1890, it was announced he had crossed the city and teamed-up with Newcastle East End. But Nelson didn't stay long at the Heaton Junction Ground either, remaining less than a season with the club.

PEARS John
Trainer: 1890-91, 1891-92
b. likely, Northumberland.
Known as 'Jack' Pears, during the latter months of West End's existence, he became trainer of the side and when the club folded moved across to join Newcastle East End with the reserve squad. He became assistant-trainer to

the 'A' side in Heaton then was appointed to look after the newly titled Newcastle United first-eleven during August 1895 at a salary, according to the club's Minutes, of "35 shillings (£1 75p) per week". However, within a year United's directorate expressed dissatisfaction with the methods of Pears and he was sacked during March 1896, being replaced in a temporary role by Willie Thompson. Pears had become an early shareholder of the club during his period at St James' Park, at the time in 1895 living on Pitt Street, off Barrack Road. Census information is not conclusive identifying the trainer, but two candidates living on Tyneside were both born in Northumberland, one in the city, the other in Alston, and living in the Benwell and Elswick districts. (Note: Newcastle United's official documents record his surname as Pears, however some contemporary newspaper and photograph captions describe the trainer as Pearce, or Pierce.)

APPENDIX

CLUB INFORMATION

During Newcastle West End's era through the 1880s to the start of the 1890s, the club played Victorian sides now long gone, teams strange to the modern football scene. Many had a brief existence as the game developed, like the West Enders. Players to appear for West End also turned out for other unfamiliar clubs around the country. Back in the Victorian era, several of these sides represented communities from districts of cities or mere villages on the outskirts of towns, a century and more later now part of urban areas. A brief explanation of these clubs is scheduled together with year of formation *(f)*, traced grounds and kit – some unusual colour combinations included. Such information is generally restricted to the 1880s and early years of the 1890s. Not included are present-day sides generally well-known such as Aston Villa, Sunderland or Celtic.

Main sources: Contemporary newspapers and club histories, Northern Athlete Directory (1883, 1884), Northumberland FA Handbook (1885), SFHA.org.uk (Scottish Football Historical Archive), historicalkits.co.uk. Note: Team colours varied over the decade while certain discrepancies exist with formation dates.

North East England

All Saints: *f1882* and titled *"All Saints Cricket & Athletic Club"* based in the centre of Newcastle with a pitch at the *"old cricket field at the back of Ellison Place"*. They played in shirts of *"black, cardinal & sky blue"* with *"rose & white knickers"*.

Alnwick: *f1879* as Alnwick Utd Services, later renamed Alnwick Utd Juniors then Alnwick Town. Played at Waggonways and the Recreation Ground during the 1880s. Sported *"maroon jerseys, white knickers"*.

Alnwick Working Men's Club: *A different club to Alnwick FC, playing during the 1880s.*

Ashington Rising Star: *f1883,* they featured colours of *"black jerseys & star, black knickers"*. Based at the Recreation Ground next to the colliery, Rising Star appeared in the FA Cup during the late 1880s and later became Ashington FC.

Backworth Hotspur: *f1884* and situated north of the pit-head, played in *"blue & white jerseys, white knickers"*.

Bedlington Burdon: *f1882* and named after a local mine-owner, they played with a kit of *"navy blue & white jerseys, white knickers"*. They had a base at Holly Mount at the east end of the town.

Birtley: *f1882 or 1883 (although also noted as 1880)* with a pitch off Station Road in Birtley, then a village outside Gateshead. Founder members of the Northern League, they also competed in the FA Cup.

Bishop Auckland Church Institute: *f1882,* the oldest club in the town and to later be one of the sides with Auckland Town to develop into the present-day Bishop Auckland. Formed originally by Oxford and Cambridge students studying theology at Auckland, they used the university colours of dark-blue & light-blue and played initially at Flatts Farm, then South Church Lane.

Blyth: *f1885* as Blyth FC with a brief period titled Blyth Waterloo Rangers, well before the Blyth Spartans club was formed.

Boundary: *f1884* when lads created a team around Boundary Street in Elswick. They had disappeared by 1887.

Brandling: *A minor club based in Jesmond; Brandling Park FC competed during the early 1880s and a decade later, Brandling Juniors existed, maybe a different club.*

Brunswick: *f1883* with a field on the Town Moor near the Blue House, then at Bath Lane. The club merged with Newcastle Association during 1887. Colours of *"yellow, blue & maroon jerseys, white knickers"* as well as *"black jerseys & blue band"*.

Cathedral: *f1883 or 1884* from Newcastle with a pitch on Bath Road, they pulled on a strip of *"chocolate jerseys, white knickers"* then *"maroon & white"*.

Cheviot: *f1883* located in Byker, they played at Byker Vicarage and amalgamated with Newcastle East End during 1887. Pulled on shirts of *"navy-blue with light-blue sash"*.

(Darlington) St Augustine's: *f1882 or 1883* from a Catholic church XI and known as 'The Saints'. They were based at Darlington Public Park, then the North Lodge Ground moving to Chestnut Grove and wore *"black & yellow jerseys, white knickers"*. The Northern League's first champions during 1889-90, they were formally known as St Augustine's FC.

St Augustine's as Cleveland Cup winners in 1889.

Drysdale: *f1883,* playing football on The Leazes near St James' Park in *"yellow & black jerseys, dark knickers"*.

Elswick Rangers: *f1886* as *"Elswick Works Athletic Club"* and associated with the Armstrong factory. Soon known as 'Rangers', they had a base at Mill Lane near Bentinck Road. A progressive and strong club to their demise around late 1891 attracting many Scottish footballers, several to work at Armstrongs.

Elswick Leather Works: *f1881* by workers of the large Richardson Leather Works in Elswick. They played in royal-blue shirts with white shorts, and had a pitch on the Town Moor, then near to Elswick Road tram terminus with a dressing-room at the Crown Hotel. The club folded during 1887.

Elswick Ordnance Works: *f1884* by employees of the armament factories in Elswick. They used a pitch on the Town Moor and wore *"white jerseys & knickers"* then *"black & white jerseys, white knickers"*. They disbanded during the late 1880s.

Gateshead Association: *f1884* as Gateshead Casuals and linked to the demise of Newcastle Rangers when many of their players moved to the Gateshead club. Grounds were at Alexandria Road, Burt Terrace, at Bensham, then Teams while they played in "white & blue" colours. They became defunct by 1890 with many of their players joining the NER club.

Gateshead NER: f1889 representing the huge North East Railway complex at Greensfield with a pitch at Park Lane then at the Old Fold Ground during the 1890s.

Hawthorn Rovers: f,c1881, a minor club which ran both cricket and football sides during the decade.

Heaton Association: f1882 as the "Heaton Athletic Association" and possibly linked to an earlier Heaton cricket club, they occupied the Heaton Junction Bicycle arena before East End moved in. They donned "blue & black jerseys, white knickerbockers", disbanding during 1887.

Hebburn: f1882 as Hebburn Juniors, dropping the Juniors tag the following year. They had "black & white" kit and a field adjoining the railway station.

Hebburn Argyle: f1882 under the title of St Aloysius Juniors with a field near the Catholic church on Argyle Street. The club became a powerful outfit during the 1890s and survived until 1919.

Ironopolis (Middlesbrough): f1889 following an amateur v professional row at the Middlesbrough club. Known as 'The Nops' or 'Washers', they played at the Paradise Ground in "maroon & green", then "cherry & white stripes". Northern League winners for three seasons in a row, joining the Football League before being dissolved in 1894.

Ironopolis, Northern League champions 1893.

Jarrow: f1882, likely as Jarrow Rangers, they were original members of the Tyneside League and folded in 1894 when Jarrow FC were formed.

Jesmond: f1883 but only enjoyed a brief life-span, disbanding during 1885. Appeared in a "maroon & white horizontal striped shirt" with a base at Abbotsfield Terrace near Brandling Park.

Jesmond FC in hooped shirts during 1883.

Lemington/Lemington Rangers: f1883 bearing kit of "black & blue jerseys, white & blue knickers".

Marlborough: f1882 and centred around Newcastle's railway station. They disbanded the first-eleven in 1883 but continued with a second-team for a period.

Morpeth Harriers: f1883 or 1884 performing on Mr Almond's field off Howard Terrace with kit of "black jerseys with gold band, white knickers".

Newcastle Albion: Playing the game by January 1889, Albion were active into the 1890s and beyond. During 1890-91 they occupied a ground "near Leazes Park".

Newcastle Association/Newcastle FA: f1880 with a ground just off the North Road at Brandling, opposite the Orphanage. They pulled on "navy-blue" then "black" shirts with "white knickers", before wearing "cardinal-red & light blue quartered jerseys". They combined with Trinity in 1881 and Brunswick during 1887.

Newcastle East End/Stanley (Newcastle United): f1881 as Stanley FC, a street on Walker Road in South Byker. They changed title to Newcastle East End during 1882 playing in shirts of navy-blue with an orange sash, then Cambridge-blue, then red shirts. Based in South Byker before moving to the Heaton Junction Ground off Chillingham Road, East End took over certain assets of West End on their demise, including the lease of St James' Park. Soon they were renamed Newcastle United, in December 1892.

(Newcastle) Rangers: f1878, the area's second club after Tyne. Began playing in Gateshead at the Drill Field, then moved to St James' Park during 1880 before relocating to Dalton Street in Byker. They pulled on kit of "dark blue (RFC on breast of the jersey)" and disbanded in 1885. Formally called "Rangers Association FC" but often referred to as 'Newcastle Rangers' to differentiate with other Rangers clubs. (A new and different 'Newcastle Rangers' was formed during 1888.)

Newcastle Rangers pictured during May 1884, the only traced illustration of one of Tyneside's pioneer clubs.

North Eastern: f1879 as one of Tyneside's oldest clubs and linked to workers at the North Eastern Railway Co in the district. Based at the Heaton cricket field next to Chillingham Road, they wore "red & white striped jerseys" in a banded fashion. North Eastern folded during the 1890s.

North Eastern FC taken from the Northern Athlete in 1884.

Ovingham: *f1880 playing in the Tyne village wearing "royal-blue & black hose jerseys" with a pitch west of the village.*

Ovington: *f1881 and located next to Ovingham, they featured kit of "black & amber" shirts.*

Port Clarence: *Based at Haverton Hill near Stockton.*

Prudhoe Rovers: *f1882 and located near to Prudhoe Castle, they displayed hooped shirts of "royal-blue & salmon" and dark shorts.*

Redcar: *f1878 as "Redcar & Coatham YMCA FC", created by local cricketers with a field at Redcar Racecourse. They changed at the Red Lion Hotel and appeared in "black & red". The club were early entrants to the FA Cup.*

Rendel: *f1881 originating from around Rendel Street near Scotswood Road, initially playing near Elswick cemetery and afterwards relocating to Normount Road in Benwell. With colours of "blue & black jerseys with red stripe on arm, white knickers" and later in stripes, they were an amateur side. Rendel disbanded during the summer of 1898.*

Rendel illustrated during the early 1890s. Joe Wardropper is at the centre of the back row, with the moustache.

Rosehill/Willington Athletic: *f1883 wearing kit of "cardinal & blue jerseys, blue knickers", based at a field near Howdon railway station alongside the Tyne. Became Willington Athletic during 1888.*

Rosewood: *f1882 in the east of Newcastle, they soon merged with the Newcastle East End club during 1883.*

Science & Art: *f1883 and representing the college of the same name based on Corporation Street and in Heaton. Wearing "black jerseys & white knickers", they played on the Town Moor then at a pitch near the Orphanage at Brandling in Jesmond. Fielded both senior and junior teams.*

Shankhouse Black Watch: *f1883 or 1884 from the pit community in South Northumberland and the local Primitive Methodist Chapel. They became the region's finest line-up for several years, reaching seven Senior Cup finals and once facing Aston Villa in FA Cup action. Operating from the Shankhouse Row Field in colours of "black jersey, red sash & black knickers", they amalgamated with Shankhouse Albion and dropped 'Black Watch' around 1888, continuing on for several decades.*

Shankhouse Blues: *f1884 having kit of "blue & white jerseys, blue knickers" with a ground at Shankhouse Field.*

Sleekburn Wanderers: *f1882 or 1883, a colliery club based at the Recreation Ground, Bedlington Station and noted as wearing colours of "black & yellow jerseys, white knickers".*

South Bank: *f1878, possibly earlier in 1868, but certainly one of the oldest in the North East. Nicknamed 'The Bankers' with an enclosure at Paradise Field then Normanby Road by 1889, they played initially in halves of Oxford & Cambridge blue.*

Southwick: *f1884 as "Southwick Cricket & Football Club". From Wearside, and then outside the Sunderland boundary, they became members of the Northern Alliance during its first season of 1891-92*

St Cuthbert's: *f1882 with an area of play on the Town Moor, their shirt colours were "red & black with blue badge on arm".*

SS Mary & James (St Mary & St James)/Newcastle Harp: *f1884 from the St Thomas' area near Leazes where they had a pitch. Sported unusual colours of "chocolate jersey & green sash", they became Newcastle Harp by 1887.*

Stockton: *f1882 and despite a fleeting period as a professional club, staunchly amateur. The 'Ancients' were FA Amateur Cup winners during the 1890s and had colours of black shirts with two (or three) red hoops, then "red & black quartered" shirts. Occupied a ground at Flatts Farm and the Victoria Ground.*

Sunderland Albion: *f1888 as a result of an acrimonious split from the Sunderland club. Playing in black-and-white striped shirts, then white shirts & blue shorts, with a ground at the Blue House Field, they were very ambitious, joining the Football Alliance and were runners-up during 1890-91. Albion competed in the Northern League but didn't survive long, being disbanded during 1892 after rivals Sunderland had gained entry into the Football League.*

Sunderland Albion as a Football Alliance club. Bob McDermid is pictured third from the left, back row, and James Hannah, middle row, first left.

Sunderland Olympic: *Playing football by 1888, Olympic joined the Northern Alliance when it was formed for 1891-92. Noted as having grounds at Ashville and Abbs Field.*

Trafalgar: *f1887, a Heaton club and originally playing at Leazes but to move to the Heaton Junction Ground in 1893 when East End moved out. Once the East Enders became Newcastle United, they changed their name to Newcastle East End during 1895. Played on into the 1900s.*

Trafalgar at the start of the 1890s featuring West End players, Patten, Nugent, Walton and McCrory.

Tyne: *f1877 as the region's pioneering club created by ex-public-school lads returning to Tyneside with the 'new' association code. For five years were the district's premier side before the working-class took over. Tyne played in "orange & black quartered" shirts, and were based at first, Bath Road,* then at the Warwick Place Ground near Eskdale Terrace in Jesmond. They had disbanded by early 1887. Sometimes referred to as 'Tyne Association' to distinguish from the rugby game.

West Hartlepool NER: f1881 by employees of the North East Railway company. They survived until 1898 when their members formed a new club, West Hartlepool FC.

Whitburn: f1881 or 1882 and founder members of the Northern Alliance and North Eastern Counties leagues, becoming the only champions of the latter short-lived competition. Played in "black & orange".

White Rose Juniors/Newcastle Rovers: f1883 or 1884 with a ground at Low Leazes, then at Bull Park. They amalgamated with West End during 1887 but reformed a year later and were retitled Newcastle Rovers by 1889 soon linking up with the Percy Ironworks club. They had folded by 1893.

Willington Athletic: See Rosehill.

Tyneside 'Wednesday' clubs:

Midweek football became popular during the late 1880s and through the 1890s when many shops closed half-day on Wednesday. Several clubs were formed in the region, initially playing friendly contests with sides generally using a suffix of 'Wednesday' such as Victoria Wednesday, Rendel Wednesday and Heaton Wednesday. Other teams were active such as the Army XI from Newcastle Garrison, and Green Market Wednesday, typical of the links to trades in the city. A "Northern Wednesday League" was created for season 1891-92.

Newcastle Wednesday: f1886 and playing their first games during December of that year, although it appears they were reformed around 1890. They were closely linked to Newcastle West End with a base at St James' Park and featured many of their players and officials. They played on until the 1920s.

England

Accrington: f1878 and one of the original participants of the Football League in 1888 playing at the Thorneyholme cricket ground. Having kit of red shirts, they folded in 1896, by then a new club, Accrington Stanley had been formed.

Ardwick: The previous title of Manchester City.

Blackpool Olympic: f,c1880 one of three secondary teams in the town after Blackpool FC, they were based at the Olympic Ground and continued playing up to the Great War.

Bootle: f1879, they became Everton's main rivals on Merseyside, founder members of the Football Alliance, runners-up in 1889-90. Bootle joined the Football League but dropped out due to financial difficulties. They were based at Hawthorne Road, playing in blue & white quarters then stripes.

Burton Swifts: f1871, one of two principal clubs in Burton upon Trent and one of the first members of The Combination. Becoming a Football League club, Swifts played at Peel Croft in red & white quartered shirts and merged with Burton Wanderers during 1901 to form Burton United.

Burton Wanderers: f1871 with an enclosure at Derby Turn and colours of blue & white halved shirts then stripes. They were Midland League champions in 1894 and afterwards a Football League side before amalgamating with Swifts.

Carlisle: f,c1884 as the "Carlisle Association Club" and occasionally mistaken for the Carlisle City rugby side. Had a ground at Waterworks Lane and won the very first Cumberland Cup during 1885-86.

Chatham: f1882 as Chatham United, but then titled Chatham Town and Chatham FC. They originally played on an army pitch, then at Maidstone Road. A founder member of the Southern League, the club are still competing, now in the Isthmian League.

Corinthians: f1882, the famous London-based amateur combination which selected top players and took the game around Britain and overseas. Played in an all-white kit and often

appeared in North East exhibition fixtures. They were based at the Queen's Club then Crystal Palace and merged with Casuals during 1939 to form the Corinthian-Casuals club.

Darwen: f1870, an early pioneer outfit which fielded several top names. Sported black & white hooped, then striped, shirts at their Barley Bank ground. Darwen reached the FA Cup semi-final during 1880-81 and joined the Football Alliance, then Football League.

Derby Junction: f1870, another club to reach an early FA Cup semi-final, they were founder members of the Midland League as an amateur club. Junction had shirts of red & navy-blue stripes and were dissolved during 1895. They played on a ground at Derby Arboretum.

Derby St Luke's: f1870 and nicknamed 'The Churchmen' with a ground at Peet Street. As amateurs they played in The Combination during 1890-91 but did not complete the season and folded during 1892. St Luke's kit featured light-blue & navy-blue halved shirts.

Fairfield/Fairfield Athletic: f, early 1880s based near Droylsden, they joined the Lancashire League in 1892 becoming champions during 1895, the same season they lost 11-1 to Sunderland in the FA Cup. Fairfield were based at the Gransmoor Road ground and played in red shirts before disbanding in 1897.

Gainsborough Trinity: f1873 and a strong Midland League team sporting colours of blue at the Northolme arena. They were champions in 1891, soon joining the Football League. The Lincolnshire club are still playing in the Northern Premier League.

Halliwell (Bolton): f1877 and entrants in the early FA Cup, they pulled on various colours during the 1880s; navy-blue shirts, white shirts then black & gold stripes. With a base at The Bennetts cricket arena, they competed in the Lancashire Combination but were expelled for failing to fulfil matches and ceased operations around 1893.

Heywood Central: f1887 from near Manchester and founder members of the Lancashire League during the late 1880s. With red & white halved shirts, they became defunct early in 1896. Central played at the Phoenix Pleasure Ground.

Jardines (Nottingham): f1884 (possibly earlier), a strong works XI from a machine factory in Nottingham playing at the Recreation Ground. Wearing red shirts & black shorts, they folded during 1919.

Liverpool Caledonians: f1892 and based at Wavertree on Merseyside, they existed only for only a few months after joining the Lancashire League. Caledonians were composed almost entirely of Scottish footballers.

London Caledonians: f1886, an amateur combination located in Holloway primarily fielding exiled Scots and an original member of the Isthmian League. They later lifted the FA Amateur Cup and became defunct in 1939. Caledonians wore black & white hooped shirts.

Long Eaton Rangers: f1881 located just outside Derby at the Recreation Ground, a club to play in both The Combination and Football Alliance before joining the Midland League. Had chocolate & sky-blue halved shirts with navy-blue shorts, then white shirts. Rangers disbanded during 1899.

Nelson: f1882, they played in the Lancashire League by the late 1880s, champions during 1896 and later a Football League club. Based at the Seedhill cricket ground and then Scotland Road, wearing blue shirts, Nelson remain in action in the North West Counties League.

Newton Heath: The previous title of Manchester United.

Northwich Victoria: f1874 as one of England's oldest clubs and during early years they featured in the Welsh Cup. Based at the Drill Field, Victoria joined The Combination then Football League but left during 1894, thereafter playing football in local leagues, recently in the Midland Football League.

Notts Mellors: f1883, a factory side from lace manufacturing business Mellor & Sons located in and around Nottingham. Playing at the Arkwright Street ground, they pulled on claret &

133

grey halved shirts then red & white, being renamed Nottingham Wanderers during 1888 but became defunct a year later.

Rotherham Town: f1882, from the Lunar Rovers side. A founding club of the Midland League, champions in 1892 and 1893 before joining the Football League, they appeared in sky-blue & brown shirts, then red. Town were dissolved in 1896, a second club being formed three years later.

Sheppey United: f1890, at the Botany Road ground they became a founding member in Division Two of the Southern League during 1894. Based on the Isle of Sheppey in Kent, United wore blue & white colours and were one of the top sides in the south, still playing in the Isthmian League.

Small Heath Alliance: The previous title of Birmingham City.

Stoke: f1868 (maybe earlier) becoming one of the original clubs to create the Football League in 1888. With colours of red & white stripes they soon joined the Football Alliance, champions in 1891, before returning to the Football League until 1908 when they were reformed, later becoming Stoke City in 1925.

Union Star (Burnley): Playing during the early 1880s as one of a handful of pioneer clubs in the town before the present Burnley FC started. They were based at the Rakehead Ground and became members of the Lancashire League but couldn't fulfil their fixtures and disbanded during 1891.

Warmley (Bristol): f1882 and founder members of the Bristol & District League, soon joining the Western League. They were champions before switching to the Southern League. From Kingswood, they were early rivals to the Rovers and City clubs but were dissolved in 1899.

West Manchester: f1884 and local adversaries of Newton Heath and Ardwick with a base at Brooks Bar. Featuring white shirts, they were one of the original clubs to form the Lancashire League before folding in 1897.

Woolston Works: f1878 as Southampton Rangers, the works team of a major shipyard that became one of the top clubs in the area during the mid-to-late 1880s. Playing on Southampton Common then at the Antelope Ground, they attracted several Scottish footballers with offers of work at the Oswald, Mordaunt company. When the shipyard closed, the club was dissolved in 1889.

Scotland

The district north of Glasgow and the River Clyde comprising Dunbartonshire and parts of Stirlingshire, was especially important in providing footballers to end up on Tyneside. It was a hotbed of early football with multiple clubs seemingly from every town and village. Prominent sides included Dumbarton, Dumbarton Athletic, Renton, Vale of Leven, Jamestown and Campsie.

5th KRV (Kirkcudbright Rifle Volunteers): f1879 from an army unit and based in Dumfries at Palmerston Park. They played in red & blue hoops, then dark-blue shirts and were dissolved in 1897.

Abercorn: f1877 and located in Paisley, they became founder members of the Scottish League. Had a home at Blackstoun Park with blue then white shirts, continuing playing until 1920.

Bathgate Rovers: f1888 one of several sides in Central Scotland just outside Edinburgh. At the Little Boghead ground, they sported white kit and merged with other clubs in the town during 1894.

Broxburn: f1880, one of the strongest of several clubs in the area around Bathgate and Broxburn. At the Sportsfield, they wore blue & white shirts, blue shorts and played until 1894.

Broxburn Shamrock: f1881, one of a number of teams in the town, they had green & white kit, also playing at the town's Sportsfield, then at Easter Road. Shamrock closed in 1888 but reformed until 1897.

Cambuslang: f1873 or 1876, one of many sides representing Lanarkshire. They featured dark-blue shirts and were runners-up in the Scottish Cup during 1888. With a club-house at Westburn Park then Whitefield Park, they folded in 1897.

Campsie: f1883 and from the small community of Milton of Campsie near Lennoxtown where several teams were playing football. They sported navy-blue kit and competed at Lennox Park before disbanding in 1894.

Carlton: f1887, from Greenock, originally a junior club stepping up a level the following year. Played in blue & white with a ground at Wellington Park and Ladyburn Park. They disbanded during 1890.

Carrington: f1880 in the Dennistoun district of Glasgow and beginning as a junior outfit, they moved to senior level during 1889 and played at Hanover Park. They pulled on black & white striped shirts then navy-blue.

Cartvale: f1878 in Busby, south of Glasgow, for a short period fielded a top line-up in their distinctive black shirts featuring a red cross & white shorts. Based at Cartbridge Park, they were dissolved in 1887.

Clydebank: f1888, one of six or seven clubs to use the title. They had a pitch at Hamilton Park and were members of Scotland's Football Federation league for a spell before disbanding in 1895. They donned white shirts with a red band.

Cowlairs: f1876 based in the north of Glasgow, one of the clubs which founded the Scottish League. Cowlairs predominately played in royal-blue then white shirts and had a HQ at Gourlay Park. They competed in both the Scottish and English Cups before folding during 1896.

Dalmuir Thistle: f1878 in Clydebank and one of several clubs to perform with credit during the 1880s. Operated from an enclosure at Castle Park in kit of navy-blue. They folded during 1895.

Dumbarton: f1872, they took over from Renton as Scotland's best during the late 1880s and early 1890s, six times in the Scottish Cup final. Based at Boghead Park, they were famed in dark-blue shirts & white shorts, then black & gold stripes. The club folded in 1901 then were reformed.

Dumbarton Athletic: f1881, second-rated of four clubs from the town, they wore colours of dark-blue & light-blue hoops, then black & white stripes, to red & black stripes before being absorbed by Dumbarton FC in 1889. Athletic played at Burnside Park then St James Park.

Dunblane: f1878, one of the top-ranked sides in their region, winning the Perthshire Cup several times and runners-up in the Midland League during 1892. With kit of blue & white hoops, then red shirts, they played at Kippencross Park and Duckburn Park. Dunblane folded in 1915.

Dundee Harp: f1879 and from the Catholic community on Tayside, Harp sported green shirts, operating from Tayside and Viewforth parks then the Athletic Ground. They were suspended for non-payment of guarantees and disbanded in 1894.

(Dundee) Wanderers: f1885 after a breakaway from Our Boys. They became Johnstone Wanderers during 1891, then Dundee Wanderers after a merger with Strathmore three years later. Wanderers played at Clepington Park, from 1885 to 1892 in maroon shirts with a navy-blue sash.

Duntocher Harp: f1887 or 1888 near Clydebank and based at St Helena Park. They appeared wearing green shirts with blue shorts. Harp folded during 1897.

(Edinburgh) St Bernard's: f1878, beginning their football life in the Stockbridge district of Edinburgh and continuing until 1943. By 1880 they played at the Royal Gymnasium Grounds, then at Powderhall, wearing white shirts & navy-blue shorts, but in 1890 they were expelled from the Scottish FA for a period for professionalism. St Bernard's lifted the Scottish Cup in 1895 becoming a noted Scottish League side.

(Glasgow) Northern: f1874 in the Springburn area of Glasgow and based at Hyde Park, they merged with Petershill during 1883 and became members of Scotland's Football Alliance league. With kit of navy-blue & light-blue halved shirts, Northern were struck off the Scottish FA roll during 1897.

(Glasgow) Thistle: *f1875 (or as early as 1868) representing the Dalmarnock area, near Glasgow Green. They were a founder member of the Football Alliance, playing with blue & white hooped then striped shirts. During the mid-1880s were based at Dalmarnock Park and Beechwood Park. They folded in the mid-1890s.*

Glasgow University: *f1877 and still playing football presently. Competed with the top sides on Clydeside and beyond during the pioneering era of the game. Based at Gilmorehill, the University XI predominately wore black shirts with a distinct gold badge.*

Glasgow Wanderers: *f1889 and dissolved in 1895. The club featured navy-blue kit, were members of the Football Federation competition and played at Eglinton Park.*

(Glasgow) Whitefield: *f1877, a side from Govan based at Whitefield Park, they dressed in navy-blue shirts and survived in the shadow of Rangers until around 1895.*

Jamestown: *f1877 from a village near Alexandria with a ground at Balloch Road, alongside Vale of Leven Wanderers. They played football until 1893 and like many sides of the era possessed kit of navy-blue.*

Kelvinside Athletic: *f1886, playing football in Glasgow's Partick district until 1891. Athletic played at Kelburne Park in white & navy-blue and once defeated Govan Athletic 16-0 in the Scottish Cup.*

Kilbirnie: *f1874 in Ayrshire, they sported colours of orange & black hooped shirts with a club HQ at Parkfoot during the 1880s.*

King's Park: *f1875 in Stirling and a well-known side during the pre-war years. With a ground at Laurelhill Park, they had all-navy-blue kit, then maroon & red shirts. King's Park folded in 1945 when Stirling Albion began.*

Leith Athletic: *f1887 and featured colours of maroon & white stripes, then red shirts, before being nicknamed the 'Zebras' due to wearing black & white by 1889. Scottish League members in 1891, they were based at the Hawkhill Ground in what was then the outskirts of Edinburgh. During 1905 they folded but reformed as Leith FC.*

Linthouse: *f1881, operating in the Govan district of Glasgow. Linthouse wore navy-blue shirts, played at Langlands Park and were members of the early Football Alliance and continued until 1900.*

Mid-Annandale: *f1877 and located in Lockerbie near the border, they had light-blue shirts then red & yellow stripes. The side disbanded during 1894.*

Mossend Swifts: *f1879 with a ground at Mossend Park in West Calder near Edinburgh, Swifts had a strip of red & white. They later merged with the West Calder side during 1903.*

Nithsdale: *f1885 in Dumfries and headquartered at Victoria Park then the Recreation Ground. Having maroon shirts, they later were retitled and took the name of the town during 1889.*

Our Boys (Dundee): *f1877, the Tayside club owned colours of dark-blue and were based at West Craigie Park. They continued until 1893 when a merger with Dundee East End created the present Dundee FC.*

Pollokshields Athletic: *f1875 in Glasgow, they twice reached the semi-final of the Scottish Cup. Having kit of white shirts and a ground at Pollock Park they disbanded in 1890, although some sources note a link with the Battlefield club.*

Port Glasgow Athletic: *f1878 or 1880 as Broadfield FC, one of several clubs in Renfrewshire. They fielded several noted players, initially part of the Football Alliance then Scottish League. Based at Devol Farm then Clune Park, they wore white shirts & navy-blue shorts and folded in 1912.*

Renfrew: *f1875 and disbanded late in 1889 or 1890. Centred at Glebe Street with navy-blue shirts.*

Renton: *f1872, during much of the 1880s wearing navy-blue shirts and shorts, Renton were Scotland's top club operating from Tontine Park. Founder members of the Scottish League, they were suspended for professionalism, while famously Renton lifted the 'Championship of the UK and the World'*

during 1888. They reached five Scottish Cup finals, but the club disbanded in the early 1920s.

Renton Thistle: *f1873, played second-fiddle to the senior Renton club but produced several players who graduated to a higher grade. With blue shirts and based in the south of the town, Thistle ceased operations during 1881.*

Shettleston: *f1880 with a ground at Carntyne Park in Glasgow, their kit changed from navy-blue to black & white stripes, then red & white stripes. Shettleston folded during 1890.*

Summerton Athletic: *f1888 in Glasgow's Govan district, Athletic occupied a pitch at Victoria Park and played in black & white striped shirts. Summerton ceased operations during 1894.*

Third Lanark (3rd Lanarkshire Rifle Volunteers): *f1872 as the 3rd LRV with a home to become famous as Cathkin Park. During the 1880s pulled on kit of blue & white hoops or stripes, then red & black stripes. They were renamed Third Lanark during 1903, the Glasgow side were one of Scotland's traditional clubs for decades until their controversial exit in 1967.*

Thornliebank: *f1875, the Renfrewshire club pulled on white shirts & navy shorts then black & white hoops. They reached the Scottish Cup final in 1880 and played in the Scottish Football Combination during the 1890s. With a ground at Heatherty Hill, then Deacon's Bank and Summerlee Park, they disbanded in 1908.*

Vale of Leven: *f1872 and the principal club from Alexandria, they were formidable during the 1870s and 1880s, reaching seven Scottish Cup finals. The Vale had all-navy-blue colours and played at Millburn Park from the late 1880s, and featured until 1929.*

Vale of Leven Athletic: *f1886 and one of several lesser clubs in Alexandria, they folded in 1894.*

Vale of Leven Wanderers: *f1883, playing at Institute Park in black & white shirts. They closed down in 1890.*

Wishaw Thistle: *f1884, they used the Old Public Park and Recreation Park in the Lanarkshire town. Originally a junior club, they sported white shirts and navy-blue shorts. Thistle ceased playing in 1900.*

135

ABBREVIATIONS

AGM = Annual General Meeting
app = appearances
Ass = Association
Ath = Athletic
b = born
BA = Bachelor of Arts
BSc = Bachelor of Science
c = circa, about
CC = cricket club
CCC = county cricket club
Co = county or company
cs = close-season
CW = colliery welfare
d = died
f = formation
FA = Football Association
FAC = FA Cup
FC = football club
FL = Football League champions
gls = goals
GP = General Practice
HQ = headquarters
Ire = Ireland
Jnrs = juniors
Lancs = Lancashire
LNER = London North Eastern Railway
MA = Master of Arts
MBE = Member of the Order of the British Empire
MP = Member of Parliament
NER = North Eastern Railway
NFA = Northumberland Football Association
NL = Northern League
NSC = Northumberland Senior Cup
OS = Ordnance Survey
Q3 = quarter 3 of year (as birth or death)

qv = cross reference
RAMC = Royal Army Medical Corps
ref = reference
RVI = Royal Victoria Infirmary
s, d = shillings, old pence
SC = Scottish Cup
Scot = Scotland
SFA = Scottish Football Association
SL = Scottish League champions
UK = United Kingdom
Utd = United
v = versus
Wand = Wanderers
Wed = Wednesday

Match Details
3q = Round 3 qualifying
abs = absent player
d = dismissed player
f = final
Fr = friendly
H, A = home, away fixtures
ICC = Inter County Championship
mins = minutes
N = neutral venue
N&D = Northumberland & Durham
og = own-goal
r = replay
sf = semi-final
W, D, L = won, drawn, lost
WE = Newcastle West End

League tables:
F, A = goals for, goals against
Pts = points

Universal abbreviations used
Months = Jan, Feb etc

FURTHER READING

PIONEERS of the NORTH

The story of how the game of association football reached the North East region; from Berwick in the far north, through Northumberland, the industrial centres of Tyneside and Wearside, and into County Durham, to the south and Cleveland.

Featuring the pioneers of Newcastle United...Stanley FC and Newcastle East End FC.

Compiled by Paul Joannou & Alan Candlish

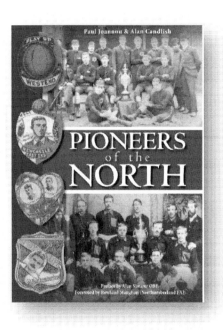

Chronicling the lively and compelling history
of
Newcastle United & North East football

www.novopublishing.co.uk

AUTHORS

Paul Joannou

For over 40 years, Paul has been connected to Newcastle United as club historian. Born and raised in

Newcastle's west end and first watching the Magpies during 1964, he also has a deep interest in the wider history of North East football, especially during the late Victorian era – a time of course when both Newcastle East End and Newcastle West End were city rivals. Paul has now compiled a mini-library covering football in the region including several definitive books including the acclaimed Newcastle United trilogy; *The First 100 Years & More, The Ultimate Record & The Ultimate Who's Who*. A regular contributor to United's match-day programme for many years, he is now retired from the day-job of a commercial director for a construction and property plc and resides in Edinburgh. Working with Alan and Bill on other projects, he was delighted to bring the team once more together to relate the story of the West Enders.

Alan Candlish

Alan was born and bred in Byker, in the east end of Newcastle, but has lived in the west end for the past 40 years. A retired auditor, he is the author of the best-selling *Ha'Way/Howay the Lads* (the definitive history of Tyne-Wear Derbies). He has also worked closely with Paul on the acclaimed *Pioneers of the North* (an in-depth record of the origins of football in the North East) and has assisted Paul and Bill on the seminal *Newcastle United: The Ultimate Record*. He is more than pleased to team up with them again with the current West End volume. Married, with three grown up children and four grandchildren, Alan has been a season-ticket holder at St James' Park for over 50 years and has been married to Margaret for even longer but, in both cases, he has declined time-off for good behaviour.

Bill Swann

From East Northumberland, Bill is a lifelong Newcastle United supporter just like

Paul and Alan. Visiting St James' Park regularly since watching his first game there in 1949, he lived in Cheshire for fifty years working for ICI, taking early retirement when his wife became seriously ill with Huntington's disease. Bill was her carer for sixteen years during which time he engaged in voluntary work supporting those with long term health conditions and their carers. He relocated north after the death of his wife and now resides in the Tyne valley from where he undertakes voluntary work in the health sector and continues to support the Magpies. A keen collector of all things black-and-white, Bill's three children, as well as grandchildren, are all United fans too. He is also proud to be distantly related to the family of his United hero, Jackie Milburn.